THE SHEEP IS WHAT
MAKES IT FUNNY

From Philadelphia to CBS,
How I Found Myself in Television

Jim McKairnes

Foreword

My father worked as a writer and performer during the experimental early years of live local television in Philadelphia. My mother loved to laugh as much as she did anything during her all-too-brief life. My aunt was born with an amazing capacity to recall dates and numbers of any or no significance. And just about every one of the male forebears on my mother's side was an unrelenting grammarian. So it seems I was wired from birth to do with my life whatever it is I've done with it and to become whatever it is I've become. But DNA met destiny in the autumn of 1977 when as an incoming senior at Father Judge Catholic High School for Boys in Philadelphia I took an English-elective course called "The Written Word and the Moving Picture." Because it opened up my world to both.

A popular and unconventional course offered to upper-classmen only, designed and taught by a seeming run-of-the-mill staff priest there at Father Judge who demonstrated with it that he was instead in a literal class of his own, "The Written Word and the Moving Picture" used music and movies of the day to teach us about the expression of thoughts and feelings, to explore the English language through our own modern uses of it. Which means that while some of Judge's juniors and seniors were conjugating never-elsewhere-to-be-used verbs or laboring over Chaucer and Milton, others of us were watching Zefferelli and George Roy Hill, listening to Bernie Taupin and Aerosmith, and coming to Vonnegut by way of Valerie Perrine's nude scene in *Slaughterhouse-Five*.

The course courted controversy with its content and, if the stories are to be believed, was a frequent target of parental and diocesan objections. But its architect stared down and won over the concerns, steadfast in a vision that saw a means of speaking *with* students rather than *at* them and in the process getting through to oft-disengaged teenaged minds. He certainly got through to mine. None of the other instructors at Father Judge -- not the wheelchair-bound Latin teacher who drilled into our heads that the verb 'to be' never takes a direct object, nor the then-newly ordained Theology teacher who employed slides of naked Greek statues to teach us about human reproduction, nor the angry Poli-Sci teacher who described 1970s feminist Bella Abzug as being so ugly "it looks like her mother threw away the baby and raised the afterbirth," and certainly neither the forever-hungover Algebra teacher with a gin-blossom for a nose nor the repressed English-instructor priest who'd one day be arrested in an out-of-state prostitution sweep – had the effect or lasting impact on me that the man behind this course had. Both he and it made poetry of the written word and stories of the moving picture. And a working professional out of me, eager to weave and display tapestries of each.

All these years later, he may not want the fame or the blame or the credit that comes from it, but anyone who went to Philadelphia's Father Judge Catholic High School for Boys in the 1970s and who was lucky enough to take "The Written Word and the Moving Picture" – or likely any of the other classes he taught there -- will understand my decision to dedicate this work to Rev. John Connery, O.S.F.S.

Because he opened up my world to both.

*

Introduction

To get to the basement laundry-area of the narrow brick Philadelphia rowhome in which I was raised, you'd enter through the front door on the main level, walk the length of the house all the way to the kitchen, and then descend a darkened and narrow staircase just off to the left, whereupon you'd double-back across the expanse of the house towards where the washer and dryer rested beneath a half-wall of glass-block windows. As you did this, you'd pass by a TV-watching area in the middle of the downstairs space -- a small black-and-white set perched atop a makeshift-stand against the green-marble-paneled wall, with an odd set of outdoor patio-furniture forming an indoor semi-circle in front of it.

If you were to make the trek any day between 1966 and 1977, you'd also pass by my mother's young fourth-born, alone in the semi-circle, staring at the small TV screen, studying its images, listening to its sounds, warming his heart against its grayish glow. Inside the semi-circle, he was also quite inside the TV – for such was the dream as he daily sought ways to remove himself from all that came with being one of nine living under his small and crowded rowhouse roof.

One night in the early 1970s, my mother, with yet another load of family laundry on her list (a half-dozen a day was not unusual), descended the darkened staircase off our kitchen and proceeded on her familiar pilgrimage to the glass-block-windowed front. As she did, she walked by the fourth-born as usual -- me, age 11 -- sitting his daily vigil in front of the electronic tabernacle. Singing along to what he was watching. Alone.

"Oh, Jim," she said, as much to herself as to me, not a break in her stride, her words tucked inside a sigh of resignation as the sounds of her six other children could be heard at play just outside the basement door. "I wish you didn't know the words to the commercials, too."

Twenty years on, in an only slightly better-furnished space, part of a small starter-apartment in Los Angeles, that same fourth-born -- me, now 31 — was once again sitting alone in front of the still-always-burning (though now slightly fancier) TV.

The town's newest transplant, I'd fled west a year earlier to start a new life in the wake of professional and personal tremors back east, determined at last to try my hand in the television industry that had held my fascination for so long. As of this Sunday night, I was still trying to figure out just how that's done. Around 10:30, the phone rang. On the line was television-producer Norman Lear, the TV-industry icon behind some of the most popular programming in television's history.

Some months earlier, soon after arriving on the west coast in fact, I'd met Lear while eking out what passed for a living as a freelance magazine writer, landing an assignment to interview him about some small-screen projects that marked a comeback of sorts to TV for him after more than a decade devoted to social causes. During the interview, the famed producer took note of my passion for television and then told me I should be working *in* TV and not writing *about* it ("Whose mail are you delivering?" was the way he phrased it, a nod to Hollywood lore of how careers here begin). I said that I'd been trying to do just that, trying to get in to CBS, for instance, for a meeting about working there, even going so far as writing a note to the network president, but that I'd never heard back. Lear offered to intervene -- to introduce me to the head of CBS, whom he knew. And then he did so just a few days later, sending his own note to him that suggested he should meet with me as a potential new hire. "There's gold in this Jim

McKairnes," he wrote. On this Sunday night, out of the blue, he was calling to see if they'd yet struck any in me, by offering me a job.

"Not yet," was my short answer, but I explained that I'd been to the network for several interviews since that note, and that I was hopeful. Which led to Norman Lear, the very person behind all the flickering images that captivated me as that 11-year-old in my family basement, the producer of all those hours that I watched, the man who all but invented modern television, saying that he was hopeful, too. Before hanging up, he said, "This'll be your year, kid; this'll be your year."

I was hired by CBS five days later.

I stayed 13 years.

I became part of the small team that programmed the entire CBS network.

My mother never lived to see that job happen. Or even to follow my move west. She never lived to see my front-facing office at CBS's Los Angeles headquarters, with a wide expanse of floor-to-ceiling windows overlooking Beverly Boulevard that, on a clear day, yielded a fairly good view of the HOLLYWOOD sign. She never lived to see me working with writers and producers and network officials and studio executives to help make small-screen history. She never lived to see the dream come true – to see me find myself in television.

But she was there when the dream was born, when the love affair with TV began. Fed and loved by my parents, educated by nuns and priests, toughened by my many siblings, I was raised by the thing I loved most, television -- a nightly escape from all that surrounded me as a child, a talisman for my lonely eyes.

Then I grew up and escaped into it.

This is the story of how that happened. And how in many ways it still is.

Like most stories, mine begins with family.

*

Before

*Six of seven McKairnes
(clockwise, from far left):
Bernadette, MaryBeth, David,
Mark, holding Eileen, me;
newborn Paul is asleep upstairs
(Philadelphia, 1968).
Neither the first nor last time
I'm seen kneeling before a TV.*

Not just because mine comes in August – though that helps – but summer birthdays really are the best kinds of birthdays to have growing up in my house.

Summer birthdays in these pre-central-air 1960s-Philadelphia days mean wide-open windows up and down the block. And on our block – one of the thousands of concrete-gray, thirty-identical-and-connected-to-one rowhome blocks here that are typical of working-class east-coast neighborhoods, with neighboring kitchens no more than a few feet apart -- that means being able to hear everything going on in the house next door. Which in turn means that when it comes time for my candle-topped birthday cake to be unveiled after dinner every fifth of August, the celebration begins in our kitchen with my parents and six siblings singing at our table ("Happy Birthday To You / Happy Birthday to You / Happy Birthday Dear Jimmy") and it concludes in the Quinns' kitchen a few feet away, with the eleven of them joining in the song at theirs ("HAPPY BIRTHDAY TO YOU," comes the last line through the window). Then from our respective kitchens all twenty of us applaud.

"AND MANY MO-O-O-O-ORE," the Quinns finish off, in a shout my way.

Happy birthday, Jimmy.

A two-family party.

Such is a day, such is the life, on the 3200 block of Wellington Street in Philadelphia's Great Northeast: Shared birthdays, open windows, involved neighbors, surrogate families -- with revolving back-doors and crowded front-stoops and perpetual conversation and endless commotion. Kid commotion. *Kids* commotion. We have seven. The Quinns, nine. The Clarks on the other side of them have eight, and then the Gravlins on the other side of the Clarks have another nine. Thirty-three kids, in just four of the houses. And the number all but doubles when the rest of the block is factored in.

Sixty-three kids at a single shot.

Thank you, *Vatican II*.

Kid after kid, cake after cake, family after family, year in and season out, it's a communal life. A participatory life. Especially in summer. Autumn is all about the unhappy single-file parade of starched-new uniforms threading a return to school out front (charcoal- and gray-slacks only for the boys, thanks; white butterfly-collars and knee-length jumpers for the girls); winter means weather-forced sequestration, wary dads staring down reluctant motors in tiny stone-cold garages, and nervous moms seeking word on school-closures from KYW-NewsRadio and then double-checking the supply of empty Wonder Bread wrappers that'll be needed for the day's shoe-insulation; spring translates into endless drab household chores centering around clogged rain-gutters and freshly seeded (and freshly sheeted) lawns. But summer makes the block – makes our families -- come alive. And it's Out Back -- the wide expanse of concrete driveway we share not only with everyone else on our Wellington Street block but also with the corresponding 3200 block of St. Vincent Street behind us, whose back-doors likewise open on to it -- where it all happens.

Here in The Drive, life begins and ends. Games of Bottlecaps and Double-Dutch by day and Manhunt and Flashlight Tag at night. Touch scrimmages on one end and hockey grudge-matches on the other. Whiffle-balls and dodge-balls battling for airspace with half-balls and pimple-balls. Metallic jacks sprinkled across out-of-commission hopscotch courts. Converse Hi-Tops thrown aloft into telephone-wire retirement. Produce sellers and scrap-collectors putt-putting up

and down in weathered pick-ups on weekly assignments.
Hungry mouths scrambling to the corner store for soft-
pretzels-with-mustard or cherry-cola Icees. Much of it framed
by a riot of colors from the neon hula-hoops, inches-high
fluorescent wading-pools, upended tricycles, and chalk outlines
of jump-rope grids. And all of it initiated each morning by the
Philadelphia "Yo" call that summons friends out to play – the
regional ritual of standing beneath a neighbor's open kitchen-
window and screaming a name for company.

"YO, Jimmmmmyyyyy," goes the sing-song-y refrain --
the *Yo* emphasized, the name elongated.

Texting for a pre-Internet age.

It's a banquet of aural and visual treats served up for
dozens of screaming mouths unhinged for the season. And it's
enhanced by the many distinct olfactory pulls of the days, from
the roofing-tar that always gurgles within blackened vats
outside one house or another to a torrent of water released
from the illegally tapped corner hydrant as it connects with sun-
scorched concrete to laundered sheets that salute the breeze
from webs of over-burdened clotheslines spun garage to garage.
All part of what local weatherman Jim O'Brien – the most
famous member of TV's *Action News* triumvirate on Channel
Six -- reminds us are the triple-H days of our east-coast
summers ("Hazy, Hot, and Humid, folks").

At this time, in this place, along with the family that
lives on it and the Catholic church that borders it, your block is
life's touchstone. It's what matters most. Like all the blocks in
what's known as The City of Neighborhoods – neighborhoods
that distinguish class, describe residents, mark boundaries,
declare bragging rights – the 3200 block of Wellington is a
home, a tribe, a safe haven, a community, a nation, and a
culture in one. All of us on it share the life and death and
sicknesses and holidays and celebrations and secrets that unfold
within it – the group birthday parties, the grocery-runs for
infirmed neighbors, the middle-of-the-night health scares that
have all eyes gawking at ambulances that pull up outside and
concerned moms convening on the scene to help out with
scared young ones. It's all about the care and feeding and
nurturing of some hundred-plus middle-class blue-collar white-
Catholic neighboring residents.

Your block's also an answer, an explanation, a modifier, for any curious outsider wanting to know more about you upon a chance meeting outside the neighborhood.

"Where you from?" ("*Northeast*")

"What parish?" ("*St. Matt's*")

"What section?" ("*Mayfair*")

"What street?" ("*Wellington*")

"What hundred?" ("*Thirty-two.*")

In the middle of that 3200 block sit the nine McKairnes by the wide-open kitchen window, applauding along with the Quinns in sugared appreciation. Mom and Dad and four boys and three girls born in a post-newlywed ten-year span between 1957 and 1967. (Factoring in a miscarriage, my mother is pregnant for 73 months in a single decade, which leads to a joke I offer in a brief stab at stand-up comedy in my 20s: "*My parents never told us where babies came from. Once a year, they'd just bring another sibling home from the car ... I was afraid to learn how to drive.*") Mom and Dad sit on opposite ends of a long and storied table, with three restless kids on each of the two wooden benches that frame it -- individual chairs are given up after the fifth born, leaving youngest Paul to sit at and eat off the portable dishwasher in the corner of the room when he comes of age for nearly all of his segregated childhood. (Don't bring it up.)

The pre-cake dinner each night is typically a meat-loaf or a roast or some other basic-red-meat-entrée roughly the size of a silver-dollar, accompanied by various mainstream vegetable side-dishes, preferably of the non-red-beet / non-lima-bean variety, as those tend to be found hours later on the floor beneath the table. Dessert accounted for, the entire dining experience lasts about eight minutes. Mom says we're finicky eaters who "eat like birds," so she comes to cook less and less for us, quantity-wise, as the years go by. My take is that the less we eat the shorter the meal -- and thus the quicker we can hightail it from the table's nightly crossfire. Sanity-wise.

The unspoken rule in our family, especially at dinner, the only time of day we're together as a group: Don't say anything unless it's funny – usually in the form of sarcasm. Biting humor floats the boat. Save the feelings and emotions for the privacy of the locked bathroom. (Or am I the only preteen boy in Philadelphia who spends 20 minutes in there at the end of *Brian's Song* on a November Tuesday in 1971, repeatedly flushing the toilet to drown out the sounds of my embarrassing sobs?) We're ruthless in our adherence to the rule, too, wielding humor against one another like the weapon we come to know it is. What a sibling says or does, or doesn't say or doesn't do, what he or she observes or thinks -- all jump balls.

Standard large-Catholic-family fare. But we upgrade the banter and the bite to an edgy art. To a way of life. To a language that only we learn and speak and understand, complete with its own syntax and cadence. "It's like a war in there," a college friend will observe one night when I dare to invite her to dinner, afterward, out on the front stoop. Half laughing, she'll also be trembling. And I'll be half proud. It's just what we do.

She'll be right, though: It *is* a war in here on Wellington Street. Fought with words. Between whom, we're not sure. Incited by what, we don't know. But it's a war nonetheless. And to mock, to ridicule, to insult – each other, friends or neighbors or strangers, even ourselves – are the rules of engagement. Thrust and parry. We learn it and refine it around that table. Night after night. Dinner after dinner. Year after year. Birthday cake after birthday cake. (If we do it well, perhaps it's too well. In still-later years, friends will recoil when I recount a charred conversation I have with youngest sister MaryBeth, each of us well into adulthood, on the morning an entire regiment of thirteen McKairnes family members flies to the west coast for youngest sibling Paul's wedding. "Everything is fine, but I have good news and bad news about the flight itself," says MaryBeth when she phones me at my California office from the Philadelphia airport. Which is? "The good news is that Mom's coming to the wedding. The bad news is that we needed to buy her three seats on the plane because she'll be lying down." Our mother has been dead for 10 years.)

Time and years of analysis will one day offer possible explanations for both the use of humor in our house as well as its darkened hue. To distance? To agitate? To displace anger? To cope? But the headline, I remind myself, is that while it can often be other things less enjoyable as the result, life here on Wellington Street is also just plain *funny*. It can't *not* be: The propensity for humor is built into the very foundation of the family -- a bequest as genetic as our skinny forms, our healthy hair, our crooked teeth, and The McKairnes Toe. A by-product of the moment in the early 1950s when Philadelphia's easy-to-laugh Mary Julia Mallon meets and then marries Philadelphia's witty onetime writer-performer Bernie McKairnes. The seven of us who follow study at the feet of masters, quick and razor-sharp each.

The more social and external-oriented of our parents, Mom is the one who likes to *share* a laugh. She seems to prefer an audience, to cause a stir and then to relish and participate in the reaction. One of six herself, she's part of a post-Depression-era household where laughs are likely hard-earned and well-appreciated, with a father who dies young and a mother who tries hard – and who knows the rush of applause from her own younger days on a neighborhood parish-stage. Whatever its roots, my mother's joy of laughter, and the sound of her own laugh itself -- a brief but loud sort of hiccup – is what frames my growing-up memories. In her late 40s, when recovery from cancer and an emptying nest yields a need for both distraction and purpose, she goes to work at a large Target-like department store in the area called Clover. For what she'll call the happiest years of her life, she fronts the Customer Service Desk, where retail complaints and consumer logistics come to die – and where she finds both her best audiences and best material.

Two shining moments come in the form of a pair of retorts during separate encounters with the type of pushy and rude customers of which she is less than fond -- the first to the man who jumps the line to demand, loudly and obnoxiously, instructions for getting to the store's lower level ("Sir, there's a silver pole in the middle of the Women's department; just hop on and slide down, and when you're done, come back to the pole, look up, and whistle.") and the other to an equally impatient customer who nearly clotheslines her as Mom walks near the Candy department during a frenzied pre-Christmas Saturday to ask "Young lady, just where exactly are the holiday nuts in this place?" ("Ma'am, today they're all over the store.")

My hunch, though, is that whatever sense of humor my mother is born with is sharpened by her exposure to the man who becomes my father, a man who loses his own mother (and bearings, one would wonder) at just six, but one with a creative streak he ends up putting to use in his 20s on a new Philadelphia experiment called television, before meeting Mom and taking on a respectable office-job that better supports a family. Dad's humor is more below-radar, more subversive. He's the more quiet of the pair, often sufficiently satisfied just knowing that he's thought up (or mumbled) something *he* finds funny, rather than waiting for any kind of acknowledgement.

Parched-dry wit, sly sarcasm, drop-and-run – these are his specialties, his targets chiefly being those of us inside the house. It's a humor that mostly orbits around putting his seven children in place. "Um, Dad," says a self-impressed teenaged Mark one Monday night at the dinner table, *faux*-clearing his throat in that obvious bidding-for-attention way, with an italicized announcement he thinks the rest around the table will envy, "I'm going *downtown* to a *concert* right after supper on Thursday, so I'm gonna need to eat *early*. So, can I eat *early*?"

Says Dad without a beat, "You can start now if you like."

That's our house with him at the helm. A sarcastic retort for every comment or question. Morning breakfast, teenaged exploits, adult plans and thoughts – his wit shellacs our every exchange. Years after Mom's gone, he'll be sitting in his small widower's apartment alongside visiting eldest son David, reviewing the day's mail, and he'll note the arrival of the formal invitation for youngest son Paul's upcoming Sonoma Valley wedding, planned for an area winery. Dad'll stare at the invite for a minute and then, to David, say, "Only in this family would my one son get married where two of my other sons can't attend." (Brothers David and Mark have their shares of addiction issues, but, proving his own genetically enhanced comedic mettle, David will follow: "Actually, Dad, that's not true. *Mark*'s the alcoholic. *I'm* the drug addict. If the wedding were held in a *pharmacy*, then I couldn't go.")

And then when the aging and deaf father-of-the-groom makes it from Philadelphia to the wedding, his wit intact, where to his dismay he sees that I have arranged a room for him that has captioned television, he'll decide he's insulted by the gesture, since as the hotel's lone unit government-mandated for the handicapped he's forced to deal with wall-rails and large-

13

print reading material and an elevated toilet, as well. ("Nice going with the room, Jim," he aims my way when I show up, before I can even say hello. "My legs dangle off the ground when I crap, it has a roll-in-shower the size of my apartment, and the bath-water comes directly from Fatima.")

I suppose that my parents would divide up The McKairnes Family Years into three eras, each according to a different shared address, all in Northeast Philadelphia: Sanger Street Days, in the mid-1950s, where they're apartment-living childless newlyweds, which lasts for about forty-five minutes; Oakland Street Days, which span the late 1950s into the early 1960s and where the first four children arrive over the course of three-and-a-half years; and Wellington Street Days, their third and last home together, which unfold from the mid 1960s through the late 1980s, where all seven of us are raised as a growing and school-bound and troublemaking brood trying to co-exist under one roof.

Home.

Here on Wellington, we seven are divided into two groups – the Older Ones, consisting of the first four born (David, Bernadette, Mark, James) and the Little Ones (Eileen, MaryBeth, and Paul, also born three-and-half-years apart after a child-free gap of four years in the early 1960s, finishing off the procreation portion of the marriage inside of a dozen married years). In such a full house, it ultimately falls to the first group to help out with the second. As in "Jim, can you go pick up the Little Ones at school?" or "Bernadette, can you help the Little Ones get dressed for sledding?" or "The Little Ones have to go to bed now; the rest of you can stay up another hour" or "I think only the Little Ones are going to go out for Halloween this year" or "Mark and David, go round up the Little Ones for dinner."

The three youngers come to detest the label, so ingrained in the family fabric that it endures well into our adult lives. Youngest sibling Paul, in fact -- and this may just be still about The Dishwasher Exile (don't bring it up) -- is quick to tell anyone who'll listen that not a half-hour after our mother's death in the late 1980s, her now-grown children are reflexively

5 Fri August 1960

7:30
8:00
8:30
9:00
9:30

Tonight's Television

CHANNEL 3—6:30, Cimarron City; 7:30, People Are Funny; 8, Wichita Town; 8:30, Masquerade Party; 9, Project 20; 10, News; 10:10, Weather; 10:15, Sports; 10:20, Movie.

CHANNEL 5 — 6:30, Walt Disney; 7:30, Man From Blackhawk; 8, Sunset Strip; 9, Detectives; 9:30, U.S. Marshal; 10, News; 10:15, Jack Paar; Midnight, News.

CHANNEL 7—6:30, Phil Silvers, 7, Queen Of Queens; 8, Detectives; 9, Project 20; 10, News; 10:10, Weather; 10:15, Jack Paar.

CHANNEL 8 — 6:30, Rawhide; 7:30, California Rodeo; 8:30, Follow That Man; 9, Twilight Zone; 9:30, Person To Person; 10, News; 10:10, City Report; 10:15, Sports; 10:20, Movie; Midnight, Movie.

CHANNEL 9—6:30, Rawhide; 7:30, California Rodeo; 8:30, December Bride; 9, Lock Up; 9:30, Person To Person; 10, News; 10:20, Movies; 1 a.m., News.

4:30
5:00
5:30
6:00

segregated into Those Who Could Handle the Funeral Details and ... the Little Ones, who were dispatched to the store for unneeded milk and bread.

To the untrained eye, our crowded-house tableau is rather conventional, typical of its 1960s-1970s era, not unlike every house on any block in this, The City of Neighborhoods. Large nuclear family, office-working father, housewife mother, neighborhood frenzy, ritual-laden Catholic church at its center. There's community feel, best friends by the score, holidays with still-in-the-area grandparents, winters of snow shoveling and summers of day-camp or the local public pool or the Jersey beach. Down the shore, around the block, up the street, on the corner, through the house, out the back, in The Drive, behind the school, over the mall – not a preposition goes unused.

Convention takes on a different shade inside, though. Seven kids, three bedrooms, three sets of bunk beds, two main bathrooms upstairs and a creepy half-bath in the basement for emergencies -- one packed three-level Philadelphia straight-through, built in the 1920s when our Mayfair community is as much farmland as residential tracts. The top floor? For sleeping and for bathing (gender-specific bathrooms) and for hormonally charged teenaged door-slamming. The bottom level, once dismissed as the dingy cellar before a 1973 remodel finds it rechristened The Basement? For watching the Bad (small black-and-white) TV and for horsing around and for bicycle repairing, as well as for the nightly drudgery that's unclogging the laundry-chute and for the late-night sneaking in after too much drinking at the high-school dance and for the spitting out of that god-awful angel-food cake that Dad insists I try at least once but which instead I tuck inside my right cheek to deposit later in the emergency toilet.

The main floor, though -- front-entry, living-room, dining-room, kitchen, all in a smooth line -- is where the action is: The meals, the Good TV, the entertaining of family guests, the twin Sunday rituals of newspaper-reading in the morning and recitation of the Rosary at night, the homework, the tossing of school-jackets on closet-doorknobs Where They Don't Belong, the smelling of incoming teenaged breath for those foolish enough not to use the basement entrance after a night out, the posting of the weekly chore-chart on the

refrigerator, and the general egress and ingress of nine people –
harder and harder to keep track of as we age that Mom
eventually institutes a sign-in system, Scotch-taped inside the
front door, with the last one home for the night in charge of
locking up.

It's also home to the large and formal dining-room
table reserved for special occasions and holiday dinners --
regular meals are eaten in the kitchen ("You kids eat like birds")
-- and on which, each and every day without fail, a greeting-
card of some sort can be found that marks the latest birthday /
anniversary / death either in the family or on the block. Each
of us is to add our signature as we pass through each morning
en route to the kitchen for breakfast. It's the first thing our
bleary eyes take note of, by rote, once out of bed and moving:
Wake, yawn, descend, sign, Cheerios.

Nine people, nine ways of thinking and living and being
and waking and sleeping. Nine moods and personalities.
Especially among the kids. Some of us solitary, some of us not.
Some of us reckless, some of us not. Some of us content, some
of us not. Some of us outsiders even inside our own home.
Maybe even inside our own skin. Each of us finding his way.
Or trying to. Supported / alienated / encouraged / enraged /
inspired by a mother and father who are parents first and
people with their own first names and personal needs rarely.

A routine weekday, with all of us in school and with
Dad still working before the deafness-causing Meniere's disease
he develops in his late 30s causes a forced retirement at 50,
begins around 7 a.m., with the kids being roused from bunk-
bed slumber, to varying degrees of success. (On weekends, we
get to sleep in, but not so late on Saturday that it's considered
slovenly or on Sunday that we miss Mass. Dad's selection of 9
a.m. on either day to power up the Hoover in the bedroom
hallway and to ram it accidentally and repeatedly into our
closed doors suggests his own personal definition. Reminder
though: No matter what time you rise on Sunday, you're to get
out of the house in time to be at Mass *as it begins* or you stay
home to await the next hour's service.) Synchronized shifts of
bathing, dressing, and eating follow. Little mingling is involved.
Little interaction. Little conversation. Little interest. For me,
there's only one must: Avoid being anywhere near eldest

brother David at the breakfast table, given his preternatural ability to chew with his mouth wide-open. I never do develop a taste for Wheaties given the amount of it I often see between his teeth.

It's the little things that unnerve me here at 3220.

By 8:30, we're each out the door and bound for school, in varying directions depending on the grade – except, of course, for Mark, still comfortably asleep under his cowboy blanket, not only having repeatedly hit an internal snooze-button during the ninety minutes since first-call but also having repeatedly ignored the subsequent pleas to get out of bed that I issue on the final walk-through of the house that Mom has me execute. The screaming his name, the kicking his bedpost, the shaking his very mattress – it's a routine employed approximately every single morning of the academic year. It's successful approximately never. Inevitably, it's up to Mom to engage the laws of physics (gravity) to tilt Mark's bed, and thus him, to the floor so that she can shoo him out the door.

Then with all of us gone to our respective schools (kindergarten, grade school, high school) and with Dad at work, Mom begins her own exhaustive day involving a lengthy to-do list uniformly compromised by the fatigue that comes from what she calls a mother's night's sleep of one eye always open and one ear always working. On the list: Cooking, cleaning, shopping, mending, laundry, calls, errands, repairs, and more -- chores that take time, take care, take a toll. If forced to guess, I'd say that the last time Mom has a full night's rest in her entire life falls sometime around Eisenhower's second inaugural.

Mid-day she's interrupted by the lucky few – me, for instance -- still dismissed home for lunch rather than banished to a school cafeteria. And she's at the ready with her pb&j on Wonder-white, with Hostess Ding-Dongs the chaser. On a good day, there's even permission for the lunch-er – still me, for instance -- to angle the TV-stand in the living-room toward the kitchen for viewings of Channel 12's *Zoom*. A bad day? Dad's home from work, and he's on lunch duty, the less-friendly menu featuring soup (*soup?!*) and the accompanying Wonder-white sandwich cut in that annoying diagonal way he favors rather than the more acceptable top-to-bottom way that the lunch-ers do. Me, for instance.

No TV. No Ding-Dongs. No fair.

Love Dad; hate his lunches.

Promptly at 3 p.m., the morning parade reverses, with the seven of us marching home from our respective academic prisons, stopping right inside the front door to offer Mom brief school-updates and then making hurried wardrobe changes for play Out Back. For a while in the early 1970s, the post-school routine also includes each of us, at one time or another, though my brothers will deny it, joining Mom to watch *Another World* on Channel 3, the hottest and most addictive soap-opera going. It's Mom's single daytime indulgence. The first to expand to an hour, the soap covers whatever sins we don't study in school. And why Lenore Curtain's supposedly loving first husband Walter framed her for a murder he himself committed or why her second betrayed her with that awful Carole Lamont I'll never understand.

Stabs at homework are made right before dinner, with us back inside and trading off workspace either in our shared bedrooms or at the kitchen table, which sees more schoolwork through the years than it does meals. So does Mom, helping with the same school-lessons night after night, year after year, as child after child moves up grade after grade, only to be replaced by another who brings home all the same assignments from all the same texts overseen by all the same teachers. Over and over again. (One afternoon well into the 1980s, Mom will, at last, fold under the repetition: Sitting in the kitchen, running her seventh and youngest through his academic paces, she'll drop her head into her hands mid-lesson, rub weary eyes, and with atypical blasphemy say to no one in particular, "Jesus Christ in heaven, I've been doing god-damned math homework since 1962.")

Between 5:30 and 6:00 each night, Dad's home, after which it's go-time at the dinner table ("You kids eat like birds"). Except for the forced recitation of the Rosary in the living-room every Sunday night, it really is the only time we're in one spot together. A nightly collection of limbs crossing and plates passing and vegetable-dropping and joke-tossing banter borne of the double helix that is a McKairnes. Except for the occasions when hard-working growing-harder-of-hearing Dad requires a calmer meal after a hectic day at the office, when we're told to keep ourselves in check by Mom who, at her end of the table and presumably out of Dad's lone-good-earshot, stares down at and pretends to study her plate, cautioning the seven of us through non-moving lips to "knock off the nonsense."

Years later, with Mom long gone, we'll tell Dad about these behind-his-back right-in-front-of-him asides, and he'll reply with a chuckle, "I heard every word she said."

Mostly deaf, I remind myself. Mostly deaf.

Our ears are on Mom, but our eyes -- mostly mine -- are on the butcher-block clock on the wall above the counter where the toaster rests, the time ticking down to 8 o'clock, the start of TV's prime-time. Beyond the undeclared but ongoing competition for Funniest in the House, the real intramural sport here at the table is the fight for the night's TV rights. Seven kids, seven entertainment preferences, one major dilemma. Who's going to get to watch what tonight – and on which TV? In our family's quasi-democracy, you have to call it if you want it, and the calls begin here.

Efficiency and timing are key. You can't be greedy, so no claiming a whole night just to watch a certain show on a particular set. Don't call too early or too aggressively, either, lest Mom and Dad become so frustrated with the in-fighting or with our small-screen dependence in general that they declare the television off-limits altogether.

"I call the Good TV at eight o'clock for *Kung Fu,*" says Eileen. The daily gauntlet is thrown.

"I call the basement TV at nine for the Flyers," counters hockey-fan Mark.

Two TVs. Two calls. First called, first viewed. It's how the rights are optioned.

Negotiations can and do follow, though, with deals usually sealed by dessert. Given my expanding TV needs as I age, I sometimes begin plotting my own calls, subversively, as soon as the milk is poured on the morning cereal. I'm always thinking, always calculating, always working the angles against the TV listings in my head. And I'm always wondering which TV will be the right one for me and my choices: The Good TV, which offers color luxury, or the small one downstairs, which promises seclusion. (The Good TV arrives in the late 1960s and assumes a living-room throne, relegating the aging and smaller set to the cellar, along with programming that Mom comes to see as more and more objectionable in changing times. In my Los Angeles encounter years later with producer Norman Lear – the man behind much of this grown-up fare, including *All in the Family, Maude, Hot L Baltimore, One Day at a Time,* and *Mary Hartman Mary Hartman* – I will tell him how *Maude,* for one, is forever banished from our living-room after its lead character refers to her husband as a "son-of-a-bitch." Quite shocking for the times, it's too shocking for Mom. "I don't want *Maude* in my living-room," is her simple incontestable edict. I'll repeat the line to Lear for amusement's sake, hoping that I don't offend. "Hardly," he'll say, with a smile. "Your mother remembered the name of the show, didn't she?")

With dinner done and the kitchen cleaned and the dishwasher stacked and the homework (both pre- and post-dinner) complete, the actual viewing begins. For me, it really is prime time in every sense of the term. Inevitably, the girls gather with Mom in the living-room to watch the lighter fare on the Good TV, and my three brothers assemble in the darkened basement to watch war-movies and sports. Me? I gravitate between the two.

Let's just say the ambiguity sets a tone.

(Dad busies himself paying the bills or making household repairs, then concludes his day with a slow perusal of the *Evening Bulletin* in the living-room, a cold bottle of Pabst Blue Ribbon – never a can -- sweating on the table beside him.)

And then, for a while, there's TV quiet the whole house over.

The long Wellington Street days begin to come to a slow close around 9 p.m., when the Little Ones are shooed to bed and away from whatever they're watching -- but only after being granted time to see coming-attractions for next week's episode. Younger brother Paul beats a retreat to the boys' room, where he'll be the first to slip in to one of its two sets of bunk beds. Younger sisters Eileen and MaryBeth are right behind him *en route* to the girls' room – severely cautioned each night as they do that they are to avoid disturbing already-retired and perpetually-exhausted older sister Bernadette, the lightest sleeper in our house (if not the state of Pennsylvania), whose slumber is never ever to be disrupted, lest the very rhythm of the planet itself be thrown off.

"Please remember to be quiet up there," says Mom, every night, as the two make their ways up the carpeted steps to the top floor. It's both a request and a warning, issued with experience. Mom once makes the mistake of poking her head into the sleeping girls' darkened bedroom late one night on her evening rounds, allowing the hallway light that is Bernadette's Kryptonite to spill across her bed. A shoe grazes her head.

Ultimately, with (most) everyone in bed for the night as the clock aims towards 11 p.m., the narrow Wellington Street living-room then converts to a expansive sanctuary for a mother of seven in search of her own daily allotment of calm. Mom tidies up the kitchen again, and then she sets her sights on her favored end of our well-worn couch to watch as *Action News* reviews another day that's sailed by without her -- a small glass of Port wine in one hand, a burning Pall Mall Gold in the other, Dad's evening paper on her lap. In doing so, she issues a quiet but full sigh that speaks volumes about the three meals and seven loads of laundry and multiple homework sessions and overall house-tending that make up her 18-hour generally complaint-free days.

I see it in her eyes, because I've stayed up, as well. And I feel it, too, her maternal fatigue and her general lot, in ways a young child probably shouldn't, in ways I will spend years trying to understand and to resolve. But rather than study and hold on to it for too long, I'm soon off to a nightly retreat of my own. I descend to the basement, my own sanctuary of choice, where I seek refuge from these and other thoughts.

In a black-and-white foxhole of my own.

*

September, 1974: Ford pardons Nixon in Washington, a plane-crash kills 70 in North Carolina, and a future Surgeon General famously separates conjoined twins in a Philadelphia hospital. Thirteen miles northeast of that landmark operation, a teenaged TV-devotee awaits the start of another new television season that'll mark his own kind of history.

Not just any new season: This is the Big One.

This September – itself a month that most teens approach with school-dread but which I long celebrate as the calendar's best (trumping even December, with its annual promise of holiday-fueled family détente) – brings with it the most anticipated and talked-about new TV shows in years. Maybe ever. The publicity drums are beating, the articles in the local papers are running, and people of all ages are wondering. And waiting. For Monday the ninth. Which is here.

It's time for the first episode of *Rhoda.*

I'm 14.

A comedy spun-off from the popular Minneapolis-set *Mary Tyler Moore* sitcom on CBS, *Rhoda* stars Valerie Harper as that show's husband-hungry and forever-weight-challenged upstairs sidekick Rhoda Morgenstern, now living on her own back in her native New York City. My whole family, if not the entire country (it'll be the first TV series to debut at Number One in the ratings), tunes in to Channel 10 at 9:30 p.m. to see her make the move. The social unity excites me as much as the prospect of the show itself.

It opens with Harper, in character as Rhoda, facing the camera, introducing herself to viewers ("My name is Rhoda Morgenstern...") in the same self-effacing and sardonic style that has made both the character and the actress so popular on the parent show since its own debut four years ago. " I was born in the Bronx, New York, in December, Nineteen Forty One. I've always felt responsible for World War Two."

It's a quick and quip-laced oral history, a primer for established fans and newcomers alike that recounts Rhoda's youth and what took her to the Midwest as a young adult and now what has brought her back to Manhattan ("New York – this is your last chance!"). As revealing as it is self-deprecating.

9

Mon September 1974

7:30
8:00
8:30
9:00
9:30
10:00
10:30
11:00
1130
NOON
12:30
1:00
1:30
2:00
2:30
3:00
3:30
4:00
4:30
5:00
5:30
6:00

Television

New 'Rhoda' Series Recommended

By ASSOCIATED PRESS

SEE THE BEST ON CBS TONIGHT ◎4

NEW NIGHT NEW TIME
Maude and Walter have a perfect love-hate relationship: she loves to win arguments and he hates to lose. Beatrice Arthur is the eminently audible Maude.

7:00
MAUDE

NEW SHOW
Rhoda's on her own with exciting new friends, a new job that's a hassle-a-minute, and a man in her life who creates a special brand of comedy complications. Valerie Harper stars.

7:30
RHODA

TV Highlights

Milwaukee Officials, Banks To Push Home Purchases

MILWAUKEE, Wis. (AP) — Milwaukee financial institutions and city officials are formulating an innovative program to stimulate inner city home purchases and financing.

Watching in our living-room, we laugh at the monologue. But one particular line, about Rhoda's childhood, more than gets me chuckling. It gets my attention. "The first thing I remember liking that liked me back," she says, "is food."

A private smile creases my face. One that has nothing to do with the character or the new show. Or food, for that matter. And everything to do with me.

In hearing it, I realize:

That's exactly how I feel about TV.

I love TV. And it loves me back.

Surely, I think to myself, as I lay sprawled out on our 1970s Tang-colored shag, that's not weird, is it? I mean, I'm not alone in feeling that, am I? Don't all of us who've been nursed on 1960s television – it being the go-to babysitting choice for our harried moms – have a connection to it? Carry with us countless overlapping memories of it from equally countless hours spent in front of it – fuzzy gray images of Good Guys and Bad, of soldiers and cowboys and doctors, of talking horses and flying nuns? Don't we all prize these mental remnants of a magical distraction that compel as they fascinate, to the point where our curious young eyes often lead us to check out whether the people seen on TV actually live in it, in the back?

That's who we all are, right?

We do, and it is.

But then again, I think to myself, which I do a lot of these teenaged days, there's a sizeable difference between interest and, well, *connection*. Between images tucked away in the recesses of memory and ones in there that actually still flicker with life. Between being merely aware of an upcoming show's debut and actually circling it on the kitchen calendar as a can't-miss reminder. Between liking TV and actually having it like you back.

In that, I fear, I am likely alone.

I really do sit down on nights like this, anxious with anticipation, and see TV as more reality than fantasy, more attraction than distraction. I really do turn to it as not just something to observe, but something to participate in. To be a part of. To get something from. Something, in fact, not just to turn on but turn *to*. To commit to. With serious affection and interest and involvement. As *Rhoda* begins, I sense the truth: In a house with eight other people to interact with, my chief relationship is with TV.

It begins many years ago -- when TV comes to me, I point out to myself, as a sort of rationale. When *it* asks *me* out. That detail seems important.

In September of 1966, *Bewitched*, a TV comedy about the marriage between a free-spirited modern-day witch and a straight-laced mortal, is one of the most popular shows in the country (and in my house). When it returns this month for a third season, it has a different look: Nodding to the times, it's no longer being shot in black-and-white. To herald the change, the star of the show, Elizabeth Montgomery herself, dressed in her full alter-ego witch's costume, pops up at the beginning of the Thursday-night season-premiere, looks into the camera, and offers this invitation:

"Stay tuned for *Bewitched*. Next, in color."

Sitting there watching this night, my 6-year-old self is wide-eyed.

Okay, I say to myself. *I will.* Thanks for asking.

Then a realization:

She's talking to us. To me.

Followed by a more transformative one:

They know I'm here.

TV as I know it changes. It's long had my attention. Now, it seems, I have its.

No longer a passive time-filler, television's evidently something that can involve me, ask something of me. To watch, to enjoy, to join in. In return, it offers something to me. Acknowledgement, company, support. Things in short supply around this crowded house. TV is recognizing me.

A relationship is born.

So now I'm there, for *Bewitched* and more. For *The Beverly Hillbillies* and its end-credit sequence, for instance, which now unfolds a bit differently for me each week: When Jed and the rest of the Clampetts emerge from the front-door portal of their California mansion at the end of each episode to thank us for kindly dropping in, it's me they're thanking. It's me that Granny is actually waving to during her weekly goodbye, as all those named credits pop on and off the screen, up to and including the moment where she uses her one free arm to support the tiring waving other one. And I'm there for *Batman*, when its narrator cautions at the conclusion of every cliff-hanging Tuesday-night episode to tune in next time to see how things resolve for the Caped Crusaders. I know it's me whose return he's encouraging. I don't know how he knows when I'm watching ("Same Bat Time!") or how ("Same Bat Channel!"), but he knows. And I appreciate that he's thinking about me.

I value the connection both with the shows and with the people in them. When Gilligan absent-mindedly thwarts yet another rescue attempt for his island-stuck fellow castaways, leaving poor Skipper to turn to the camera and roll his eyes in frustration, it's me the portly leader is seeking sympathy from. And I'm there for him.

I can't believe he did it again, either, Skipper. I just can't.

TV and I are speaking to each other.

Someday I'll learn that much of this is part of something called "breaking the fourth wall" – the theatrical device that finds actors directly addressing their audience. I'll probably even realize that my shows aren't the only ones on TV that are employing it. But they're the only shows I'm watching, the only ones that have gotten through to me, that have paid me heed, that have asked me to share. And I find comfort in the sharing. And in the asking. I like that Gilligan and the Skipper and Batman and Samantha and all the others in there are noticing me out here, acknowledging me, inviting me, thanking me, appreciating my loyalty. I like the reaching out, the asking of me to enter their space, the linking of our two worlds.

And so I stay nearby to both -- in the basement (mostly), waiting for connection (always). On point, watching and waiting. For Jack Lord to wish me goodnight at the end of every episode of *Hawaii Five-O* – but only after showing me scenes from his next episode ("Be There...Aloha"). And for the equally commanding voice behind *Dragnet* to tell me to stick around through the final commercials now that the show has ended to learn the fate of the week's criminals ("In a moment, the results of that trial"). And for the helpful narrator behind every Sunday installment of *The F.B.I.* to explain the nature of tonight's crime. And for that oversized animated eye that looks out from the depths of the genie bottle during the opening credits for *I Dream Of Jeannie* to wink at me.

Just me.

Which it does every week.

Yes, I'm here.

I stay there as often as I can, anyway: Mom and Dad sometimes impose a TV moratorium on school nights. But I try my best to maneuver around it: I need the daily dose of inclusion. And the more I watch the more I feel not just part of what I see, but of the process behind it. I'm compelled by the many pieces that seem to make up TV's whole -- the actors and the stories of course but also the various acts of the shows, the commercials, the coming attractions and other trailers and promos, the main- and end-credits and the differences among the elements of variety series and one-hour dramas and half-hour sitcoms.

My young mind reels. There's so much going on in there. Amid the distraction of weekly fun that comes with Lucy and Andy and Gomer and Lassie, with *McHale's Navy* and *Flipper* and *My Favorite Martian* and *The Flintstones* and *The Mothers-in-Law*, with both the *Man* and the *Girl from U.N.C.L.E*, with Daniel Boone and the Cartwrights and the men of *Rawhide* and *Combat*, with Ed Sullivan and the Smothers Brothers and Dean Martin, there's a whole other world revealing itself to me. A world to marvel at, to live in, to learn and dream about.

And to connect to -- in obvious and direct ways like being waved at or being reminded to watch, and in more subtle and indirect ways like with sly humor and toss-away jokes that I feel I'm alone in catching, crafted by people who seem to be having as much fun making their shows as I'm having watching them (and who know that I know that they know.) Which only makes me want to join them all the more.

Jokes like the kind found in a genre-stretching scene from the presumably silly yet alarmingly clever *Beverly Hillbillies*, featuring this exchange between dim-bulb Jethro Bodine and a con-woman named Emaline who lures him into helping her elude the police and then enlists him to craft a new identity for her:

Emaline: What I need is a city name.
Jethro [thinking]: Well, how 'bout Chicago?
Emaline: No, I mean a Christian name.
Jethro [thinking, then triumphant]: What about St. Louis?!

I laugh and laugh and laugh. As much at the thought of the writer conjuring up the exchange as at the joke itself. Clearly, I think to myself, there's some cleverness going on behind the bucolic nonsense of *The Beverly Hillbillies*. This silly fish-out-of-water tale can find itself on very dry land. And I for one, here in the basement of my Philadelphia rowhome, appreciate it. I appreciate the winks and nods, here and on *The Monkees* and on *Get Smart* and on *Hogan's Heroes*. The way they can live outside their lines. Satire's a word I don't know yet, either; but I do sense these and other shows are operating on two different levels, being broadcast with twin signals. I tune into each. Alone in my crowded house, alone with my crowded thoughts, there's an immersion underway. A growing sense of being in on TV.

If *The Beverly Hillbillies* whispers a cleverness and sophistication hidden beneath its broad strokes, I know that *Green Acres*, a comedy formed from one of its ribs, outright screams it. An inversion of that show's stranger-in-a-strange-land formula, *Green Acres* pops up on CBS in 1965, four years after the start of *Hillbillies*, mining its comedy not from Ozark rubes who move to Beverly Hills but from the idea of sophisticated Manhattan-ites transplanted to a tiny hayseed southern town. A parallel universe called Hooterville, this is a place that revolves around a sun of absurdity.

The show's an instant hit. I find it almost halfway through what will be its six seasons, at around age eight, its lunacy having mushroomed into flat-out comic anarchy. Any live-action TV series that roots itself in reality yet features a (subtitled) talking pig, which no one in the town finds at all strange, is more than worthy of my time. Black is white here in Hooterville. Up is down. And everyone on both sides of the TV screen knows it. Including me.

It's the kind of self-aware television that finds an eight-year-old tuning in each Wednesday night desperately hoping for one of the show's occasional scenes that begins with the brain-addled lead female character actually acknowledging the on-screen credits that appear at the top of the show:

> **Oliver** (in bed, to his wife, upon waking to
> see her sitting wide-eyed next to him, staring
> into space): "Lisa, why are you just sitting and
> staring like that? What are you doing?"
> **Lisa** (silly question): "I'm waiting for the
> names, Oliver. The names."

And sure enough, to her childlike wonder, up they pop ("Written by Paul Henning") -- but only after non-believer Oliver resumes his slumber, missing it. And I roll and roll in laughter on the floor. Here's a TV character that actually refers to the TV credits that I myself am seeing on-screen at home. *It knows it's a TV show!*

I feel in on the jokes, in on the action, in on the show. It feeds my appetite for more. Looking for it often, finding it only sometimes. Gems are like that.

The crowning moment of my search comes in February 1969, during an episode of the long-running ABC comedy *That Girl*, starring Marlo Thomas, the real-life daughter of 1950s TV star Danny Thomas. Called "My Sister's Keeper," the episode features Marlo Thomas's character scurrying down the hallway of a parish-church building and accidentally bumping into a priest. In a blink-and-you-miss-it unbilled appearance, the priest is played by a collar-wearing Danny Thomas. The resulting dialogue is this:

> **Ann**: "Excuse me, Father."
> **Priest** (smiling): "That's alright, my child."

And then each continues on.

Seven words. And once again I'm elated -- by the inside joke, by the blurring of the line between TV and reality, by the producers and writers tossing out a comic bone to the audience. One that evidently I'm to be the only one in my family who

30

cares to catch and then gnaw on. "Wasn't that funny?" I say as I look around my living-room. "It's her father, dressed as a Father, and she calls him 'Father'."

Nothing.

"Get it? Her father is a Father! And then the Father says 'my child' to her, and she's his child in real life!"

Silence.

My TV fascination is a solitary one. No one seems to share in my absorption of these moments, to plug into these moments of connectivity. Not to Elizabeth Montgomery's invitation; not to Lisa Douglas's anticipation; not to Danny Thomas's ordination. And I'm okay with that, I guess, maybe even embracing the isolation my immersion provides. I wonder what else is out there, or in there, just for me.

Then two things happen late in 1969 -- key developments as both my first decade and the world's latest come to a close -- that make the immersion complete. A pair of new TV shows arrives that fully drag me into and then behind the screen. One lasts much longer than the other, but each leaves a permanent mark.

The more successful one shows up on Friday, September 26, on the heels of a wealth of feature films and a rolling wave of TV series this decade, from *The Andy Griffith Show* years ago to the fall's fellow freshman comedy *The Courtship of Eddie's Father*, that redefine the concept of family at a time that it's evolving off-screen, too. A time of change. *The Brady Bunch* punctuates it. A light comedy about the blending of two single-parent families, it's maligned in the success it quickly finds (as it will be in perpetuity), but with its relatively more realistic depiction of TV family-life, its portrayals of easily resolved and relatable conflicts, its innovative focus on its young stars in equal measure to that of its adult cast, and especially with its fantasy suburban-house large enough to land a Cessna, I'm a fan from the start. More significant, so's every kid on my block.

Out Back where the various family-nations of Wellington Street gather to play, everything and everyone stops on Friday nights for the start of *The Brady Bunch*. It's must-see peewee TV, and all of us have to be there when the small-screen subdivides into those nine familial squares. It's a first for my young eyes -- this mass appointment-television to plan for and around and then to talk about after. Until now, TV is something I enjoy on my own in my basement or take in as part of a default family routine on the Good TV upstairs. But with *The Brady Bunch*, I'm seeing how television can be a collective experience, a national campfire around which many can and do warm their hands and hearts – especially with episodes like the Christmas one featuring young Cindy Brady asking St. Nick himself to restore her mother's laryngitis-affected singing voice in time for holiday services. ("He's better than a doctor, Daddy; he's San-ta Claus.")

I'm seeing the power of shared TV. The ability for TV to create community and to stir conversation. That it can unite, provoke passion. Not to mention generate no small amount of ire among loyalists whose father picks 8:22 every Friday night to come back from the supermarket with a week's worth of groceries in the paneled Ford station-wagon that the whole family is charged with emptying *right now*.

That I ever get to see how Bobby and Cindy find their ways in the Grand Canyon is a small miracle.

(Not insignificantly, *The Brady Bunch* also finds me further caught up in the business part of TV, too, when after watching it on Fridays I frequently sit down to watch *Mission: Impossible* on Saturdays to see that some of this drama's scenes take place in what is quite obviously the Brady living-room, despite attempts to disguise it with oversized houseplants and re-positioned furniture. Eventually, I sleuth out how and why by staying through to the end of the spy-show's closing credits, discovering that, like *The Brady Bunch*, it bears the Paramount Television logo, which means the two series are produced at the same studio and, evidently, on the same soundstage. So the re-purposing is understandable. But it's also annoying. Are we expected not to notice the telltale Brady staircase on another TV show?)

A week before *The Brady Bunch* unpacks on Friday nights to redefine the TV family sitcom and my own TV experience, another new series shows up that to my now-nine-year-old eyes redefines television itself. *My World and Welcome to*

It lasts not nearly as long (one season to the Bradys' five), but it resonates in a way that no other show has and that few others will as my love affair with TV grows.

Cut from a wildly different bolt of creative cloth, it's a comedy loosely based on the work and life of contemporary humorist James Thurber, and it stars William Windom as Thurber-esque writer-illustrator John Monroe, a husband and father with a rather conventional family existence. But Monroe's highly imaginative mind yields a life that's anything but. Much of the half-hour show, in fact, takes place in his head.

Whether he's trying to figure out his changing role in a changing world or how to help his daughter with her homework assignment on Robert E. Lee or merely greeting the morning milkman, whatever Monroe is doing (or thinking or feeling) often springs to life in fantasy sequences that employ an intentionally cheesy mix of live-action and animation.

It's emotion brought to surrealistic life. And it's as strangely hilarious as it is unusual -- made all the more so by the fact that it's only we the viewers at home who see the fantasy elements. They're meant just for us. Even better? Sometimes there's dialogue just for us, too. Some scenes feature Monroe talking *directly to the camera*, right in the middle of a conversation with others on screen, who *stand there unaware*. Verbal asides that only we see and hear.

Monroe is confiding in *us*. In *me*.

My World and Welcome to It breaks as many rules as it does fourth walls, up to and including the moments when John Monroe actually notes when the show he's in starts to fade to black in transition to a commercial break. "Wait, I'm not finished," he'll say to the camera. "Where you going?" Or "Okay. See you in a minute."

With its asides, with its only-for-us explanations, with its creative experimentation, with it very title, it actually calls for viewer involvement. No winks or nods or subtle nudges. The invitation is clear. It really is Monroe's world. And we really are welcome to it. I stand at the ready to oblige the invitation each week -- not just into John Monroe's life but also into the world of a TV series that knows it's a TV series.

With this comedy, I find myself fully inside the TV. And, as I look around, I like what I see. (Sadly, few others accept Monroe's invitation. *My World and Welcome to It* is one of the lowest rated shows on NBC. It's different; it's challenging; it's on against *Gunsmoke*; it lasts just 26 episodes. But it does win Best Comedy at the 1970 Emmy Awards for its lone season. It's my choice this year, too.)

Whatever promises television makes when it first asks me out in 1966 have been realized by the end of 1969. Now we're going steady. I like TV, and I feel very much liked back, rewarded with its company and attention, hope and inclusion. TV has come to make me laugh and to think and to be aware, to encourage me to feel and be exposed to others' feelings.

Small-screen emotions reach out to touch me -- the disappointment of young daughter Dodie on *My Three Sons*, fearful that the hand-made gift she's conjured up for her parents' anniversary doesn't match up to all the store-bought ones given from other family members; the crushing sadness behind *The Littlest Angel*, an eight-year-old new to Heaven, when he's allowed to return to Earth one last time to hug his grieving mother (a hug she senses but cannot see); the frustration felt by the heroes of the *Time Tunnel* as they're transported everywhere but home; the satisfaction behind another successful shift behind the wheel of *Adam-12* for Officers Reed and Malloy; the exhalation of relief that settles in when order is restored in the wake of mayhem conjured up by witches and genies and ghosts and Munsters and Martians across all of prime-time.

TV's an amazing place that exposes me to all these feelings, takes me to all kind of places, shows me all the ways it can unify, introduces me to all kinds of people who seem to care about one another (and about me). Clearly, this thing is a huge landscape of promise, of possibility. I roam its acreage, taking in every site. A switch has been triggered, a button pressed. I now have to be part of it all. I know there's something in there for me -- and out there, off Wellington Street -- as the rest of my life begins to unfold.

There's a calling. And I'm listening.

*

It doesn't happen every day, just often enough for it to be predictable. And often enough for me to say that I'm bothered by it. (Which I'm really not.)

I'm a year or two shy of adolescence, in a house that now claims three full-fledged teens. A house that feels more crowded than ever, if only because at least half of the nine of us are, I don't know, *taller*. A house where I nonetheless still feel as alone as ever, with thoughts and feelings and worries that are taking up more than their fair shares of room, too -- closing in on me with as much strength as I can find to bat them away. About the world and about myself. About stuff I don't understand and about stuff that I fear I do.

But when and where possible, I have TV, so I'm not really alone. I'm not entirely without aid or comfort or support or company. Where there is TV, there is escape. So I continue to escape into it. Often.

And that's why it happens.

Not every day but often enough for it to be predictable and for me to say that I'm bothered by it. (Which I'm really not.)

"Go find Jimmy and ask what's on TV tonight!"

The voice belongs to just about any member of my family, on just about any given night of the week – usually heard around two minutes before 8 o'clock, two minutes before the start of prime-time, with dinner long since over and with whatever homework of the day complete (or, on weekends, with whatever post-dinner games played Out Back at an end). It comes from the living-room, where the Good TV that's been exiled in silence on a cart against the wall for most of the day has now been wheeled to its more viewing-friendly angle in the middle of the room, warming up. And where my brother or my sister, or my other brother or other sister (or my *other* other brother or *other* other sister), or even my mother, is in a panic because the television supplement untucked from the two-inches-thick *Inquirer* newspaper each Sunday and then kept atop the set for week-long reference, as well as the TV-section of tonight's daily *Bulletin* -- picked up at the corner-store only an hour ago -- are both missing.

No one knows what to watch tonight, because no one knows what's *on* tonight. Here in the crowded house smack dab in the middle of the 3200 block on Wellington Street in the Mayfair section of Philadelphia's Great Northeast, chaos looms.

So the all-points-bulletin goes out house-wide:

"Go find Jimmy and ask what's on TV tonight!"

The clock on the living-room mantelpiece, centered directly under the Green-Stamps-purchased oil painting of a backlit Jesus, threatens 7:59.

"And hurry!"

"*Laugh-In* and *Gunsmoke* at eight," I yell from the basement, in response to the impassioned question thrown down at me from the top of the kitchen stairs. "And there's a special on Channel Six, so whatever's normally on isn't on tonight. It lasts an hour."

The hustle of feet is heard overhead, rushing from the kitchen back to the living-room. The news is relayed.

Downstairs, I roll my eyes.

"Weirdos," I say out loud to my young self.

Then I re-take to circling and reviewing the TV shows from both the *Inquirer* supplement and the *Bulletin* listings in my lap.

I pretend to be bothered by the nightly APBs, but I'm really not. If anything I'm irritated by the never thanking, not by the always asking. And by the marginalizing that comes with all of it (Jimmy = TV questions only). But I suspect that part's mostly my own doing. The asking part actually gives me a feeling of power at the center of attention, refreshingly different around here for me.

I do *know*, after all: I do study the listings and I do read the TV articles and I do watch the small screen incessantly. Intensely. I do crave and eat up all the information I can find about it. I do memorize the statistics and the trivia. Throw me a day, toss out a timeslot, I'll give you a title. (If needed, I can help with next week, too.) In this house, I *am* the *TV Guide*.

The continued small-screen devotion confuses some of those around me. Like my father, for instance, when I approach him with solemnity on a summer Saturday night in 1972 – I'm 11 – concerned about why after airing on Thursdays for as far back as I can remember ABC's *Bewitched* is now found on

Saturday nights opposite CBS's even-more-popular new-ish *All in the Family,* where it's getting crushed in the ratings.

> **Me:** "Dad, are they trying to kill *Bewitched* by moving it here, or is it already cancelled, so they don't care where they air it because it doesn't matter, since it's not coming back?"

> [Long pause]
> [Staring]

> **Dad:** "Shouldn't you be outside playing?"

Please. As if there's a point in *that.*

It strikes me as not at all odd that I'm not out there with my friends and family on this late-light weekend night, that I'm the only one I know who's inside squaring off against a Huge Television Dilemma that's forcing me to choose between favorites. Like school and homework and eating and sleeping, playing has its place. But, let's face it: TV, with all its promise, has priority.

Loyalty wins out: I choose *Bewitched.* But I'm right in my supposition that ABC has abandoned the long-running series. I later read that it has indeed been cancelled, and the network really is just running out its remaining episodes in the Saturday berth, the best bet it has against CBS's juggernaut. By September, *Bewitched* is gone, sentenced to rerun jail. And I join the entire country in making Archie Bunker my default choice on Saturday night.

Bewitched's diminishing returns alongside the meteoric ascent of *All in the Family* isn't lost on me, even at age 11. In fact, it reinforces what my vigil-like viewing has been telling me about TV: There's an evolution, a revolution, in the works, not just in material -- from broad to more realistic sitcoms – but in the power of TV to create passion, create conversation, create change, on a level bigger than here inside my house. The power to create mass viewing that will leave the kind of *Brady Bunch* commitment I notice only a few years ago in the dust. *All in the Family* opens my eyes. The Norman Lear-produced series is actually one of two new shows – the other being *Mary Tyler Moore*, which shows up four months before the Bunkers, during the same landmark 1970-71 television season -- that change what and how and why I watch as my double-digit years begin. With them, I begin to see that TV, sitcoms especially, can be more than something to enjoy, more than just a half-hour's worth of silly situations. TV can be *about* things. It can be about people and stories, not just circumstances. TV is in fact becoming more and more about storytelling. About *writing*. And in that relatable element, TV can unify, on a large scale.

For both shows, I surrender the isolation of the basement to join the upstairs crowd. Everyone in my family – everyone everywhere -- is watching Archie's and Mary's shows. If *The Brady Bunch* illustrates TV's potential to be a communal campfire, *All in the Family*, in particular, is a national inferno. And sharing it makes it even better. Funnier. For a half hour each Saturday night it also quiets life at 3220 as it puts all nine of us on a rare same page (which also makes it a minor miracle). Mindful of the daily din around here, that offers me peace as it gives me hope. TV is helpful that way.

All in the Family brings all of us to TV and brings TV into the real world. It's the first show to incorporate into its storylines what seem to be the simplicities of everyday life. The Bunkers' is a home we recognize, that we've been in. We cringe in familiarity as we laugh and (sometimes) cry, watching scenes unfold in one place, on one stage set, incorporating real conversations similar to the ones we pretend not to hear our parents have in other rooms of our own homes – about money and sickness and sex and politics and marriage. It's a whole new small-screen reality, down to the sound of TV's first flushing toilet.

Funny and popular and relatable though it is, however, *All in the Family* is also loud and caustic and angry. It pivots on conflict, my least favorite state. It also shoots on videotape, like the local news and the daytime soaps, to look and feel even more real, more *actual*. I watch; I laugh; I appreciate. But almost always I also squirm. It's uncomfortable. The show makes me nervous.

Mary Tyler Moore, on the other hand, which airs later in the night, is a more gentle experience, about people who co-exist more peacefully in an equally real world, more in support of one another. People who have lives they seem to enjoy. It fosters hope -- mine -- for a world in which we all get along, laughing as we do. Filmed, not videotaped, it allows for a softer on-screen look and thus a softer thirty minutes. I like *Mary Tyler Moore* better. Watch it more faithfully, more fully. I care more about these players than I do any other small-screen team. I'm stationed on the living-room shag every week for their show for every one of its 168 episodes from September 19, 1970, a month after my tenth birthday, to March 19, 1977, a few months shy of my 17th.

(Confession: I'm actually there for only 167 of the 168. On October 25, 1975, I succumb to teenaged curiosity and opt to skip the sitcom in favor of a scandalous and highly publicized movie airing on NBC's Channel 3 at the very same time, which we're told in school and at Mass not to watch -- *Born Innocent,* about a rebellious teenaged girl sent to a reform school where, among other abuses, she meets a certain plumbing-related fate. Fan of irony that I am, the lone episode of *Mary Tyler Moore* that I choose to miss in favor of it, a blacker-than-usual outing about death entitled "Chuckles Bites the Dust," is hailed by the *New York Times* as "the funniest half-hour in television history" and ends up winning multiple Emmy awards. I have to settle for the repeat.)

Mary Tyler Moore also deepens my burgeoning interest in the business end of TV. With each episode, I find myself taking note of and filing away the names of writers and directors and producers that come on screen in the opening and closing credits – more and more aware that TV is a product of work and effort. Of people doing stuff, not just actors saying stuff. I keep track of who's who and who does what. I like the way the whole creative team behind the show seems to be crafting a world that slowly unwraps itself to us a scene, an episode, a season at a time. Adding up to a distinctive whole. I see more evidence of a TV recalibration: Comedy is getting quieter, subtler, slyer. I see it more and more on other sitcoms around the dial -- "Dr. Hartley," says a handsome guy seeking counseling from shrink Bob Hartley on *The Bob Newhart Show* because he feels the world only notices him for his looks, "you have no idea what it's like to be incredibly good-looking" – but

I notice it chiefly on *Mary Tyler Moore*. Comedy is less obvious, mined more slowly. Sometimes even darker. Shows are employing humor, not jokes. More irony, more conversational sarcasm, more laughs crafted for the ears than for the eyes. Forced to help her boss out with a baby's birth when a friend goes into labor at her apartment, a panicked Mary Richards says, "...Mr. Grant – a delivery room is no place for a woman!"

Comedy is coming from interactions and conversation and even inflection, not necessarily situations and words. Courtesy of a influx of new young writers with a whole new approach to TV writing, characters are beginning to talk to, not at, each other -- just like real people do in real life. More subtext and grounded stories, episodes that play out in more organic ways. Characters develop over the course of episodes and seasons, with those behind the show trusting that we'll care enough to follow along and pay attention as to how. Eventually rewarding us for the time spent. Thus with *Mary Tyler Moore,* I come to admire and appreciate the quick wit that is Rhoda, the lost ego that is Phyllis, the happy naiveté that is Ted, the gruff patrician that is Lou, the common-man frustration that is Murray, the passive-aggression that is Sue Ann, the childlike wisdom that is Georgette, and all that is Mary, the calm in their imperfect storm. But I also come to see that each is more than what they bring to the situation of the week: Each is a real person, contributing to the telling of a real depiction of real and evolving lives.

I also see that the show is breaking ground in other more technical ways, too, from its regular use of establishing-shots -- city skylines, residential landscapes -- that denote scene locations (*Lucy* doesn't do that on a regular basis, nor do *Dick Van Dyke* or *Andy Griffith* or the other shows I'm familiar with) to closing-credit sequences that incorporate storyline footage from the just-ended episode -- a sort of summary of the show that I look forward to as much as the body of the show itself. It even features something that decades from now will be a sitcom staple -- living-credits, scripted action that continues the night's storyline under the crawl of usually-ignored end-credits. In the future, the technique will have a cynical use -- to keep viewers sticking around as long as possible through one show so that they find themselves by default watching the one that follows it. But here and now, it's employed because it's clever. It's funny. It's in service to the story. It's to entertain, not to manipulate.

These and other little things perhaps mean nothing to some, but they mean the world to me. They confirm that TV is made by people who seem always to be thinking of new ways to innovate, new things to bring to the screen, new ways to tell a story, new ways for me to have fun. These people really *are* having fun in there, I think. The kind of fun I wouldn't mind being a part of.

In my house, both *Mary Tyler Moore* and *All in the Family* are seen on Channel 10, our city's CBS station. It's the channel and network that more than any other (of the admittedly few there are these days) is fostering my relationship with TV. It just seems to be where all the good and popular shows *are*. Certainly it seems to be where most of them have always *been* -- from *I Love Lucy* and *Gunsmoke* and Ed Sullivan in the 1950s to *The Dick Van Dyke Show* and *The Beverly Hillbillies* and *The Andy Griffith Show* and Red Skelton in the 1960s.

Now it's overseeing a revolution, sparked by the arrival of the game-changing pair of the 1970-71 TV season and then fully lit late in 1971 when in a move to disentangle itself from what it sees are the weeds of older-skewing unsophisticated programming (leftover from the 1960s), the network cancels a litany of still-hit shows, ratings be damned. The *Hillbillies* and their spin-off kin (*Green Acres, Petticoat Junction*), the *Andy Griffith* sequel/spin-off *Mayberry R.F.D*, variety shows from *Hee-Haw* to *The Ed Sullivan Show*, even *Lassie* -- all gone, overnight, to make room for new shows and a new look and a new feel for a new decade. It's known as "The Rural Purge." The industry joke is that CBS is getting rid of any series with a tree.

Even the days of longtime untouchable stalwarts like Lucy and *Gunsmoke* are numbered. TV is now in the hands of a new generation of writers and producers and executives – the first to grow up with TV. Newer and edgier and younger and worldlier shows – *real*er series -- are becoming the aim and currency of prime-time TV.

Eleven years old, I don't fully get why. But I sense and am excited to be caught up in what seems to be a movement. I like the simple shows from the simpler 1960s, but I'm growing up as television does. I welcome the new fare and the new ideology washing ashore. That much of it springs from the now-powerful and in-demand producers and writers behind *All in the Family* and *Mary Tyler Moore* helps.

From the Norman Lear factory, I discover, like the rest of the country, *Maude,* then *Good Times,* then *The Jeffersons* and *One Day At a Time.* Back to back to back to back hits, it's a remarkable string of shows that comes in a four-year period. They're all videotaped to reflect that everyday look; each is about what my young eyes and ears take to be consistently provocative issues. I don't always get the political references in *All in the Family* or the racial ones in *Good Times* or the sexual ones in *One Day at a Time* or the social ones in *Maude* (a show I really don't even know to watch until we're told at Sunday mass not to, by boycotting its famous abortion episode). But I know I'm watching Big and New. I realize change is taking place. I get that TV's reach is now extending beyond its grasp.

Likewise, I ferret out any of the new stuff on Channel 10 marked by the meowing MTM Productions logo that accompanies *Mary Tyler Moore.* It's blazing new trails, too, just less in anyone's face about it. The thriving production company is offering smart and character-driven writing -- on film, not videotape, just like that seen in the mother-ship show. Writing that encourages viewers to come to and *discover* the comedy rather than just sit back and have it handed to them, as sitcoms have long done. Less topical, they're less controversial as a result, though it's obvious even to me that single Rhoda's not a virgin and that Bob and Emily Hartley enjoy their marital bed. Standouts do include *Rhoda* and *The Bob Newhart Show,* but lesser lights like *Doc,* too, if only for this sole line from the short-lived sitcom, from a confused first-time dad who thought his pregnant wife would be delivering twins, right after the arrival a lone baby girl: "Just the one, Doc? Have you checked everywhere?"

With my consciousness raised and my interest stoked (and my homework usually done), I'm a TV-watching machine the whole week long: I'm learning more, watching harder, digesting fuller. Sometimes with family members, sometimes alone, I'm tracking who and what I see on the small screen, how it plays off-screen in the newspapers and among my friends, sifting and sorting through and filing away the storylines and the names that crawl by. The crime-solving on Sundays (*Mannix, Kojak NBC Mystery Movie*), the comedies on Mondays (from *Here's Lucy* or *Doris Day Show* early in the decade to the empowering trifecta of *Maude / Rhoda / Phyllis* in later years, TV's female leads changing as women change in real life), the made-for-TV movies on Wednesday and Thursdays that always star familiar TV faces moonlighting from their day-jobs, the family magnets on Friday (*The Brady Bunch, Donny & Marie*) – I'm there for all of it.

But it's Saturday that serves as the divining rod in my TV education. It leads me to the best of television, ground zero of the ongoing revolution, wave after wave of 1970s reform, all of it on Channel 10. I study it, appreciate it, consume it. *How does all this great stuff get here?* I wonder. *Who and what is behind it?*

From stem to stern, from opening- to closing-credit sequences of each series, from the transition into and out of and between shows to the commercials that break them all up, I don't dare look away. I take it all in. I'm starting to see how it all fits into something called a TV network, how each piece represents parts of a greater whole, with a brand or identity or connection that link the series to each other and that connect to viewers like me in the process. I notice how it uses the linchpin comedies (*All in the Family, Mary Tyler Moore*) to secure the 8 o'clock and 9 o'clock hours and then to support newer or weaker comedies that it places after them (*The Bob Newhart Show* and *The Jeffersons* and *Doc* and *Paul Sand in Friends and Lovers*). And how it caps off the night with its prestigious *Carol Burnett* variety series, resulting in a three-hour block of comedy that locks in viewers for an entire night.

It's a successful strategy year after year and season after season these heady days, no more so than in 1973 when the network assembles its five most acclaimed series – *All in the Family, MASH, Mary Tyler Moore, The Bob Newhart Show*, and *The Carol Burnett Show* – to air back-to-back. A line-up so stellar that at the Emmy Awards towards the end of the season virtually every comedy-related statue goes to a show from this night (fourteen total). A landmark achievement, featuring artists and other craftspeople working at the heights of their powers and talents, the lineup is anointed "TV's Greatest Night" – a title it will still hold decades from now. Taking it in each week, I know I'm watching history.

No longer just a viewer of individual series, I'm now seeing the pieces that make up prime-time programming strategies, by people who seem to be charged with thinking them up and then executing them (and getting paid for it). Strategies not just for excellence or survival but also for victory. For bragging rights. Each of the TV networks wants to have the most viewers. And they employ these strategies to get them. CBS does so well on Saturday, in fact, -- a night on which it plays from strength and scores the most points -- that it leaves only defense for the other networks to play. The formula becomes clear, maybe even simple, certainly fun to follow and analyze. The programming and counterprogramming, the zigging against the zagging, the use of existing shows to launch and promote new shows, the race to grab uncommitted viewers – high-stakes thinking, all around, it seems. A high-stakes popularity contest.

But in the night-by-night three-network race that is the TV popularity contest, appeal can be transitory. Take Friday, for instance, where longtime favorite *The Brady Bunch,* ABC's strong night-opener, luring viewers to come for it first and then to stay for the night, is being challenged by newcomer *Sanford & Son,* on NBC's Channel 3. Personally, I hate the Redd Foxx comedy. Too much conflict and scenery chewing, too many unappealing characters, a setting I don't care about and situations I can't relate to. But I understand why it's a hit: Not only is it another timely effort from the Norman Lear factory, it's the ultimate zig opposite the wholesome *Brady* family zag. And I get more than a little excited when it starts to become the timeslot's bigger draw -- bigger than *The Brady Bunch* ever dreams of being – and thus eventually starts to lift NBC as a whole from also-run to victor on the night.

Clever scheduling and careful strategy add up to success. Even I join the exodus from ABC for a period, though my boycott of *Sanford and Son* means I don't cross over to Channel 3 until *Chico and the Man* starts at 8:30. Once there, though, I'm on board for the rest of the night -- staying tuned for *The Rockford Files* and *Police Woman* and, later, on non-school-nights, *The Tonight Show*. I never have to switch the dial. Smart thinking, NBC. On Fridays in 1974, this is the place to be.

(It's also the dumb place to be a few years later, offering up offer a telling lesson in what seems to be the nuttiness that can be the TV business, even to my outside-the-business eyes, when after the death of the 23-year-old star of *Chico and the Man*, Freddie Prinze, from a self-inflicted gunshot wound mid-way through the show's third season, NBC decides to continue with the show anyway. Prinze, who *is* the very show, is replaced by an unknown and unproven child actor, also Hispanic and also to be called "Chico" -- because that nickname can apply to "any Latino boy," we're told in the press. Thankfully, whether uninspired by the change or offended by the racism, America never really takes to the revamped show or to the new Chico opposite the old man, and the comedy is soon cancelled.)

The viewer in me is at the head of the well-stocked TV table these days, enjoying the banquet; the business-curious side of me sees all the food and can't learn enough about how it's made and where it comes from. Mid-decade, though, a seismic shift upends the whole restaurant.

It begins slowly, in the early months of 1974, when I'm in the eighth grade. First, inside of the same month and airing in the same timeslot, ABC and CBS introduce similar-sounding family sitcoms -- *Happy Days* and *Good Times*, respectively. The optimistic titles and the shared Tuesdays-at-8 berths are the only things the pair have in common, however: *Happy Days* is soft-focus nostalgia show, shot on film with a single camera (no live audience), about a WASP-y Milwaukee family living and thriving in the 1950s; the grittier *Good Times*, videotaped in front of a studio audience, with a multiple-camera setup, from (no surprise) Norman Lear, is about the barely-getting-by black family living in a modern-day Chicago housing project.

Talk about zig meeting zag.

I gravitate towards *Happy Days*, if only because 14-months-older brother Mark reports that the premiere episode talks about hickies (whatever *they* are). But both shows find an audience, albeit a modest one.

A year-and-half-in, though, after a successful one-time experiment with shooting in front of a live audience, *Happy Days* changes its format permanently to multi-camera. It also promotes the thus-far supporting character of Fonzie, who has started to gather a following, to a starring role. The result is that the show morphs from a moderately successful sitcom to huger-than-huge ratings bonanza, becoming the Number One show in the country.

I'm hypnotized, not by the episodes themselves (fun and relatable but mediocre at best) but by how wildly popular they now are, seemingly overnight – in my house, on my block, around the country. Lines are being repeated Out Back. Cast lunchboxes pop up at the store. Fashions change to ape the show's nostalgia. And characters on the series are getting wild applause from the studio audience just by *entering* a scene, not even having said a word. I've never seen this before in all my years watching TV. There's something about the way the new format is creating intense relationships between its cast and its audience, both in the studio and then at home. Such unity and connectivity. (*Happy Days* reinforces in my eyes how important and necessary live audiences are for most comedies: The live laughter coming at us as we watch in our homes enhances and enriches our own, creating that communal experience that I think TV is envisioned as. Famous film-producer Walter Mirisch says, "Movies don't exist in a vacuum; they exist in conjunction with their audience." I find myself feeling the same way about sitcoms.)

Happy Days becomes so successful that, naturally, it almost immediately leads to a new cousin-comedy called *Laverne and Shirley*. It, in turn, becomes TV's *second* most popular show. (These are becoming the Days of the Spin-off: With *All in the Family, Mary Tyler Moore* and now *Happy Days*, the concept is becoming a powerful new source of TV success – and revenue.) Juggernauts each, *Happy Days* and *Laverne and Shirley* are paired back-to-back on Tuesday nights. Now watching *both* is a way of weekly life in the country. And suddenly everyone is talking about and watching ABC instead of longtime national favorite CBS. I can feel the ground moving beneath me, the shift is so big. TV habits are changing, and so are TV fortunes, the news tells us, with reports coming in that perennially low-rated ABC – the network that spawns the 1960s joke that all President Johnson needs to do is put the endless and divisive Vietnam War on ABC and it'll be over in thirteen weeks -- is now TVs newest powerhouse.

I'm spending even more time in the periodicals room of the nearby Northeast Regional Library tracking it all -- seduced by the business behind the business as ABC launches hit after hit from its perch, amazed to see how TV success can be built on the back of a single hit. Happy days indeed. When copies of *Time* or *Newsweek* are passed around in History class for us to read about and then to discuss, my eyes go first to the Table of Contents for entertainment stories. Never mind Capitol Hill. Tell me about TV. About the *Kojak* trial. About executives like Grant Tinker and producers like Aaron Spelling. These are *my* current events.

And at the center of the storm is the biggest name of them all – that of Fred Silverman, the rock-star architect of ABC's ascension. It's foremost in my mind with anything I read at school, at the library, at home. In bold print everywhere, the man behind the name is crowned the king of all prime-time, and I'm fascinated that TV is his *job*. The stuff I think about all the time at home? The picking and scheduling of TV shows? The dreaming up of spin-offs? The fostering of a network *brand* and creating nightlong blocks of TV shows night after night? That's work? He gets paid to do all that?

In joining the exodus over to ABC, I feel a bit guilty -- that I'm cheating on CBS. But the lure really is seductive. ABC is hosting a nightly party these high-school days. It's a happy place to be, a whole new destination with all-new people and all-new kinds of fun. *Welcome Back, Kotter* fun. *Charlie's Angels* fun. It marks a break from the realer worlds found on the other channels.

Somewhere in all of this, I do tend to school. I do have homework. I do fulfill my non-academic family obligations – getting the trash to the front curb each Wednesday night for Thursday morning pick-up, shaking Mark awake on school mornings, triple-checking each night before bed to ensure that the basement space-heater and the kitchen stove are each shut down for the night, worrying and analyzing in general. But none of any of it has the hold on me that TV does. Comedy, variety, hour-long dramas, movies – it's all good.

For a while in the winter of 1976, the whole house joins me at the party, at least on Monday nights. Everything stops inside our four walls – as it does across the country, leading to reports of deserted streets and early restaurant-closings -- for a new form of TV called the mini-series. A full year before *Roots* makes the term a household word, *Rich Man Poor Man* rivets us to our seats, all nine of us, as it spills the sordid secrets behind the rise and fall of the Jordache family. Mom and I are its most ardent fans. We watch every installment during its eight-week run – routine for me but nothing short of a miracle for Mom, given her endless to-do list as well as her distaste for being a slave to TV. To offset the venial sin that is her appointment-viewing, Mom reserves all her sewing chores for Monday nights, darning away as the show unfolds.

It becomes our weekly ritual in front of the Good TV: I sit in the rocker by the non-functioning fireplace; Mom settles in to her usual end of the couch, hands fast at work color-coding her four boys' socks and T-shirts -- sewing single threads of different hues into the labels of our various whites to ease post-laundry sorting.

I like the alone time with her, the sharing-an-experience time, even if it does center on television. Or maybe because it does. Connection without intimacy. That's how it's done here – at least for me. Real life experienced through the reel one. Olivia Walton's miscarriage, Brian Piccolo's cancer, Lou Grant's divorce and Ted Baxter's infertility, Mike Stivic's impotence and Mr. Brady's sex change, Richie and Potsie's friendship -- life experienced and explained by way of the small screen.

All of it except for the tough stuff, anyway. The landmark gay episode of ABC's new drama *Family*? The one in which teenage son Willie's best friend comes out to him after years of private turmoil? The one that the network buries during the "dark week" between Christmas and New Year's Day when fewer people are watching television, and thus, fewer might become aware of and bothered by its frank and sympathetic portrayal of homosexuality? I watch that in the basement, alone. Just as I seclude myself down there four years ago to watch the even more revolutionary *That Certain Summer,* a movie about an actual gay relationship between two adult men. I'm compelled and fascinated by both pieces, as I am by the few other attempts, such as *Steambath* on something called public television, to cover the topic in these my teenaged years. Curious, too. But I'm alone in my curiosity, as alone as I am in my skin and with my thoughts. So I watch alone, a fleeting sense of solidarity as I do, though – which disappears as abruptly as the images themselves when I shut off the set. More confused than ever.

I guess I could take my questions about life's issues Out Back. That's where I get all my other explanations for the stuff on TV that befuddles me -- and about which I know I won't learn inside my house. The references to Gloria's "playground" being closed during her pregnancy on *All in the Family*, what it means when Rhoda tells her sister that she's late, why Richie Cunningham gets excited when Potsie tells him the new neighbor is "hot-to-trot", what exactly is being referred to on *The New Dick Van Dyke Show* when the young daughter "walks in on" her parents, the underlying bigotry behind the comic tension of *Bridget Loves Bernie*. But I don't think the subject of homosexuality is going to get its due here in the driveway amongst my friends. There's danger even in just broaching it: If you ask, you are.

Television is my primary educator, and I've got nothing but time to learn, because these days TV really is just about all I do. Not only does it continue to offer the connection and company it always has, now it offers protection, too.

Not unlike Willie's friend from the controversial *Family* episode who opts to cope through isolation, I close myself off, too, using TV as my walls. Isolation both for myself and *from* myself, perhaps. I rarely even leave the house from ages 13 to 16. My view of life is one seen in the black-and-white shadows of the Wellington Street basement. I do join in some of the family viewing upstairs on occasion. Some of it's inevitable. Some of it's even enjoyable. But mostly I isolate.

Viso, ergo sum.

I watch, therefore I am.

Or I'm not, depending.

The result? Beyond the safety? A brain swelling with small-screen information and facts. ("Go find Jimmy and ask him what's on TV!") Dates past and present. A charting of the rise and fall of every show and their every writer and producer. A personal home-scheduling board with my own network line-ups, replete with strategies and promotions. A mental file of main-titles and end-of-show credits and theme music and production logos. A nightly private prayer that a series or a movie end a few minutes short of its allotted timeslots so that leftover minutes be filled with coming-attractions for still more programming. And an all-out panic that greets Premiere Week each September, with a bacchanalian-esque private consumption of *TV Guide*'s Fall Preview edition that for some reason I purchase in secret from a corner-store outside my neighborhood and then bury for safekeeping beneath the red-threaded Fruit-of-the-Looms in my dresser drawer.

Using my unwieldy and primitive-looking new reel-to-reel tape recorder –roughly the size of a TV-set itself -- I supplant my small-screen fascination by audiotaping shows, sitting Indian-style on our living-room floor in front of the Good TV with the recorder's hand-held microphone aimed towards the speaker. All so that I can re-visit whatever I'm watching an hour later in bed. *The Poseidon Adventure* loses none of its punch coming through my pillow later on the night ABC brings it to TV for the first time ("You see, Mr. Scott? In the water I'm a very skinny lady").

I watch as successes yields successes, trends beget trends, hits spin off hits, ideas launch and fly, concepts crash and burn. I watch the fat crime-solver (*Cannon*) and the bald crime-solver (*Kojak*) and the blind crime-solver (*Longstreet*) and the sloppy crime-solver (*Columbo*) and the unlikely crime-solvers (*Charlie's Angels*) and the middle-age sexy crime-solver (*Police Woman*) and the senior crime-solver (*Barnaby Jones*) and the cowboy crime-solver (*McCloud*) and the Agatha Christie crime-solvers (*The Snoop Sisters*) and the *noir* crime-solver (*City of Angels*) and the Alaskan crime-solver (*Kodiak*) and the supernatural crime-solver (*The Night Stalker*) and the Nick-and-Nora crime-solvers (*McMillan & Wife*) and the forensic crime-solver (*Quincy*) and the real-world crime-solver (*Serpico*) and the high-tech crime-solvers (*S.W.A.T.*) and the reluctant crime-solver (*The Rockford Files*) and the wheelchair crime-solver (*Ironside*) and the motorcycle crime-solvers (*CHIPS*) and the mystical crime-solver (*Kung Fu*).

I watch as families live through the Old West (*Little House on the Prairie, The New Land*) and the Great Depression (*The Waltons, The Family Hovak*) and the 1950s (*Sons and Daughters*) and the far-off future (*Logan's Run, Planet of the Apes*). I watch the superhero shows like *The Six Million Dollar Man* and *The Bionic Woman* and *Wonder Woman* and *The Amazing Spider-Man* and *The Man from Atlantis* and *Gemini Man*.

I watch the series based on or inspired by movies, like *Bob & Carol & Ted & Alice* and *Paper Moon* and *Alice* and *Logan's Run* and *Alias Smith and Jones*. I watch as *Network* begets *W.E.B.*, *Star Wars* begets *Battlestar: Galactica*, *Chinatown* begets *City of Angels*.

I watch the shows that are trying to cash in on both the times that are (*The Mod Squad, Room 222, Getting Together, The Bold Ones, The Girl with Something Extra, Lucas Tanner, Get Christie Love, Carter Country, The Sixth Sense, Project UFO*) and the hits that be (*Beacon Hill*, straining for shades of *Upstairs Downstairs; Flying High*, straining for shades of *Charlie's Angels; Buck Rogers in the 25th Century*, straining for shades of *Battlestar: Galactica; Supertrain*, straining for shades of *The Love Boat;* and *On Our Own*, straining for shades of *Laverne and Shirley*).

I watch as the variety-series, introduced at the dawn of television, starts to die a slow death as tastes and times change and against the rise of a whole new kind of comedic sensibility that springs from late-night TV in the form of *Saturday Night Live.* I watch as comedian after comedian is recruited to bring his star wattage or his stage persona or his sizeable following to weekly TV – some succeeding (Redd Foxx and Freddie Prinze and Jimmie Walker and Gabe Kaplan) and others failing (David Brenner). God help me I even watch *The Brady Bunch Variety Hour* and *Saturday Night Live With Howard Cosell*.

To a single one, they're all important to me -- beginning to end, top to bottom, front to back. They speak of and about the TV business, how creators and producers and writers and network executives think – how being derivative is sometimes as successful as being innovative, how sometimes trends are set and at other times they're followed, how sometimes it really is best to zig where others zag.

And if I'm avoiding learning anything about me or my life or even the world in the process, I remind myself that it's not as if there's no learning going on at all with my TV consumption. After all, I'm the only one in my house who's developed PBT (Perfect Break Timing) – the art of knowing just how long to be away from the TV during a commercial break without missing a single frame of a show.

At 16 I'm introduced to the real world outside the basement when I acquire both a part-time job to go to (at the local brand-new McDonald's, the first all-electric franchise in the whole of Philadelphia) and a group of friends to hang with (high-school classmates from the neighborhood), but I still seem to view it through the prism of the small screen. I'm amazed – shocked, at 16 -- to discover that unlike the good and chaste girls I see on TV my female McDonald's colleagues, well, aren't much of either; and I often lament to my new social circle that it's a shame we don't seem to be having the kind of adventures "that Richie and Potsie and Ralph have."

The curtain that exposes the real world with these twin developments is parted even wider around this same time, when I enter my senior year at Father Judge High School ("A Tradition of Excellence!") and the second-floor classroom reserved for the English-course elective "The Written Word and the Moving Picture." It's the talk of the school, if truly the bane of the Philadelphia archdiocese if the stories are to be believed, due to its incorporation into the syllabus of contemporary music and sometimes R-rated movies. It's a back-door means of getting indifferent 17-year-old minds interested in reading and writing. (And if only the Philadelphia Archdiocese knew just which of the complained-about nude images of co-stars Olivia Hussey and Leonard Whiting in Zefferelli's *Romeo and Juliet* were the ones of chief interest to me.)

It's a sort of re-booting of my life. Each afternoon, I race to the second-floor, anxious to see whether our blue-plastic wood-veneer-surface-top desks are facing towards the front of the room where giant speakers rest (thus signaling we'll be listening to Top 40 music) or towards the back wall where a silver screen is hung (thus signaling a movie's on the docket). I'm good with either. Music and movies each fuel my passions, make me come a little bit more alive. Anything with stories and images. Listening to The Band or Joan Baez or Kansas or Aerosmith, dissecting the lyrics of Bernie Taupin or Paul Simon, uncovering the backstory of and then discussing the messages in *Inherit the Wind* or *Slaughterhouse-Five*, researching the making of *Gone with the Wind*, parsing *West Side Story*'s re-telling of Shakespeare – it's all an education. It's all about examining the impact of language, the resonance of words and images, the value of storytelling.

SECONDARY SCHOOL SYSTEM OF THE ARCHDIOCESE OF PHILADELPHIA

REPORT CARD	MCKAIRNES JAMES JOHN					FATHER JUDGE HIGH					1977/78
	3220 WELLINGTON										
784150	PHILA		PA 19149	A09		MATT11461					
STUDENT NUM.	NAME			HOME ROOM		PARISH					
SUBJECT	TEACHER	FIRST	SECOND	SEM.		THIRD	FOURTH	SEM.	FINAL		
		GRADE COM.	GRADE COM.	GRADE		GRADE COM.	GRADE COM.	GRADE	GRADE		
WR WD&MOV PIC	2 CONNERY	96	98	98	96	96	98	97			

The course also provides structure and clarity for the abstract world I've been immersed in all these many years at home. Its analyses of the business behind all this entertainment brings understanding of and increased appreciation for how TV and movies come to *be*, how (and where) it all comes together. It tells me so much more about how the words and the images have people and jobs *behind* them. And how the work in their world affects me in mine. It's not just the best class of my senior year; it's the most rewarding of any in all my time in school. Time that's fittingly coming to a close. In my 18th year, The Written Word and the Moving Picture invokes a life for me, brings it into focus, shows a future in which the fantasy that's been TV speaking to me for so long now can, in fact, become reality.

An image comes to mind as I close in on my June graduation. It's a TV image, of course, carved from the memory of sitting with my father to watch Jackie Gleason's long-running variety show in the 1960s-- Saturday nights, right before *My Three Sons*.

Every week, I watch as the Florida-produced show begins with a dramatic main-title sequence, opening with the camera far out over the silent Atlantic Ocean and then, accompanied by a hint of anticipatory music, starts a slow move to shore just above the surface of the water, picking up speed as it skims the waves, the music building as the camera gets closer to land, a crescendo forming, until with a smash of timpani it finds the beach and then dramatically shoots upward into an azure-blue sky, where we see the show's title spelled out in big bold letters and hear an announcer say:

"From Miami Beach, it's *The Jackie Gleason Show!*"

Approaching my final days in school, I feel a similar rush to land, a similar sweeping that's taking me to the shores of a new world – one that my senior year has told me is as real as the passion I feel for it. I've been watching and studying and reading and learning about and communicating with TV for as long as I can remember. Wondering more and more as I age, and with increasing intensity, how my life could include still more of it. How *it* can include more of *me*. Now, I feel ready to find out. To see if everything In There is actually Out There for me. A timpani smashes in my ears as I graduate Father Judge High School for Boys. I look upward to an azure-blue sky for a sign that it will welcome me in big bold letters.

And I move to Hollywood.

Four thousand seventy six days later.

*

The eleven years that separate high school from Los Angeles are neither the result of my not being ready for the move (though I'm not) nor of my not knowing how to accomplish it (though I don't). They're more about life. And how it has a tendency to happen. About how we often find ourselves in places we don't foresee. Places where we're likely meant to be instead of where we plan to be, doing other things we're evidently meant to be doing. At least for a while.

Like Temple University, for instance, at 18, for a journalism education, when out-of-state and away-from-home translate to beyond our means, and I find myself staying local for college instead, commuting daily from Wellington Street to the urban jungle of North Philadelphia some eleven miles away. Still bunk bed bound at night. The result is a schooling that ends up exceeding my expectations thanks to what turns out to be one of the nation's premiere media programs.

I am meant to be here, so that I can have that.

Or like the large Philadelphia-area retailer called Clover, for a part-time job that I turn to at the start of that education and to last for all of it, because financial need demands it. Which finds me working alongside my now-full-time toiling mother, herself a newbie to the recently opened place. The result is extra time with her, richer days, some of the best, in fact, of what will be our 27 short years together as parent and child, her clock ticking down as it is, unbeknown to all of us. A gift not every child gets — to know a parent as a colleague, to experience a mother with a name and an identity other than the one used and seen at home.

I am meant to be here, so that I can receive that.

Or like Hahnemann Hospital in downtown Philadelphia, for example, for the unlikely surgery that comes my junior year, when complaints of fatigue and weight-loss lead to a battery of tests and then to exploratory surgery at the direction of an alarmist and somehow-licensed family doctor who tosses off the prospect of cancer to my frightened parents. The result is a non-issue as pertains to the disease, but a life-changing experience in that I almost lose mine at the barely there age of 20 due to a massive recovery-room infection, followed by a four-day vigil of torment for both me and my family -- only somewhat mitigated by incidents of comic relief, the first coming in the form of a bored and disinterested orderly who enters my room before my procedure, where I rest alone, with instructions for me to change into a paper gown he hands me and then to *void* before surgery, which paralyzes me with fear since I have no clue what the word means ("Just piss, man," he says to me with an impatient sigh when I meekly, and finally, after four minutes, ask from my side of the bathroom door. "Just piss"); and the other in the middle of my coma-like recovery from the infection, as my mother pitches in to help the nurse change the linens of my fever-soaked bed but only after first using the soiled ones to strap me to a nearby chair to wait out the change, lest my limp and semi-conscious form slide to the floor, which it does the first two times she deposits me there. I'll always wonder the thoughts of those walking past my room at that particular moment, looking in from the hallway to see an unconscious patient tied by his sheet to a chair -- head down, outstretched arm tethered to an IV-pole, hospital-gown bunching up to reveal his white briefs.

I am meant to be here, so that I can remember that.

Like the Leo Twin movie theater in Philadelphia's Far Northeast section, for example, a theater I hardly ever go to given the wealth of screens closer to home, but which for whatever reason I find myself choosing on a dull and rainy February Sunday during my college senior-year for the 2:15 showing of *Night Crossing,* a new release I actually have little desire to see. I show up early enough to notice a kiosk in the corner of the theater lobby that offers free copies of a just-launched film magazine called *Moviegoer,* whose contents I hungrily devour in my seat before the movie and whose masthead I turn to the next morning in search of a name and address for a what-the-hell hand-written fan-letter in which I state the dream it would be to work at a magazine like it when I graduate from journalism school.

The result is an unannounced internship-application in the mail a week later with instructions to ignore the expired deadline, a phone-call two weeks after that extending an invite for me to join the summer roster, and a move to a southern state I'd never heard of seven days after commencement, at 22, where I stay for seven years. An out-of-the-blue offer that comes from a random day at the movies. A hand-written note that launches a career. And a life.

I am meant to be here, so that I can write that.

Like Knoxville, Tennessee, of all places, where the internship brings me and which I come to call home when the temporary position become permanent. My first real job. And in my chosen field no less, as a writer and editor on a show-business magazine. (*Look*, I say to myself: *Who I am combined with what I love*.) In a place where I break free and spring alive and come out in every way but the most important one, if only because knowing how still eludes me. Where I make a home, make friends, make money, make a name, make a life. The result is a life-long love affair with a city I adopt as my second home.

I am meant to be here, so that I can feel that.

Or Like Whittle Communications, in downtown Knoxville, the company at the heart of the love affair, which publishes *Moviegoer* and which welcomes me into its heart and then introduces me to colleagues and friends whose love and support surround me in coming years, most tellingly during the one when my old life back home in Philadelphia begins to come to an end. The result is the ability to endure the slow decline I witness from a distance as my mother's cancer returns with an unleashed fury, and then the strength and permission to return home close to the end, for as long as it takes, to stand by her bed, in silence, with my father and six brothers and sisters, to watch her die at 58. At an age wholly too young for any of us. The combustible laughter and the daily laundry and the dinner-table-asides and the Christian life-lessons and Ding Dongs-capped grade-school lunches and the *Rich Man Poor Man* Mondays and the shared retail-days and all that math homework since 1962 come to a slow and agonizing end in a darkened hospital-room made heavy with unimaginable grief -- the hair gone, the breathing labored, the limbs swollen, the lips cracked, the eyes pleading, the time gone.

The last of her to shut down is the maternal concern, wrapped as it always is in curiosity: Alone with me near the end one afternoon, for six hours, her hands finding comfort under mine as I sit alongside the bed, she manages an out-of-nowhere question. "Do you think you're going to live in Tennessee the rest of your life?" -- a normally casual inquiry made anything but when I realize she's referring to the rest of a life she's given me but won't be around to see. As I search for a significant answer, the only one that comes to mind is that, at 27, I just don't know. But in this Sunday's gloaming, I come to suspect that the answer is I won't. Mom's caution since we're all young is to make full use of the life we're given; her want for us is to get up and *do*. "You're going to be dead a long time," is the occasional reminder behind her gentle push. I've heard it for years. Yet as I sit here beside her bed with my eyes closed and I count the endless seconds during the widening gaps between her breaths, praying for just one more inhalation *("...five...six...seven...")*, I'm hearing it for the first time.

Whittle Communications in downtown Knoxville, Tennessee, a company I've never heard of in a town I've never thought about, affords me the chance to be with her for this exchange. And then when I return to its embrace afterward, it makes easier the burden of moving on without a mother.

I'm meant to be here, so that I can experience that.

I am meant to be all of these places, doing all these things, if only for a while, in my 20s.

For these four thousand seventy six days.

Before Los Angeles.

Because it's only through these events in an early life that I'm able to go in search of the rest of it. Only now am I able to go where I meant to go and to be what I am meant to be, to have my heart touch its destiny.

Only now I am meant to be in Hollywood, so that I can do that.

*

During

CBS's 1995-2005 "Christian Scheduling Team":
Jim McKairnes, Andy Kubitz, Kelly Kahl
(Television City, 2003)

On the day before my 29th birthday, in August of 1989 and at the close of another decade, I end my comfortable Tennessee job, pack my comfortable Tennessee life into my comfortable Tennessee car, and move across the country to start over again in the completely uncomfortable unknown that is Los Angeles. I arrive on the sunny west coast late on the same hot summer Sunday afternoon that soon-to-be-infamous Beverly Hills teenaged brothers Lyle and Eric Menendez shoot and kill their millionaire parents as the older couple sits watching television and eating ice cream (strawberry, reports will say) in the den of their expansive home – a rampage the siblings will blame on the Mob as they gleefully go about spending their newly inherited fortune.

Greed. Murder. Ambition. Junk food.

All in all, not a bad introduction to the place.

I come here because I've decided to shake up my life as I stare down both at age 30 and then forward toward the rest of it. My emotions are bobbing in the wake of loss, and I am coming to view life in general through different eyes. In a word, it seems short. I feel the need for change. To live and be elsewhere. To live and be *more*. So I set off on the course to Hollywood.

To do what, I don't know, other than it has to relate to TV. I know that part of me wants to be a TV writer. To be *Dick Van Dyke*'s Rob Petrie. To be a guiding force behind small-screen comedy. But I think a bigger part of me yearns to be a guiding force behind TV as a whole, whatever that it is and however one gets to do it. Whichever the career, I'm on a course that I seem to have been charting for most of my 29 years. I need to be here to find out where it leads.

Two tangible things support the otherwise existential decision to live outside the lines as I've drawn them – or as they've recently been re-drawn for me. First, I find that I'm less happy in the day-to-day that is my Knoxville publishing job after seven years here. The powers-that-be, the culture that is, the colleagues who are – it's all changed from the early days when I arrive straight out of college and see a small company doing big work with nice people. The movie magazine that brings me here has shut down; its fun staff has dispersed; the editorial work I'm commissioned to do afterward is less rewarding, less interesting, and less genuine. The company itself is getting larger in what I view are unhealthy ways, exposing corporate avarice and internecine rivalries. And un-truths and suspicion. For the first time, mistrust is part of the job. It's now the kind of environment where a direct-report questions my work not to me but to her own boss, who then calls me into his office to confront and to chastise me, then has me return to the direct-report to make amends, who in turns denies saying anything about me to the boss in the first place. ("I don't know what he's talking about or why he says that to you," she says. "You and I are doing fine together.") Life's proven to be too precious to be spent under these dark clouds.

Second, during this period of late-20s reassessment, I receive a call from a woman I know as one of one of my four fellow interns at the company from the summer I arrive long ago. A reporter and editor now, she's based in New York. We haven't talked in years. "Jim McKairnes is still in Knoxville – what's *that* about?" she says, almost immediately. "Jeez, from what I saw and heard seven years ago I thought you'd be running Hollywood by now."

I have little desire to run anything, especially Hollywood. But her well-intentioned words somehow sting. When I hang up, I hear myself asking the same question:

Still in Tennessee – What is *that all about?*

So, within two short weeks I give notice on my job. And then three weeks after that, with an affectionate farewell from colleagues, it's over. I board a flight to Los Angeles the next day – part one of a two-part move -- with a mission to find a new home so that when I return by car in a few weeks I'll at least be arriving at a place I know. (From among the city's many communities and neighborhoods, I pick the notable TV-friendly Studio City in which to look and to settle, because that's where *Mary Tyler Moore* and other classic TV series from my youth are produced, on a famous production lot that, as things tend to turn out, will become a major part of my future life.) After two eye-opening and frustrating days of searching, I sign a lease on a new place literally on one last swing through the area before I head to the airport for my return flight to Knoxville. A new address secured, I go back to Tennessee to pack up both my life and my car. And then on August 13 -- townhouse emptied, furniture shipped, directions printed, farewells said, IRA liquidated, stomach knotted, bowels blocked – I point my car towards I-40 West.

Beyond the occasional brief business trip for *Moviegoer*, my only other exposure to California is the summer I'm 12 and I accompany my two-years-older sister on a trip to see relatives in the L.A.-adjacent city of La Habra -- an experience remembered primarily for the unfortunate carsick-incident during our excursion to Orange County, when the swallows returned to Capistrano right around the same time my lunch did all over the back of Uncle Jack's Cadillac. But these days I'm game for anything. I'm going. The transmission's in Drive. I pay it heed.

Before I do, there's a final parting gift from a friend as I sit behind the wheel – a copy of the current *Newsweek*, its cover-story devoted to the state I'm about to adopt as my own, with a collage-illustration supporting it of the many disparate images that define the place. The cover-line screams

CALIFORNIA:
AMERICAN DREAM, AMERICAN NIGHTMARE

A week later, after a cross-country drive in a tiny red Mazda hatchback so densely packed that I'm left with just two inches of space to see the east fade into my rear-view's memory – the result of which is that for the entire 2700-mile trip I switch

20 | Sun August 1989

7:30	
8:00	**SUNDAY EVENING**
8:30	
9:00	
9:30	
10:00	
10:30	
11:00	
1130	
NOON	
12:30	
1:00	
1:30	
2:00	
2:30	
3:00	
3:30	
4:00	
4:30	
5:00	
5:30	
6:00	

	7:00	7:30	8:00	8:30	9:00
8	Trans-Antarctica Expedition		MacGyver		Movie: "The Spy
10	Magical World of Disney		Family Ties	Saved by Bell	Movie: "Irreconci
12	60 Minutes		Murder, She Wrote		Movie: "Nick Kni
19	60 Minutes		Murder, She Wrote		Movie: "Nick Kni
20	Living Planet: Earth		National Geographic		Great Moments
25	Trans-Antarctica Expedition		MacGyver		Movie: "The Spy
26	Magical World of Disney		Family Ties	Saved by Bell	Movie: "Irreconc
33	Evening at Pops		National Audubon Society		Masterpiece The
AMC	Come to	Movie: "The Ox-Bow Incident"			Movie: "Lloyds c
ARTS	Decades: 70's		Joe Louis for All Time		All Creatures Gr
BET	Paid Program	Paid Program	Paid Programming		
CBN	Our House		Campbells	Snapshots	In Touch
DIS	Movie: "Springtime in the Rockies"			Disney Album	Carol Burnett Sp
ESPN	SportsCenter	NFL Kickoff	NFL Preseason Football: New York Jets vs. Philad		
HBO	Movie: "Overboard"				"Tailspin: Behind
LIFE	Cardiology	Milestones	Physicians' Journal Update		Cardiology
MAX	Movie: "Rocky II"				Movie: "First Bl
NASH	American Sports Cavalcade			Inside/Racing	Trucks Power
NICK	in. Gadget	Looney Tunes		Right Back	Room-Daddy
NOST	Rogues		AARP's Mod	Nostalgia	Movie: "Sweet F
PLAY			Electric Blue		How to Fill a Wi
PTL	R. Lee	Oral Roberts	Heritage Village Church Service		McDonough
SHOW	Movie: "Hot Pursuit"				Movie: "Gung H
TMC	Movie: "Salsa"				Movie: "Throw N
USA	Miami Vice		Movie: "Peggy Sue Got Married"		
WTBS	Movie: "Shadow Mountain"				National Geogra

freeway lanes only at night, guided as I can be by the presence or absence of headlights -- I arrive in Studio City to start my new Hollywood life right around the same time that Jose and Kitty Menendez's lives are coming to a bloody end fifteen minutes away.

American Dream, American Nightmare.

Then I see that my new apartment is actually in the same neighborhood as the real-life *Brady Bunch* house.

And I know I'm home.

My first week as an L.A. local revolves around two things: 1) introducing myself to and girding for the many area freeways; and 2) rocking back-and-forth in the corner of my small apartment and muttering, "What have I done?" The overall tone is set by two encounters with two separate neighbors on my third day: The first is with Rosita, a tough but tender sixtysomething native who immediately opens both her door and heart to me, offering up a written list of area restaurants and traffic shortcuts, as well as general warnings about the city culled from her forty years clerking for the police department; the second is with Unnamed Guy, to whom I offer my hand and identity when he pulls up alongside my car one day near the garage, who fails to offer either of his own in return, and who when I say I'm a writer mutters "Oh another one" before moving on to his own place, never to acknowledge me again.

Okay then.

Renewal is underway. It's intimidating to live here, especially alone, but I quickly gather that Los Angeles is a place of adapt or perish, so I choose the former. I adapt. To the traffic. To the summer heat in the Valley where Studio City daily bakes. To the challenges of street parking and to the irony that is rush hour and to the nightly aerial sprayings of the Malathian insecticide being used to battle a critical fruit-fly infestation. To the self-interested Show Business hum that vibrates citywide with an alarming obviousness day and night. (Why is there no humidity in Los Angeles? Because the city is already so self-absorbed.)

I adapt to all of it: It's paradisiac California, after all. The sun is a brilliant yellow. Humidity is a memory. The sidewalks are clean and defined and guarded over by towering postcard-ready palms. I settle in. To the culture, to the mood, to the styles and attitudes, to the people. In no time at all, I'm one of them. Lickety-split. Wide-eyed become ho-hum, my cynicism and detachment all but a Welcome-Wagon gift. And I begin to let it all roll over me. Whiz by. Barely noticing.

The newspaper listing for a hair-pullers support group? Nothin'. The ads for "scrotum enhancements" and the one placed by a Universal Studios attraction looking for "in-shape men and in-shape black men"? Whatever. The sign outside its main store during the popular local run of the Tutankhamen Exhibit proclaiming Sees Candies as "The Official Chocolate of King Tut"? Meh. Heck, I hardly even arch a brow when, driving through downtown, I notice an enormous electronic billboard promoting both a local stage production of *The Ten Commandments* and a soon-to-be-decided state-ballot initiative, which blinks:

VOTE YES ON MEASURE A!

VOTE YES ON MEASURE A!

VOTE YES ON MEASURE A!

VAL KILMER IS MOSES!

VAL KILMER IS MOSES!

VAL KILMER IS MOSES!

I'm good with all of it. I have to be.

The whole welcome-to-LA feel is nicely capped about three weeks after my arrival, courtesy of a small drama I watch unfold as I pull into a Sherman Oaks gas-station on Ventura Boulevard, where I see that an evidently heated in-store confrontation between its foreign-tongued owner and an irate customer has moved outside, with the customer hurling insults over his shoulder as he re-takes to and peels away in his car, the owner chasing after him.

"Sir! SIR!?" the proprietor screams as he runs, extending a telltale hand-gesture towards the disappearing Miata's taillights. "Fuck ah-you, sir! Fuck ah-you!"

Fuck you, *sir*.

I get it: Los Angeles is a polite middle finger.

Los Angeles is a place of constant contradiction. Where black is white and wrong is right, the thinking turned upside down.

Los Angeles is a place where cars brake uphill, sit immobile at green lights. Where the busiest most congested day of the long workweek comes on what's dubbed Rideshare Thursday, the workday set aside by the state to encourage car-pooling. (It's not unlike, say, a prison instituting something called "Sodomy Free Saturday" – well-intentioned, but impractical.) A place where ninety minutes behind the wheel can add up to a stressful ten-mile drive across town or a 100-mile jaunt up the coast to Santa Barbara, depending on the day of week and time of day. Where freeway signs for North also mean West and South actually stands for East. Where there are any numbers of fun places to be at any number of times of day, just so long as it doesn't involve *getting there*.

Los Angeles is a place where the heat's turned on at home upon waking and then the air-conditioning in the car an hour later for the drive to work. Where billionaires buy beachfront homes and then install treadmills in their new windows overlooking the scenic mile-long walking path below them. Where a local community-college actually introduces a course called "Goodbye to Shy" that promises "to help you learn how to reduce anxiety, build self-esteem, strike up conversations with others, win friends, and act confidently" – but offers it only online. Where the air is proclaimed both the cleanest in the city's history and the dirtiest in the United States. Where the Department of Water and Power spends $1,000,000 on a campaign to promote the quality of city water and then $89,000 on bottled delivery for its own offices.

Los Angeles is a place where dreams and nightmares co-exist. Where the choices are either to be someone or to be no one at all. The land of the haves and have-mores. It's a company town where people work but don't live, making movies and TV shows they don't watch. Where failure leads to success, firings to promotions, and job-scandals to bidding wars for the disgraced worker's next services.

It's "raw, uncouth, and bizarre," says director Werner Herzog, "but it's a place of substance." Where "all the crazies end up in a migration west," according to comedian Bill Maher, "like a bowling ball headed to the gutter." A town, says a fellow newcomer whom I meet upon my arrival, "where people walk the streets as though they are starring in their own infomercials."

It's all of this.

I'm learning and learning more during these first few months, but I'm still very much alone in my new town. It's hard to create connections from scratch at age 30, especially without a job to go to. I've given myself until the end of the year to get one. My savings will likely take me only that far. Nearing the deadline, I luck out: A TV-producer friend of one of the two semi-contacts I do have in town is looking for an assistant. Am I available?

The renewal continues. A one-time magazine editor, I become a producer's secretary – and a bad one at that, given that each time the phone rings I ask my boss if she wants me to find out who's calling. But it's an actual job in Hollywood (Culver City, more precisely) on an actual prime-time TV show, *In the Heat of the Night*. Four months an Angelino, I get to tell myself I'm already working in television. And if it means a tortuous daily commute from Studio City in the Valley at least it ends on the same acreage where *Gone With the Wind* is made more than fifty years ago, all about which I know thanks to a certain influential high-school movie class.

Tara *firma*. Full circle.

In the Heat of the Night, a hit NBC drama starring *All in the Family*'s Carroll O'Conner, is actually shot far away from Culver City: It's done entirely on location in Georgia. The less-glamorous behind-the-scenes stuff (scripts and schedules) is what's handled back here. My boss, a one-time actress enjoying her own flourishing second act as a writer, has worked her way up to co-producer, which is inspiring to me. Encouraging. My role is to man the desk outside her office, tending to clerical and administrative duties, which seem to include dropping more calls than I forward.

There's education all around me. I get to see how a one-hour TV show comes together, from idea to script to raw footage to air. And I learn bits and pieces about the business-side of the industry in the process. Salaries and budgets, formal and informal roles. Gossip, too. One producer on staff loathes O'Connor; writers finagle script-assignments through questionable means; two highly paid staffers literally do nothing but wait for their daily 4 p.m. ice-cream runs to the studio commissary. And I learn politics. "I don't know how I feel about it," one of my boss's colleagues says to her one morning about a just-submitted script, "since I'm the only one whose read it so far."

Okay then.

Here on the lower rungs of Hollywood ladder, I find a sort of caste system in play. An assistant with whom I work when I start on the show -- and with whom I enjoy friendly daily chats -- moves on to a different job on the lot not long after, and when I see her at the commissary a week later to say hello to she looks straight through me, without a word of response. *That was then*, is the message; *this is now.* Some of the caste-roles breed tension: Veteran career-assistants (mostly female) seem to resent the newer hires (right now, mostly male), eyeing them as short-timers looking to hop up to better digs and gigs -- and over them in the process; fellow newbie assistants subconsciously compete with one another to see how best to position themselves with bosses; and mailroom employees don't like anyone in any administrative position, unhappy to be at the very bottom of the ladder after being rejected for the assistant jobs they've yet to qualify for.

More than once I'm on the receiving end of each group's issues, grateful for the thickened skin that comes from all those Wellington Street family dinners. And my genuine entreaties of friendship or even acquaintance-ship lead to reactions that fall somewhere between rebuffed and recoiled.

Being an assistant proves instructional, but it does little for my wallet, despite having a boss who generously supplements my lean MGM-payroll check with one drawn from her own funds. So I decide to do some supplementing of my own.

Back in Tennessee, for *Moviegoer* and a few of its sister magazines at the publishing company behind it, as well as for a handful of other newspapers and magazines that the job exposes me to, I wrangle some fun writing assignments to go along with my primary role as junior editor, from on-the-set reports of forgettable 1980s movies (*Firestarter, Weird Science, SpaceCamp, King Kong Lives,* and, most notably, *Howard the Duck* – a bomb of a superhero film whose top-secret set I'm invited to and then inside of twenty minutes escorted from, lest I discover and reveal the secret of how the duck comes to life) to interviews with newcomers like Lea Thompson and Molly Ringwald and Kevin Bacon to business pieces about the film and television industries as wholes. I work just enough to make me feel at last the writer I fancy myself to be ever since scoring a grade of "Very Good" in January of 1967 for my landmark first-grade four-line essay "My Dog Did Not Ate Bones." (Copies available upon request.)

Here and now in L.A., where money is tight, I'll pick up my pen again as a writer for hire. I hope for assignments that excite me, but I know I'll settle for any that come my way. In the most literal sense I can't afford not to. Thus, there's a rasher of less-than-thrilling interviews -- with performer Sandra Bernhard, touting her latest movie but more interested in herself than I can ever imagine myself to be; with one of the tween stars of the hit family-sitcom *Full House,* about the mind-numbing hot-button topic of her hair ("Oh, you prefer bangs?" I hear myself ask, on the direction of my assigning editor. "They don't get in your way?"); with 1972's seven-time gold medalist Mark Spitz about his plans to return to Olympic competition (which never materialize); with notoriously eccentric actress Cloris Leachman (*notoriously eccentric* subbing for *crazy off her nut*), whose answer to my innocuous ice-breaking first question to her is, "Oh, I don't know the answer to that -- How about 'Fuck you?'"; with the five members of a brand-new teen singing group as they assemble for a video-shoot on the helipad of downtown Los Angeles's sky-high Bonaventure Hotel, my own fear of heights and the start of the 1991 Persian

Gulf War earlier in the day be damned. I say yes to these and many many others.

But they're offset by ones that compel and even thrill me: Movie- and TV-set reports, sit-downs with comedian Jerry Seinfeld and with singer Clint Black and with director John Landis and with old-school music icons like David Bowie and Rod Stewart and Don Henley. (At a record-industry party I'm invited to as research for a newspaper piece on Henley, I'm introduced to a cheeky Stewart, who upon hearing why I'm there and without warning calls Henley "a cunt" – which causes a wide-eyed reaction just this side of *Roger Rabbit* from Henley's publicist, there alongside me and also a Stewart friend, who rushes to say, "Rod! Rod! This is *USA Today* asking, Rod. *USA Today*" and which then leads to Stewart looking at me and saying, "Well, he's a *nice* cunt, Jim.")

Both types pay enough to get by on, even if between the secretarial gig and the writing assignments my combined income these days is less than half what it is in my peak earning years in Tennessee, where it's significantly less expensive to live. My income for all of 1992, in fact, living alone and still trying to re-create a life for myself at age 32, three years into my move, is $8,870. My rent for the year? $6,500.

I become highly skilled at paying last month's bills with next month's checks. I eliminate luxuries. I re-classify laundry as an entertainment expense. But I'm not deterred. I can't be. Poverty is temporary, even the kind that finds me on my most humbling day eating vending-machine crackers as my sole lunch entrée, purchased at the Universal Studios employees' store (my TV-producer boss's latest gig has taken us here for a season) courtesy of five quarters shaken loose from the change-jar at home, and which I exit to see none other than same-aged Kevin Costner pulling his movie-star convertible into as VIP parking space in front.

Oh, but what a few years apart in age and a millennia in circumstance can mean.

There's no option but to wait it out, though. I know things are meant to be. I know TV success of some kind awaits. A reason for being here. I know it sure as I'm alive. Sure as I'm tracking the industry and reading the trades each day. Sure as I'm sitting in the audience at the town's annual TV festival two springs in to my move, staring at a stage full of people gathered to celebrate the best of TV, envisioning myself as soon among their ranks. As someone who works to get TV made.

Soon, I tell myself. *Somehow.*

In these pre-smartphone days, I create at home what I call an Emotional Rolodex – a collection of business-cards kept on a spinning black wheel that adds up to Los Angeles contacts of all stripes that I make, for me to learn from and lean on and expose myself to and be advised by and remain in touch with either through my boss or fellow assistants or friends of friends or my freelance-writing work. Everyone and anyone. Each day's simple goal is to add at least one more name to the wheel.

I also purchase an oversized whiteboard to hang on my bedroom wall, on which I list another group of names of people I *hope* to meet. More and more, I'm realizing that the business I want to break in to has no real breaking-in place, that "TV" is as much concept as it is reality -- a tall and heavily populated building filled with all kinds of people doing all kinds of work but one devoid of any ground-floor entry or even windows for those of us who are lining up outside to look to as possible ways in. These names just might get me inside. If I have to, I'll force an opening.

The thought turns in action when I hatch a plan: With my freelance contacts looking to me for show-biz related stories to publish, why don't I pick some of the names on the board to pitch as possible interview subjects? I'll find a hook that makes one or more of them newsworthy, suggest an article, and then set up an interview that yields a piece for the magazine and then a contact for me? Win/win. It's how I come to spend invaluable time with some of the town's bigger TV names, including producer and former executive Grant Tinker (currently writing his memoirs, the hook I use to pitch his name) and legend-in-the-making Bob Iger (currently resurrecting ABC in prime-time), among others. I'm intimidated by the stature of each of the names I reach out to, and I feel slightly guilty for manipulating my way into their worlds, using my journalism cover. But I've learned that this is how it works: People get jobs and establish careers by working the Hollywood system.

My plan is fortified by advice from my boss's boss at Universal, a veteran TV producer to whom I turn one day with deepening concern that despite the access my twin jobs here are providing me I just still can't seem to crack the Show Business Building. I'm here several years, I say to him, and I don't know how to do the selling of self that's required to get me all the way through.

"Learn," he says, without hesitation, a look of seriousness on his face that I seldom see. "You've got to act as your *own* agent in this business, Jim. *You* represent *you*. No one else will. No one else *can*." And as for whether it's in my Catholic low-self-esteem Wellington-Street nature to talk about and promote myself? "*Get* it in your nature. Everyone here does it. It doesn't have to be *who you are* -- just *what you do* to get and stay in the game.

"And don't be concerned with how you're coming off as you're doing it. The very fact that you're even thinking about that in the first place says that you're probably coming off just fine. And it also sets you apart from most of the people who really do come off otherwise and can't see it. The people you're trying to get advice and favors from in this town know the difference. They know who's worth listening to and who's just hustling them."

Fair enough.

And advice that comes in handy very soon after.

In 1991, producer Norman Lear, already a TV icon, having come out of the medium's early live days of the 1950s to go on to revolutionize it in the 1970s with *All in the Family* and scores of other landscape-shifting prime-time hits, is returning to series-television after a decade off the front lines. He's behind two new shows -- a political satire for NBC called *The Powers That Be* and a "spiritual sitcom" for CBS titled *Sunday Dinner*. His name is high atop my whiteboard-list – someone I'd kill just to get time alone with. So I pitch the idea of a story about him and his return to prime-time to one of my editors, who bites. So a call to Lear's publicist the next day leads to an appointment for me to meet the famous man himself in his office a week later.

With the advice from my day-job producer-friend in my ear, I try to act the part of a bold and self-possessed journalist who represents himself when I drive to the historic Sunset-Gower Studios in the heart of Hollywood the following Wednesday. I feel anything but, however: I'm about to sit down with television history. After a brief introduction in his office – a modest room made memorable by an oversized piece of wall-art that pays homage to Michelangelo's "The Creation of Adam" in the form of an arm reaching out of living-room chair and connecting with another arm reaching out from a TV -- I sit down with Lear in a nearby conference-room to talk.

For journalism purposes, the conversation that follows is relaxed and productive and informative. For selfish purposes, it's affirming: The producer seems impressed with my familiarity of his long career. (I'm surprised that that surprises him – after all, he's *Norman Lear.*) When I cite a lesser-known TV project that he worked on in the 1950s, almost 20 years before *All in the Family* brings him his fame, he raises his eyebrows and smiles.

"Whose mail are you delivering in this town anyway, kid?" he says. It's a joking reference to the storied way of how show-business careers can (and do) begin in a Hollywood mailroom. "You need to be doing more than what you're doing here." Frozen in the moment, I manage only to respond, "I'm trying" -- at which precise moment, in an ode to bad timing, our conversation is interrupted by an assistant who tells Lear he's needed elsewhere. So, with apologies, and after little more than 45 minutes, the interview is shut down. At its most critical point, the door to Norman Lear closes. And I'm crushed. It just hasn't been enough time – for either an interview or a connection.

The disappointment is somewhat mitigated by Lear's saying on his way out of the room that I should meet one of his colleagues ("Have Patricia come in here -- she's just got to meet this guy") and then by his asking me to stick around the complex to watch episodes of his yet-to-air series. Which I do, happily. But in what seems like no time at all I'm back in my aging and wheezing hatchback, the time with a whiteboard-name over before it begins. *The window to a career just opened*, I think to myself, *but I didn't climb in.*

I drive north up Cahuenga Boulevard, and I see the famous HOLLYWOOD sign teasing me in the distance, telling me that I'll never be a part of what it represents. And then I'm back in Studio City, back in my small cinderblock one-bedroom apartment with its well-worn whiteboard and its STEPS TO GET A JOB IN TV chart and the name NORMAN LEAR crowning it. And with a sigh I move to cross it out, to turn to the next name, to the next note, to the next call, to the next day, to the next round of hopes.

And then the words come back to me:

"You've got to act as your own agent. You represent you. No one else will. No one else can."

Two years in Los Angeles, refining my ambitions and desires, watching at a distance from the stands as people play ball on the field I need to claim as my own, barely getting by with a secretarial job, buying food with spare change and tiring of waiting for the freelance-phone to ring, I decide I'm not going to squander the very best opportunity I've had since coming here. I'm not going to let go. I'm not going to let this chance pass me by. I'm just not.

I walk to my living-room, past the *TV Guide* collection spreading kudzu-like in the corner, and I head to the phone, the number for Lear's publicist in hand.

I dial.

When the woman gets on the line, I thank her for setting up the morning's interview with Lear, tell her how wonderfully it went, explain how our interview was interrupted halfway through. And then I close my eyes. I exhale. And I ask her for another appointment so that I can finish it. I owe as much to the magazine that has hired me, I say.

I act as my own agent.

I represent *myself*.

Which is how I end up back at Sunset-Gower Studios two weeks later to sit down again with Norman Lear. Window? Meet Jim. I'm coming through. (The guilt over my seemingly naked ambition is eased somewhat later on the day I first meet Lear when the man himself calls me at home to ask my opinion of the shows that I stay behind to watch. "I can't talk to someone who knows as much about TV as you do without asking what you thought," says the TV titan.)

Okay then.

My second session with the producer finds me both more relaxed and more intent on Seizing The Moment. But because I do possess a conscience, I seize it only once the official interview's over, since that's what brings me here. It's what I am being paid to do. I ask an hour's worth of additional questions, explore Lear's past and present work, get some great quotes about the state of the TV business. And then when I'm done, when all my interview questions are asked, I turn off my recorder, close my notebook, and thank him for the information and the time. Then I steel myself, offering an awkward smile.

"Okay," I say, trying to remember how I rehearse the pitch alone in the car earlier. "I'm no longer here representing the magazine that hired me to talk to you. But, if you don't mind, I actually do have a few more questions to ask that have nothing to do with your career or the new TV series. They're about me. And I feel a bit awkward asking them. I really don't know how this works."

Lear himself now smiles. It's one of recognition, I sense. I prattle on.

"I guess I want to say somehow that I can't have this kind of access to you, to be around you, without telling you what I want to do with my professional life and then asking your advice on how to get there in general. But I don't know how to say that or how to make myself sound any different to you than every single other person who comes in here to ask the same questions and tries to get the same help. I don't know how not to come off like a jerk hustling you for a job. I know you're busy and you must get this all the time. And this is awkward for me – asking for help."

Lear leans back in his chair, and the smile, sympathetic and warm, widens. He takes only a few seconds before replying. "I know exactly what you are saying," he says. "But by the same token you are never going to get anywhere in this business unless you ask." He looks directly at me.

"So, ask."

I look directly back at him, and I do.

"I want to get into TV programming, but I don't know how. Or even really what that exactly means." Totally focused now, my eyes becoming as wide as the crack I know this conversation represents, I lay out for him my passion for and desire to work in network television. How I grew up studying it. How I spend time writing about it. How I moved here to be a part of it. A part of CBS, in particular. How I want to work there. But how after two years living here I still have no idea what to do to make that happen.

"What have you done about it so far?"

"I sent a letter to the president of CBS, introducing myself. But I have no clue if he got it or read it or how to follow up."

The simple request that follows:

"Go home and find the letter. And send it to me."

With that, our time is at an end. But the exchange I needed to happen has happened. The crack has widened. A connection has been made. I thank Lear again for the extra time and for the offer to help, and then I head home to print out and send to him a copy of my CBS letter.

A week later, an envelope bearing the logo for Lear's company shows up in my mailbox. Inside is a copy of a note that Norman Lear has sent to CBS president Jeff Sagansky on my behalf, writing that having met me recently he "couldn't have been more impressed by this guy." He reminds him that he has a letter from me on his desk, and then he urges the CBS executive to read it and then to meet with me.

A short note, but one that will soon hang framed in my apartment next to the whiteboard that has both Lear's and Sagansky's names on it, it concludes this way: "Jeff, he's a programmer. He's a developer. He's a whatever. But I believe there is gold in this Jim McKairnes."

I sit down in my apartment after reading it, and I cry.

The next day, CBS president Jeff Sagansky calls me at home. A week after that, I'm in his office for a meeting, and seven days later he calls again to tell me I'm "at the top of the list" of future hires for the network, after which the future becomes the present when I'm invited to join CBS Television as its newest programming executive. I stay for thirteen career-defining dream-realizing years, leaving as Senior Vice-President.

Because of a chance encounter.

And because I ask.

Twenty-five years after Elizabeth Montgomery reaches out to me from the TV screen, fourteen years following a high-school class that gives focus to my passion, a decade after nearly losing my own life in surgery only to watch that life re-shape after my mother loses hers shortly thereafter, two years into a Los Angeles renewal built on hope and desire and woven with loneliness and confusion, I'm here.

The TV world. And I'm welcome to it.

My slavish lifelong devotion to CBS isn't just rooted in the fact that it's where most of my childhood favorites are to be found when the love affair with TV begins, but also in the fact that based on what I see and hear as I watch them it seems to be the actual home of television itself. TV is its very *address*.

"From Television City, in Hollywood" is what I hear time and again at the beginning of sitcoms like *All in the Family* and variety-shows from *The Smothers Brothers Comedy Hour* and *The Jim Nabors* Show to *The Glen Campbell Goodtime Hour*, from Sonny & Cher to Tony Orlando. Plus, "Recorded at Television City, Hollywood California" is stamped on to the end-credits of just about every other program on my roster, from *Maude* to *Good Times* to *The Jeffersons*. One of my most-loved shows even gives me an actual glimpse of the place every week in its opening credits -- albeit in cartoon form -- as it depicts a familiar-looking cleaning-woman with a pronounced jaw standing outside an enormous building that bears the letters "CBS" high atop it, watching as they drop down to spell out *The Carol Burnett Show*.

Clearly, CBS is where television lives, I think to myself. And my young mind can't conceive of a more exciting place.

It's an awe that never wavers as the series roll by and the TV seasons roll on. Through childhood and adolescence and beyond. Not even when I'm an adult finally living in Los Angeles and I get my first up-close peek at it the day I'm called in for the meeting that Norman Lear brokers. It really does exist, I see. It really is called Television City.

And then not long after, I'm its newest full-time resident.

Of course, this being Hollywood, the full *full* story behind my getting here isn't as neat as the compressed one I tend to recount. The months that elapse between the network president telling me I'm atop his list of future hires and then my *becoming* that future hire number nearly twenty-two. However successful my initial encounter with the CBS head, it comes the very week of a massive company-wide layoff and hiring freeze. I'm told to be in touch as the network waits out the thaw, to be patient, not to worry.

It's all quite sincere. And periodically thereafter I'm summoned to meet with various department heads to see where and how I might fit in at the network when the time finally comes. (My joke is that I'm at CBS so often I'm the only job-candidate with a parking space.) But there is much waiting to be done – and life to be tended to as the waiting goes on.

I continue my assistant job, which is on-again/off-again as it is. I take a night class or two in TV practices (where the Hollywood pecking order further reveals itself on the first night of one of them when someone sits at an empty desk next to mine, makes small-talk with me, initiates a more detailed conversation about what I do, and then when told I'm a mere assistant actually gets up and moves to another seat.) I continue to write freelance articles, too, for more well-needed pennies – continuing to hope for assignments that introduce me to or that get the attention of TV higher-ups, which some do.

I try every door that seems only slightly open and every window that appears unlocked, acting as my own agent, introducing myself everywhere I go and to everyone I meet. I even withstand a withering encounter with a longtime executive at Paramount Television who meets with me only as a favor to a friend and then, face to face with me in his office, looks over the top of my journalism-heavy resume and says to me, "There's nothing about this resume that leads me to believe you are remotely qualified to do what you want to do."

But I also never let my eyes drift from the CBS prize. I keep in touch with the network and with the executives there that I go in to meet with. I try to avoid thinking that time is whipping by, that in many ways I'm still starting from scratch out here, at now nearly 33 years old, still dirt-poor.

Then, finally, during the memorable week that begins with Norman Lear calling *me* at home for an update on my career and saying, "This'll be your year, kid," it becomes just that. I get the CBS call at last. I'm given a job in network television.

The hiring process, once it officially begins, is smooth: Paperwork, drug test, orientation. Routine matters. Very little that telegraphs the glamour of TV or of Hollywood. Two things trip me up. First, in the call that comes with the actual job offer, I'm asked to think about and then get back to CBS representatives about my "package." I hang up clueless about what that means, feeling every bit a 20-year-old hospital patient again being told to *void*. (*There's a package involved? And I give it to them? Shouldn't* they *be giving it to* me?) Even when a helpful friend explains to me later that night that I'm being asked to name my salary request based on my current quote, I'm still flummoxed: I make $500 a week as a producer's assistant (but only when my boss is working), and I earn a dollar a word writing magazine articles on a freelance basis. How exactly do I convert that into a TV-level salary request? (I settle on an amount calculated on how much I'd make if I were to work as an assistant year-round, while also writing an article a week every week for a year; when CBS bites without blinking, I wish I'd gone higher.)

The other hiccup comes by way of an introduction to the nerve-ruining game of Waiting for Answers in the Corporate World. Getting an official sign-off is a weeks-long ordeal with lots of internal moving parts that on my end feels like years, during which I convince myself, daily, that every single person at CBS even remotely connected to my being hired will either be fired or accidently killed before I'm made official – and I'll be forgotten in the mix.

It's just the way I think.

Finally, on Monday April 12, 1993, 74 days after the Thursday on which I get the first official call from CBS, I report for work. The weepy cancer-movie *Steel Magnolias* airs on CBS the night before, and I wonder what it means.

That's just the way I think, too.

"You picked a good time to start," says the network's Number Two when he sees me in the hallway my first morning and welcomes me with a shake of the hand. And so it seems I have: This Monday marks the first day of the annual multi-week process here at CBS – and at all the networks -- devoted to screening the just-made series under consideration for the new fall schedule, to be announced next month in New York. It's a period that strikes at the very heart of the TV industry, and given that it's also what draws me into TV as a child – the comings and goings of TV shows and the science and strategy of scheduling a network – my level of excitement is chart-high.

So while I'm curious about what I see and hear as I'm hurriedly introduced around the non-distinguished third-floor executive wing at Television City, any real exploration of the place or even of the new job itself -- I'm given a sort of hybrid entry-level position that straddles both what's called the Current Programming department and the Scheduling department – takes a back seat to the screenings, which will number as high as four a day for at least the next two weeks.

Down in the small ground-floor screening-room of the 45-year-old TVC building, I attempt to blend in among the sea of seemingly nice overwhelmingly white young faces – certain that wherever I position myself in here I'm violating some form of seating-protocol. I'm a bit taken aback by how non-incidental it seems to everyone to have a new colleague (me) in the room: Rather than another all-in-this-together hand-on-deck, I guess I'm just another passenger along for the ride. I'll learn that, in Hollywood, executives come and go with a swiftness that leaves little wake.

Once I do sit, I make an earnest and not altogether successful effort to banish from my head the words of what are supposed to be support that I receive days earlier from a friend to whom I confess my nervousness and whose writer-husband has dealt with many of these and other TV executives in town through the years:

"Just remember, Jim: They're all idiots."

It takes little time at all to discern that the purpose of these daily dimly-lit convocations is two-fold: To watch and to evaluate the potential of proposed new series for a berth on the new fall schedule, yes; but also to establish bragging rights as Funniest Person in the Room, if not the Company.

12 Mon Apr 1993

	8:00	8:30	9:00	9:30	10:00
7:30					
8:00	Fresh Prince	Major League Baseball: Baltimore Orioles at Texas Rang			
8:30	Fresh Prince	Fresh Prince	Blossom	Mad-You	Seinfeld
9:00 AM	Movie: "Young Guns"				News
9:30	FBI-Story	Detective	Movie: "Class of '61"		
10:00	Shade	Bob	Murphy B.	Love & War	Northern Expos
10:30	Shade	Bob	Murphy B.	Love & War	Northern Expos
11:00	FBI-Story	Detective	Movie: "Class of '61"		
1130	Washington Capitals at Montreal Canadiens				
NOON	Fresh Prince	Fresh Prince	Blossom	Mad-You	Seinfeld
12:30	Travels		Medicine at the Crossroads		
1:00	ange	Wholey	Destinos	Ch. Care	Americas
1:30	Movie: "Young Guns"				News
2:00	Movie: "Native Son"				Movie: "The Gl
2:30	Movie: "Flowers in the Attic"				Hunter
3:00	Movie: "Young Guns"				News
3:30	Great Journeys		Medicine at the Crossroads		
4:00			Movie: "Sweet Charity"		
4:30	David L. Wolper Presents		Sherlock Holmes Mysteries		Lovejoy
5:00	Sanford	Comicview	Video Soul		
5:30	Country Music Television		Country Music Television		Country Music
6:00	Avonlea		Movie: "Thoroughly Modern Millie"		
	Major League Baseball: Minnesota Twins at Chicago White Sox				
	Young Riders		Father Dowling Mysteries		700 Club
	Movie: "If Looks Could Kill"			Movie: "The Punisher"	
	: Semifinal – Teams TBA			Olympic Showcase	
	L.A. Law		Movie: "Fatal Judgment"		
	Movie: "Lunatics: A Love Story"			Movie: "Frankie and Johnny"	
	Get Smart	Van Dyke	Dragnet	Lucy Show	M.T Moore
	Movie: "Unlawful Entry"				WWF Wrestlen
	ague of Their Own"				WWF Wrestlen
		Movie: "Sunset Grill"			
	Battlestar Galactica		War of the Worlds		Magician
	Movie: "A Kiss Before Dying"			Movie: "Q & A"	
	Archaeology	Silk Road	Ancient Journeys		Operation
	Crook	Texas Conn.	Nashville Now		Warner Bros. I
	Movie: "Major Dundee"				
	Murder, She Wrote		WWF: Monday Night Raw		Matrix

Unfortunately, this is where my being the new guy does play a role: I'm a prime target, fresh meat, for the attacks of biting humor.

I set myself up for a hard fall and quick first lesson as soon as the lights come up following the very first screening of this my very first day -- a crime drama about an ex-con-turned-private detective, starring former *21 Jump Street* heartthrob Richard Grieco. A discussion begins when the screening's over, as will be the case following each of the pilots, I'll come to see. In time, I'll learn that the more lengthy and earnest and even heated these discussions are the more potential the shows in question have to be picked up as weekly series – they're the ones that are taken most seriously. This first pilot generates little to no discussion at all. It's not very good; the verdict is obvious. Rather than take that as a cue, though, I feel the need to weigh in.

"I don't buy Grieco as an ex-con," I offer. "He just looks too well-groomed and tanned and fit to have spent any time in jail."

Silence.

Then, from the back of the room:

"Not necessarily -- it really all depends on whose bitch he was on the inside."

Raucous laughter erupts. In my direction. At my expense. It's a good line, but I feel humiliated. My comment is dismissed. Harshly. We move on. Afterward, back upstairs on the third floor, my new direct-report boss takes me aside. A nice guy, he has advice to offer, phrased in what will be his hallmark pointed way.

"Jim, about the screening?"

"Yes?" I ask, expecting some kind of providence or wisdom.

"Don't say those kinds of things."

And then he moves on to his office.

Okay then.

I follow him and try to explain that my comment comes from the *If I don't buy it, I won't invest in it* school of TV-watching -- that the actor in the pilot needs to have credibility from the outset for me to believe him, care about him. "I know, I know," the boss says, his words over mine. "But just don't." In every sense, he moves on. And I'm left standing there alone in the hallway outside his now closed door.

I come to see both his point and my own naiveté. The Grieco pilot is already *made*. It's cast, shot, completed, delivered. What's up on the screen is *it*. An actor's looks at this point are irrelevant; comments about them are needless and wasteful, if not the mark of an amateur (and, evidently, embarrassing to a boss). These screenings are about evaluating *potential* only: Does the pilot offer a story and character worth following from week to week? They're not about grooming. Lesson learned. (And besides: Who's to say that I'm even right about the note to begin with?)

Three more screenings unfold this Monday, with about 25 more to follow over the coming two weeks. They pass in a blur. Some pilots are better than others; some are bad beyond measure. (The ratio comes to apply to the whole process each year.) It seems a bit crazy as I look around to see that so much rides on the feelings and actions of so few, some of whom don't even take the process all that seriously. I notice a personality to it all – diplomacy where needed, ridicule when warranted, earnestness and practicality however they apply to the art and science of crafting a prime-time network schedule. Common sense usually, but not always, prevails: A non-fiction medical documentary-type pilot that features a dead child in its opening minutes is screened at 8:30 on a Friday morning. Tears pour forth. Pity the producer of the pilot that has to follow it.

Some executive can't hear enough of their own voices; some are enervated by the ritual; some are bored; still others seem to have endured one pilot-season too many. One afternoon, late in the second week of screenings, a colleague rushes in at the last minute and sits next to me just as the lights dim. We're here for a proposed sitcom starring camp cable-TV siren Elvira ("Mistress of the Dark"). It's so god-awful from the outset that about twelve minutes in, the executive allows his head to fall into his hands, fully defeated by what he's watching. He leans my way. "A million dollars," he whispers, with a shake of his head and a gesture towards the screen. "A *million*." (I discover later that before he works here he works as a schoolteacher, which begs a theory I cultivate that those who come into Hollywood jobs with non-Hollywood experience seem to bring to them the most real-world and valued perspectives.)

Still, I remain awed by the fact that I'm part of the proceedings. Ebullient. I've waited so long to be here, to be doing what I am doing.

The whole ritual is over by early May, and in the end, just two pilots prove uniformly popular in the room, standing out as having the most potential to be successful long-running series – the sitcoms *Dave's World* and *The Nanny*. (Stinging from my first-day lesson, I say nothing about either on the days we view them.) Then nearly everyone I've met so far, which is just about the entire third-floor executive wing (department heads and other members of the inner circle), disappears to New York, where the annual rite continues on its path to an east coast conclusion. There, as it's done every year, Development executives and Sales executives and researchers and various bosses analyze and debate the strength and weakness of all the pilots, as well as those of some existing shows, and use that information to build a revised prime-time schedule, which is announced soon after amid much fanfare in a two-hour ceremony called the Upfront presentation. (Most all the networks, likewise locked down here in Hollywood and then in New York, announce their new schedules during the same five-day period referred to as Upfront Week.)

Back in Los Angeles, I'm a bit surprised when the new CBS schedule is officially unveiled. Some pilots that generate little excitement during our west-coast screenings have been ordered to series; others that seem semi-sure-things for pick-ups are nowhere to be found; a few existing shows that I think are all but cancelled still stand. Clearly, much can happen between Los Angeles and New York, where it seems other factors are taken into account when building a schedule. As expected, *Dave's World* and *The Nanny* are among the comedies that have been ordered to series. (And, as expected, each goes on to become a multi-season hit for CBS.) Two other comedies that I don't recall generating any excitement at all join them: *Family Album*, which won't last long and whose producers will do better a year from now at NBC with *Friends*, and a romantic-comedy called *It Had to Be You,* starring no less than Faye Dunaway – in so mediocre an effort that I can only assume it's ordered for the car-crash potential of seeing its famously mercurial lead in what is her first TV series.

In fact, *It Had to be You* – a horrible title, which doesn't bode well -- really seems to get on the air based on what I can only describe as Pilot False-Positive Syndrome, which involves a pilot that's ordered to series as a result of a single stand-out scene that often has little to nothing to do with the actual series storyline. Here, that's an Are-We-Really-Seeing-What-We-Think-We're-Seeing scene that shows the Academy-Award winning star of *Bonnie and Clyde* and *Chinatown* and *Network* in conversation with her co-star while standing on her head. It's so jarring and strange an effort -- and presumably so admirable -- that the studio audience applauds wildly as it plays out, triggering the false-positive in the screening room.

Thus, *It Had To Be You* goes into the Upfront meetings as the sitcom pilot that generates huge audience reaction, despite the fact that the spike has nothing to do with whether the series itself will work, which – come fall -- it doesn't. Because it's just not very good in the first place. And sadly neither is Dunaway. (Pilots often emerge from executive screenings or test-audience previews similarly inflated, based on single-scene false-positives that accentuate sight-gags or feature babies or employ popular music – memorable warm fuzzies that have nothing to do with the actual show. Years off, the pilot for what will become a long-running CBS success called *Yes, Dear* gets picked up to series in much the same way, offering up a sight-gag that's so stupidly funny and elicits such loud laughs that it nearly brings down the ceiling tiles in the CBS screening-room, mostly courtesy of an infectiously loud cackle on the part of one particular influential executive. It's all but guaranteed placement on the fall schedule that very morning. Good thing, too, in this case: *Yes, Dear* proves to be a subversively witty long-term success for the network.)

Among the one-hour dramas announced: A promising and warmly received modern-day-western called *Harts of the West*, and, to my raised eyebrows, a low-rent detective buddy-show called *South of Sunset*, which to me provides the final nail in the coffin of TV's private-eye-genre. (Neither will last.) Cancelled to make room for these and other new titles as the CBS schedule is rebuilt are *Designing Women*, *Knots Landing*, and

Major Dad, a family sitcom that I think has more life to it and should be renewed, and the *Golden Girls* spin-off *The Golden Palace*, which doesn't and rightfully isn't. To my amazement, *Hearts Afire* and *Love & War*, two existing sitcoms that I think are all but eliminated from contention when everyone heads to New York, survive to battle another (final) season each.

Again, the wonder: Is there more than popularity or even quality that makes a TV series get renewed?

With just about every top-level executive from the third floor gone to New York for the better part of this May, including my boss, I have less oversight and thus more time to explore a new workplace that to date I've barely seen. The magic that is Television City. Here on the executive floor, but for the black-and-white cast photos that hang on the walls, I'd never suspect I'm working in Hollywood. It's a generic kind of office space on a floor subdivided by the usual collection of grey-fabric cubicles and black-metal lateral files, with benign looking but nonetheless highly prized window-offices marking the perimeter. And it's populated by surprisingly small numbers of mostly friendly people involved in self-evident though un-labeled departments (Development, Scheduling, Current Programming, Late-Night, Daytime, Promotion). All very nice. All very ordinary.

But a scouring of the rest of the building reveals its true personality and history as it takes me into the heart of television. On the cavernous ground floor, for instance, nearby to the screening room that I've gotten so familiar with lately, there are walls full of vintage photographs that chronicle the construction and early days of the mammoth complex, the building and its players, as well as photos of the recently completed expansion that added two soundstages to the East. This, on top of multiple shots of what claimed the whole property even before CBS did (Gilmore Field, home of the Pacific Coast baseball league's Hollywood Stars). And in various other parts of the labyrinthine four-level structure, especially in the wing where most of the really old stages are, I see other photos that document the productions and

performers from the early days of both CBS and the industry itself. Art Linkletter, Burns and Allen, Danny Kay, Judy Garland, Carol Burnett. Walking around, I take in wall-murals dedicated to *Playhouse 90* and other historic live dramas of the 1950s done here, when TV was new and ambitions were high. Their home is now mine.

Up and down back stairways and all along lengthy hallways, I pass stage after stage, each in use for decades and now home to our daytime dramas and various game-shows. I pass an area sectioned off for Costume and Scenic Design, and I notice a pallet-rack and a pushcart off to the side, collecting dust. Each is stenciled with the words JACK BENNY SHOW. My mind wonders as it wanders. TVC is imagination and history come to life.

It's well into summer before the realities of my day-to-day duties upstairs fully present themselves, with me, at 33, still very much feeling the new guy around here – the guy who may think he knows TV but who really doesn't know what he's doing, working alongside those who do. It doesn't help that whispers and speculation trail me when I walk the third floor to and from my unadorned office. My arrival here is greeted with suspicion on two fronts, as a) I'm mistaken for a new employee who's rumored to be a pet-hire of the second-in-command, and b) I'm held in complete contempt by an admin-level person in my own small department who resents my being given the executive position she feels she's herself earned.

Dealing with the former is easy: Having met the real so-called pet hire, I remind myself that I'm not an African-American woman. Handling the latter isn't as simple: The colleague is unfriendly to the point of nasty, and she's enlisted two friends on the floor, assistants each, to hate me as well. In fact, all three spy on me and look for ways to enable a fall. I dub them the Macbeth Witches.

"Be careful," a fellow executive says to me one afternoon in an aside, when word gets around the floor that I've made an embarrassing mistake in one of the weekly reports I'm charged with compiling. "The three of them are watching you, and they want you to fail."

Watching me? Seriously?

And they actually want me to fail? To lose my very job?

The scrutiny and the drama make for discomfort and frustration during what should be celebratory days. But as these things tend to do, the childish exploits of the Witches die down, and I get to focus on my work and duties. They overlap two departments: Scheduling, which is responsible for the planning behind and the placement of the many series that make up the networks' 22 hours of nighttime programming each week, and Current Programming, the area that oversees the production of the shows themselves (with the exception of those that fall under the News division, based in New York).

The work of Scheduling demands most of my time at the start, given the time of year: Pilot screenings and the May announcements are the orders of the days; few series are even in production (and thus require no oversight) during these hiatus months of April through June. I'm given Scheduling-related assignments that are mostly of an administrative or research nature. Filing, ratings, and the mundane like -- some of which, unfortunately, orbit around my least favorite subject of math. Which is why anyone stumbling into CBS headquarters late at night during the summer of 1993 can see the network's newest hire, the one with the high self-impression of his TV knowledge and who's been enlisted, he thinks, to help build a winning and profitable CBS schedule, on the phone with an east-coast childhood friend tutoring him in fractions.

I also track and share competitive changes (what's newly scheduled or rumored to be scheduled on FOX and ABC and NBC), read any stray script I can get my hands on, and study the magnetic board on the wall of my office that displays all the networks' schedules. It, too, keeps me humble: One of my other charges is to order and pick up the show-title strips for it and for all the other magnetic boards on the third floor.

No real decisions made about the network's fate involve me. I'm part of very few strategy discussions. Understandably, I tell myself. I'm new. I remain intimidated and nervous, but I don't let on. And I keep to myself. Lunch-hours are spent alone in the TVC commissary or at the outdoor mall ("The Historic Third Street Farmer's Market") found behind our building. At an end-of-season employee gathering on one of the CBS stages, I hug the perimeter of the room, by myself, knowing in my heart that I'm where I'm meant to be, working at this network and at this time, yet still wondering what the many things are that I don't yet know about how it all works. Or how I fit in with all these secure-looking people. Only the absence of the 1970s treacle "Color My World" by Chicago on the sound-system keeps me from convincing myself that I'm back at another Father Judge High School dance, clinging to the walls.

When our many series do go into production come mid-July, the other half of my duties as a member of the Current Programming department are revealed. I'm to be assigned real series to cover – to act as liaison for, between CBS and the studio and producers behind the shows. I'll be a point-person for their questions and requests and complaints, network representative at tapings or shootings, note-giver on scripts, referee and counselor and problem solver and confidante for the writers -- the person who tries to blaze a smooth path between a show in production at a studio and the network that's airing it.

The role involves tracking a show from first script reading to rehearsal through to taping and delivery of the rough- and then final-cuts. And other than figuring out that it'll require knowledge of the quickest ways around Hollywood since I'll be spending half the workweek in the car speeding from stage to stage …

… I have absolutely no clue how to do any of it.

I do hope I'm assigned to oversee comedies, however. Sitcoms aren't just TV's lifeblood. From *Bewitched* and *Green Acres* to *All in the Family* to *Mary Tyler Moore* and from *MASH* to *Barney Miller* to *Cheers*, they continue to be mine. Since landing in Studio City in 1989 and quickly discovering that I'm within walking distance of the famous TV production-facility known as the Radford Lot -- with a history that dates back to silent films and where seminal TV efforts from *Mary Tyler Moore* and *Gilligan's Island* to *The White Shadow* and *Lou Grant* are made, along with countless other shows -- I've surrendered many of my weeknights to standing in the first-come-first-serve lines outside its gates hoping for a bleacher-seat at any one of them. Living this close to where they're made, I long to see how. I luck out most frequently with tickets for *Newhart* and *Seinfeld,* securing a small role in TV history the night I attend the taping of latter's infamous and award-winning episode called "The Contest" in 1992, a ribald outing that opens up the prime-time floodgates to more and more adult material -- to be written, unfortunately, by those who don't seem to get what makes the episode works so well, that less equals more.

When the Current assignments are announced, I'm grateful mine do indeed include a handful of half-hours. For some, I will serve as backup to some of the department's full-time Current executives. I'll shadow and learn from them, and I'll even fill in for some when needed. Other shows will be mine to cover alone. And if the combined result isn't enough to quench my comedy thirst, there's always the set-visit privileges that my new employee-badge will yield for whatever free nights of the week are leftover. I can go to tapings of any one of CBS's comedies. (I mostly end up settling for attending the four shot closest to home, for easier commutes after: *Evening Shade* and *Dave's World,* each shot at Radford -- no more lines or bleachers! – and *Designing Women* and *Murphy Brown*, done on the Warner Bros. lot in nearby Burbank. On the *Murphy Brown* set I end up spending most of my time not near the cast or producers or even video-feeds of the various cameras – the best part about attending tapings as an executive is that I can stand on the stage floor -- but alongside the show's script coordinator when I discover that her resume includes the same duties on *Mary Tyler Moore* and *The Dick Van Dyke Show*.)

Yet I still have no clue how to be a Current executive.

"I have to go over to a rehearsal this afternoon and give notes for the first time," I say to a longtime Current person I've come to trust, on the day of my first assignment. "How do I know what to say?"

"You'll know," is the reply, which seems to constitute the entirety of my training, if not the training all over in a town where today's bewildered newbie is tomorrow's emboldened company head. But the advice is spot-on. Instincts take over later that day when I join a small cabal of writers and producers and studio executives after the show's first rehearsal, for a discussion about what we've seen.

I observe, listen, contribute, with what I hope is tact and care – and still tamed by my first-day screening ridicule months ago. I stand there with full awareness that I speak for and represent CBS and my boss, which I'll always want to handle with a gravity I take seriously, perhaps often too seriously. I head home afterward happy to have survived the day, especially given the irony of this first-time experience: The show in question this afternoon is a soon-to-launch (and even-sooner-to-be-forgotten) comedy called *704 Hauser*, a spin-off of sorts warmed from the embers of long-gone *All in the Family*. And the person who stands listening to my notes after the rehearsal is its producer, Norman Lear, the man who makes my CBS job possible in the first place.

Again I am amazed that not only am I here, but that I am anywhere even nearby.

Most of the comedies that I'm to cover alone are of the lower-profile or limited-order (six episodes) type that seem less pressured and more conducive to on-the-job training. But short or long season, an episode of TV is an episode of TV. Each week's work on even these limited-run series is a study in how a show morphs from first draft to final shot in just five days – as well as in the practice in walking the sketchily drawn line between being a network representative and an ally / advocate for the series you're covering, a series whose participants often need reassurance. It's a multi-tasking role that incorporates elements of diplomat / counselor / fire fighter / referee in dealing with fragile creative egos. And it's typified by a strange call I take in my office one afternoon from the star (and producer and head-writer and, were she able, chief caterer) of one of the comedies I'm overseeing.

A sweet-talker to the world at large, she's calling to introduce me to a whole other side of her personality, because she's heard that one of the show's staff writers has come to my office earlier in the day (at my invitation, extended a week earlier when I meet him briefly backstage). The light-hearted tone she works in public is gone. "Jim, what is [writer's name] doing up there in your office?" she demands to know, a freaky menace in her voice. And before I can even formulate a thought that will lead to my answer, she follows with, "I tell you if he's up there talking about this show, I'll fucking fire his ass."

For talking to me.

Okay then.

One other day, on another show, after its rehearsal, the female co-star approaches me with a *faux* sense of casualness to ask who it is at the network she'd talk to about a recent *TV Guide* advertisement for it that's she "just noticed." I tell her that I'm not sure but that I will find out and get back to her.

"I'm just wondering, is all," she says.

Happy to help where I can, I think.

"I mean," she continues, as I walk away, "my name is supposed to be the same size as [co-star's] in all advertisements. That's all. No big deal."

Apparently, though, it's a *huge* deal to her.

I keep walking.

"So who do I talk to about that?" she asks again.

(Indeed, her contract does stipulate equal billing, which she'll get on her next show a year from now when this one dies after a handful of episodes. It will be called *Friends*.)

Still another show sends word my way that if I'm to come to its tapings on Friday nights and I wish to venture out of the network Green Room and on to the stage floor, I'm to wear black clothing only, along with everyone else there. And I am not to appear in the star's sightline. (In fairness, neither is an uncommon request on movie and TV sets.) And another conversation one afternoon at yet another show finds the two men who produce it -- each a multi-Emmy-winner and neither short on self-regard -- arguing *about* me *in front of* me when I offer notes following a rehearsal.

"We're not taking that note!" / "The script is fine as is. Period." / "He can't tell us this isn't great comedy." All said just two feet from me, the executive who represents the network that makes the show possible. To them, though, I'm a hologram.

These solo Current assignments are for brand-new shows. None last beyond their initial short orders. Among them: *The Trouble With Larry*, starring recent *Perfect Strangers* alumnus Bronson Pinchot, which provides an excruciating test of my network loyalty the night of the first taping when I mistakenly think I'm to stick around until the final shot of the night, which comes at 2:45am, following a 7:00 start the night before (sitcoms typically take from two to four hours to shoot);

The Building, starring Bonnie Hunt, the chief memory of which, besides its self-destructive lead, is a premiere-night party on the patio of its director's hillside house that midway is attacked by rock-throwing vandals in the scrub above us and which prompts fellow partier George Clooney to assign himself the role of crime-stopper, by sprinting up the hill's dusty paths towards where the rocks seem to be originating (his last quite-serious words before escaping the living-room in which we've all sought cover from the assault, issued from a crouch position: "Cover me!"); *Muddling Through,* an above-average personal favorite with a sharp and seasoned showrunner but a lousy title, to be remembered if at all as the failed series Jennifer Aniston does right before she, too, moves on to *Friends*; and *Daddy's Girls,* starring Dudley Moore, whose frequent memory lapses and flubbed lines on tape-night, always during the second of the show's two back-to-back Friday tapings (typical of the time), has all eyes on the control-room clock, since we know that it means a very late night of re-shoots looms. (Fives years after the show's merciful cancellation -- just three episodes air out of the thirteen produced -- Moore is diagnosed with a memory-impairing neurological disorder called Supranuclear Palsy, from which he dies in 2002. I'm not the only one in town who wonders, sadly, if it begins undiagnosed during the run of the show.)

The different series that I cover make up a mixed bag of projects that offer their shares of challenges, but I do revel in attending the comedy tapings, being part of and witnessing the process either from the network Green Room off-stage or on the actual stage-floor with the casts and crew. They provide the kind of rush I can only wonder about as a child, when I sit at home and pretend to be behind the cameras. In on the action. In on the jokes. And though the truth is that most of the hands-on work of a Current executive is already done by tape-night, with notes offered through the week leading up to it on the script's various incarnations, watching it all come to its feet on show-night is like seeing it for the first time.

To me, the role of Current executive is chiefly one of support, especially on show-night. But questions and crises do arise that need attention and solution. One Friday night, I'm asked to fill in at a taping of *The Nanny* for the show's regular Current executive. I've shadowed her all week anyway, observing and listening as she handles notes-sessions and addresses network concerns after the first cast-reading and subsequent network run-through rehearsal. I've been introduced to the show's various producers, too. So I feel comfortable agreeing to step in. The show is well run.

Halfway through the taping, though, as I sit alone in the network viewing-room backstage, tracking along with my dog-eared copy of the night's script as the four monitors on the wall show what's being filmed by each of the floor's four cameras, I see that a small huddle has formed on the set among the (many) producers and writers. At first it looks like a typical between-scenes time-out, to discuss how the most-recently shot scene has gone. But it lasts for an atypically long length of time. Brows are furrowed. I wonder why. Then, courtesy of the stage microphones that are fed into the Green Room, I hear, "Is the CBS executive here?"

Me? I think to myself, looking around the empty room.

"Can the CBS executive make his way down here, please."

No, seriously — me?

And so I make my way to the scrum, in the process walking past several hundred pairs of eyes in the audience bleachers, trained on me, making me feel both important and intimidated. (There's a certain amount of prestige and power and ego-inflation that comes with being even a lower-level TV or studio executive in Hollywood, especially in this kind of position. It's a heady high at times. But it's also illusory -- a by-product of the position and not the person. The distinction will become clearer to me as I move in and around and outside The Business in years to come, as will the awareness that many in town often mistake the value of their positions for their own as people.) *What exactly am I being called on here to resolve?* I'm thinking. *It's not even my show.*

The question when I approach the circle of players: "We're about to shoot the scene, and we need to know one way or another whether we can say 'Jew.' That hasn't been decided yet."

Hmmm, is what I think.

"What?" is all I manage.

It seems that despite being in on this week's script's evolution, despite shadowing the regular Current executive to and from the soundstage, what I don't know is that this episode of *The Nanny* has involved a behind-the-scenes tug-of-war all week between the producers and CBS over the planned use of the word "Jew" in a key scene. To date, to this minute, in fact, with filming underway, it's apparently gone unresolved.

Interesting, I think. *Now what?*

"So can we or not?" one of the producers asks.

All eyes, both on the floor and in the bleachers, are on the (Catholic) onetime McDonald's fry-cook from Philadelphia. The clock is ticking. The pressure is mounting. I spark to a solution.

"Wait a minute," I ask. "According to the script, Fran [the nanny] is the one using the word, right?"

Right, I'm told.

"And isn't she herself, the character, Jewish?"

She is, they say.

Problem solved.

I leave Culver City later this night confident in the small role I play in keeping Hollywood peace if not in world politics as a whole, happy with the issue-solving pronouncement that still reverberates in my head.

"Well, then," I say to them. "Keep the 'Jew'."

The Nanny lives on.

Other series, not so much.

In late 1994, about eighteen months into my two-headed time-splitting job in both the Scheduling and Current Programming departments at CBS, with Scheduling still much more an administrative gig than a creative one, I'm assigned to be the Current executive for a new series to star Dolly Parton, in her first sitcom. She's to play Betsy, a mid-level career-focused entertainer who's accidentally electrocuted one night in her dressing-room, then dies and goes to the gates of Heaven, where she's told by an afterlife escort that she's to be denied entrance based on what has been her life of self-involvement. She's sent back to Earth to seek redemption, by doing better among the people in her life, in order to earn her wings. *Heavens to Betsy,* starring Dolly Parton as an earth-bound do-good angel, is the result.

The experience will not be as simple as the concept.

To begin with, the sitcom is scheduled to be shot not at any one of the number of available soundstages in Los Angeles, but in Orlando.

The one in Florida.

Rumored reason: Parton's fear of earthquakes. (Full disclosure: The rumor is never substantiated, though if it's true I can't say that I blame her.)

Then, the pilot shot for the series – essentially the first of its six-episode order, which establishes the premise, ends up so bad that it's completely scrapped, and a new pilot is ordered. (The only good to come of the rejected pilot is the story associated with the reaction to it by a high-ranking CBS executive who questions the casting of an African-American as Betsy's heavenly escort. "Really?" he's heard to ask, as if the idea eludes him. "A black angel?")

With a modified storyline, a second pilot is shot, completed, and delivered. And then it *too* is thrown out. The electrocution / afterlife angle just doesn't seem to be working, though in my book it's the least of the project's hurdles given the way it's borne of little more than a star and title in search of a series. (Not the first project that suffers from this approach, it also won't be the last.) So the premise is abandoned altogether, and a third iteration of *Heavens to Betsy* is crafted.

A more conventional sitcom, it'll be about a perky and successful singer who returns to her small Southern hometown to co-run a diner with a caustic and freshly transplanted New York. Naturally. Theirs will, of course, be the standard oil-and-water relationship, with hints of romance to come. (How Parton's singer and the New York chef, perfect strangers, come to open a business together in this small town, let alone how they manage to do so in the three weeks that make up the pilot's storyline, is never explored.) Gone are any traces of death. Or afterlife. Or making amends for a selfish life. Or confusing black angels. Only the title and star remain.

Third time being the charm, the rather unexciting and formulaic new *Heavens to Betsy* is deemed acceptable enough to complete a six-episode order at last.

Which is when the gates of heaven truly open.

In Orlando, the show gets underway. Cast-readings and rehearsals are fed *via satellite* back to our offices in Television City. My direct-report boss in Current Programming and I watch as it all unfolds, and I find myself wondering if we should blame its continued overall badness on the oft-malfunctioning hardware on the roof. The sad reality is that no matter the title or the premise this project is just not good. It's not funny. It's not interesting. And Dolly Parton, undeniably a star, is not a sitcom lead. At least here.

In an effort to salvage the show, writers and producers come and go backstage with impressive speed, as do I, to Orlando, sent for various rehearsals and tapings and general moral support often enough over the course of these handful of episodes to serve as a one-man testament to the concept behind the Residence Inn where I stay. My visits are met on set with a sea of smiling faces, frozen in place; behind them are whispers and eye-rolling among the staff and crew – though if members of the cast seem dazed by the experience they're never less than friendly. As for Dolly, she's consistently what seems to be her gregarious and upbeat and affable normal self. (Another unsubstantiated rumor: On the first day of production, Parton comes to the set, throws open her jacket – she's wearing a top – and says to the assembled staff, "Okay, folks, here they are; now let's get to work.")

But every visit, up to and including the one I make only to be told upon arrival by a low-level crew member that the show has shut down for a few days ("Hmm, did no one tell you that, Jim?"), has the feel of a slow-motion freeway wreck. Which comes to a head one Friday when, in a scene straight out of series television in its own right, the sitcom's (latest) pair of writer-producers, a longtime and successful comedy team with multiple long-running series to their credits, come to actual blows in their locked office – an inexplicable knockdown fistfight of such fury and animus that a younger staff-writer is forced to break down the office-door, with others rushing in to separate the pair.

Sitting in the rear of the production-office complex, I know nothing of the cage-match underway no more than fifty feet from me; admin personnel are charged with monitoring my whereabouts and then distracting me if I seem to be heading too close to the melee, since no one wants me to witness and report the incident back to CBS headquarters.

Because when you think of a Dolly Parton sitcom predicated on the concept of an angel doing good deeds, you think of a fistfight between its producers in the Magic Kingdom.

Heavens to Betsy somehow manages to complete its six-episode order more or less on time. Outside of a marathon screening for its (final) writing staff months after it wraps, in the Pasadena apartment of its CBS Current executive, it never sees the light of day. On CBS or anywhere else. Except for the 2001 afternoon when I exit the Subway sandwich-shop across the street from Television City, awkwardly stumble, hit my head, and knock myself unconscious on the sidewalk – face-first on the concrete, one arm up, one arm down, sandwich clenched in-hand, for I don't know how long, in direct sight of the office of the network president who could very well glance out his window at that very second and wonder why exactly one of his executives is currently unconscious in the curb across the street – it's my most surreal CBS experience.

These are my early years at CBS, the new guy becoming not so new, the intimidated guy trying to become more assured, the quiet guy trying to speak up more. Helping not a small amount: A dinner one night about a two years into the job with a longtime CBS-er who stares quizzically at me when I confess my feelings of inferiority among some of the higher-ups, and says, "Jim, Jim, Jim. *Why?* These are guys who go to Vegas for a weekend and sniff cocaine off hookers' *asses.*"

I continue to split my time between the Current and Scheduling departments. I value the Current-based work: It really does lift a curtain to the creativity and the collaboration and the shared TV experience that I long to be a part of. But Scheduling taps an even deeper passion – to learn how a prime-time network line-up comes together and how the decisions are made behind the scenes and between the seams. I'm not part of any real decision-making group yet, though. But I am picking stuff up.

In my specific role in the department, there is information to disseminate, competitive changes to track, reports to compile. (Daily, weekly, monthly, internal and external, Status Reports, Production Reports, Development Reports – the third floor is an archipelago of paperwork in an ocean of administration.) So there's definitely a curiosity being satisfied. There are also competitive calendars to maintain and to distribute in this not-yet-automated world that chart what's scheduled to air this and in future months on all four (and then five and six) broadcast networks. And there are people and departments and divisions for me to interact with and speak to.

Unlike most areas at the network that have single self-evident focuses – Development, Daytime, Late-Night, Current – Scheduling maneuvers around and interacts with just about every strata of the company on both coasts, by nature of its role. Internal information is released, made official, through us; external information comes in to and then is disseminated by us. Changes come and go. The essence of the department is apparent from the first days: Of the seven new series announced for that first 1993-94 TV season, only two (*Dave's World* and *The Nanny*) survive a freshman year, demonstrating not just the ability to withstand competition but also to support their respective timeslots and nights of air, with the promise of building a constituency that'll follow it if moved to a new timeslot. The very definition of success. Scheduling sees this and analyzes the rest – the other new series that fairly limp through the year before being cancelled.

One, *South of Sunset*, disappears overnight. Literally. It
offers the quickest case-study to date in how TV can work.

A light-hearted buddy-detective show that for some
reason feels the need to bring The Eagles' co-front-man Glenn
Frey to series television, *South of Sunset* is one of the last of the
new 1993 shows to premiere, saved to begin after (and thus
promoted during) the Toronto-Philadelphia World Series being
broadcast on CBS. The thinking is that the fall classic will
provide heavy exposure for the new show's many promos and
that its huge and male-friendly audience will then want to tune
in to watch the action-comedy hybrid. So after six highly-rated
World Series games, *South of Sunset* debuts at 9 p.m. on
Wednesday October 27, 1993.

It's cancelled 12 hours later.

The show's fate is sealed in our regularly scheduled
Thursday morning staff-meeting, when the network head
comes in, sits at his usual spot at the first-floor boardroom
table, is handed the overnight ratings, notes the abysmal if not
shockingly low number for the first *South of Sunset* (despite all
the promotion during the World Series, of course, which begins
my push-pull relationship with Research and Promotion), and

then turns to the Current executive in charge of the show with a single question before the meeting even officially begins:

"Are they still making this show?"

Flustered by the out-of-context inquiry, the executive shuffles through her paperwork in search of an answer. "Well, yes," she eventually says, the shooting schedule now mapped out in front of her. "It's a thirteen-episode order. They're up to the eighth one."

The president's four-word response:

"Tell them to stop."

And *Sunset* goes south overnight. Never to air again. Based solely on the overnight ratings. (The overnights are viewership estimates gauged from about a dozen major-market affiliated stations.) The insult heaped on the injury of cancellation: The show never even airs in Los Angeles, the city where it's made and in which it's set, as CBS programming is preempted here on October 27 for local coverage of area wildfires.

Much of the time in Scheduling is spent evaluating similar dilemmas – though not always as hastily. Evaluating ratings and research, competitive as well as our own, to make decisions about what's working and what's not. Scheduling, I see, really *is* about the playing of prime-time offense and defense that I deduce it to be back in my Philadelphia basement. It really is about when to lead with your strengths and how to protect your weaknesses in order to build a killer team and have a winning season, about the careful placement of the twenty-two to twenty-four episodes produced for each of twenty or so weekly series that make up a prime-time line-up.

For this, my direct-report introduces to me the concept of harvesting, the populating of the now-standard 35-week broadcast-television season with that relatively limited number of episodes, so that each night and week seem fresh (and watchable) despite the inevitable reliance on repeats. The challenge comes from having anywhere from eleven to thirteen weeks of the season, not counting summer, built-in with these reruns, which the math dictates. (The scheduling of specials, movies, sports, and short-order replacement shows help flesh out the season and even fortify timeslots that likely won't stand repeats of less-popular or of serialized series.)

This show-harvesting -- the physical mapping out of season-long runs of these dozens of episodes of multiple series, taking pencil and eraser to large oversized blank grids to be filled in week by week, title by title -- becomes my favorite part of the job. It's math, I suppose; but it doesn't involve fractions.

Scheduling benefits from a sort of medical approach: Part of the job is devoted to emergency-room triage, evaluating shows and time-periods that need immediate attention and treatment; the other part is spent on administrative work and tending to less urgent-care patients and issues. Fairly cut-and-dried – as is the overall system behind TV itself these days, more or less, be it here at CBS or at the other broadcast (non-cable) networks. It'll change in the very-near future, as TV itself rapidly does, becoming more 24/7 and year-round and less reliant on next-day ratings. But for now it follows a system, a calendar, a pattern, a timeline. It revolves around a yearly cycle of LATE SUMMER/EARLY FALL (when new series are introduced, while ones for the following fall begin to be pitched/developed/bought), WINTER (when some among this next round of pitched ideas are picked up to pilot), LATE WINTER / SPRING (when the pilots are made and screened and tested and then either selected or rejected), and SUMMER (when the schedule that this new batch is to be a part of is sold to advertisers and marketed for a fall debut). Then the cycle begins anew.

Comings and goings, orderings and cancellings, building and rebuilding, salvaging and protecting – sometimes it requires a deft touch, sometimes a smackdown. Sometimes it involves delicate deal-making and ego-handling, protracted analyses and intense research, multiple pitches and endless meetings, and calls and return-calls from producers and writers and studio executives. Sometimes there's little involved but contractual guarantees or backroom politics. Sometimes there's agony over a show's cancellation. Sometimes there's a network head pointing to a failing show's ratings and saying, "Nothing would give me more pleasure than to cancel this fucking thing." And sometimes there's a phoned-in plea to do just that, from a star herself of a show that's withering on the vine ("Somebody over there please get this piece of shit off the air").

The whole of it – from development to air, page to stage, birth to earth – is at once as precise and exacting and as carefully strategized as I always imagine it to be and as random as I always suspect. Stars and careers and fortunes can be made or saved or lost based on a zig, a zag, a personal bias, a preference, a hunch, or, as is the case with one project when I first join the company, a casually listed rasher of names doled out at a torturously long casting meeting that ends with the head of Drama Development saying with a huge sigh, "You know a new show is in trouble when you're considering both Bob Euker and Albert Finney for the lead." (It goes to Tom Conti; the show lasts seven episodes.)

In another meeting, the topic is a pilot for a quirky and unconventional office sitcom underway that's to feature a mixture of live-action and animation -- a cartoon sheep is at the center of an otherwise all-human cast. The executive overseeing the project reports to the head of the network that the ambitious effort is proceeding smoothly but, like any show that features animation, it already portends to be an expensive endeavor if picked up to weekly series. Praising the script, he carefully suggests that perhaps the project is strong enough to work without the animation, as a conventional office comedy.

"No!" interrupts the normally mild-mannered president, his palm slapping the conference-room table for emphasis. "The sheep is what makes it funny."

Life, death, success, failure, career-fame, obscurity – so much can ride here on so few only-in-Hollywood words. (The president turns out to be right about the animated project: Shot as conceived, the pilot is well-received in executive screenings a few weeks later. The cartoon sheep does indeed make it funny. Just not enough for the show to make the spring cut.)

I'm still learning. There's more to development than ideas and scripts. There's more to shows than weekly ratings. There's more to renewals than what is written or said. Two years in, with me settling in and more comfortable in my role, I observe and grapple with and try to understand all of it. The in-office politics, too. The careful orchestration of executive careers. The backroom maneuverings. The smiles that belie the insecurities. The ferreting out and the guarding of information. The passive-aggression. The nastiness behind the friendliness.

A third-floor assistant leaves the company under a black cloud for a better position at another company, deleting all her department's computerized records on her way out the door. A vice-president stages a sickout in protest of a new parking space that she feels is beneath her standing. A high-level executive's name is rumored to be among those listed in the Black Book of a famous and recently arrested Hollywood madam. A colleague reacts to my latest office-move with a rage that amuses as it frightens me, given how nice he is to me face-to-face. ("*Fuck that guy!*" I hear through the walls, about me, after hearing that I've been given yet another office, this one perceived to be better than his. "Who does he think he is?") Employee lawsuits dealing with job discrimination and financial mismanagement are quietly settled. Adulterous affairs amongst staffers become open secrets, their selections of area motels for lunchtime assignations a shared joke by the rest of the third floor.

It's not hard to look, listen, and follow the backstage action of this town's daily theater, where knowledge is power, weakness is seized upon, and image is everything without picking up basic tips of survival. In even the most casual of conversations, "You're right" comes out instead as "I don't disagree" -- three words that cede the point without relinquishing power, predicated on the speaker's "I" rather than the listener's "you." A subtle distinction. My growing understanding begins to allow a level of comfort in *being* here that matches what I know are the reasons for my *getting* here.

I am a network executive.

I speak up more about things that merit attention or change, buoyed by the reaction I get to my first real attempt. It comes one spring morning when I see a promotional campaign planned for airing during our annual March Madness NCAA basketball tournament.

In an apparent attempt to appeal to its multitudes of male viewers, a series of spots has been filmed that spoof the popular *Siskel and Ebert* movie-review show, here "reviewing" a slate of upcoming action movies planned for airing on CBS in the weeks after the tournament. The promos employ a pair of Latinos who are seen sitting in movie-theater seats, offering critiques of the upcoming films.

108

I don't get the math behind the campaign – college basketball? Siskel and Ebert? Latinos? – but what I see in its execution worries me: The Latino pair (and I'm not all that certain if they're actual Latinos or just white actors pretending) affect exaggerated old-school English-mangling accents, mispronouncing the names of the actors and titles they're touting, sloppily chewing on popcorn as they speak -- spittle and kernels projected with every other syllable. It's like stepping into a bad 1970s movie. To me, it's also startling in its racism.

When I bring the spots to the attention of my two direct-report bosses for a sort of reality check, each of them thinks they're part of some kind of internal joke. But I show them that they're actually airing already on the network, and the two race to confer with the head of our division, who, equally appalled, pulls the spots and cancels the entire campaign immediately. They're not just offensive, he says, a look of incredulity on his face, they come at the most inopportune time imaginable. In a bizarre twist of irony, CBS this very week is being recognized with an award from the national Imagen Foundation for its positive portrayal of Hispanics in prime-time.

For some reason, around this time I'm assigned to oversee two unusual specials that are being shepherded to life by the Scheduling department, each a documentary-type pet-project for the stars involved. One is from Kevin Costner, pitched and ordered on the heels of his Oscar-winning success with *Dance with Wolves* in 1991 and now finally coming to life. It will focus on the Native American settlement of North America. My role is mostly limited to watching all eight hours of the noble but incredibly staid narration-heavy project that his company turns in. (Costner hosts each installment.) In the highly commercial big-tent world of broadcast-network entertainment, it seems destined for failure, a fate it more than meets when it finally airs to record-low ratings. I meet the Oscar-winning Costner just once, in a group setting. He seems perfectly nice.

The other non-fiction effort I'm saddled with comes from talk-show host Montel Williams, here presenting a variation on the landmark 1970s documentary *Scared Straight*. The daytime talker is bringing his fire-and-brimstone motivational-lecture approach to inmates at a medium-security prison outside Las Vegas. It, and he, mean well. But the special is ultra-contrived and overly staged, to the point where producers single out camera-friendly faces from among the prison population to act out pre-written "personal testimonials" about the hard life within their cement walls. All too eager to be on a TV show, the prisoners selected are given their lines and then prompted off-camera by producers about how to deliver them. They're shot in mocked-up mini-prison-cells for effect. In a word, it's icky. As is the show. CBS never airs it. But the experience does leave me with a conversation-stopping anecdote for parties, about the day I spend in prison with Montel Williams.

I report to two different network-presidents during my first two years at Television City. In mid-1995, the forever spinning office-door that fronts nearly the entire entertainment business spins yet again here to welcome a third. A high-profile born-to-win former studio-head, he comes to a once-thriving now-struggling CBS – fewer new hits, aging existing ones, disparaged older audience -- as one of the most successful and powerful executives in television. The word is that he doesn't take kindly to losing. Anything. And he's set to change both the network and us with his aggressive attitude. So, what has been, to me at least, a game of sorts here -- a high-stakes game, but a game nonetheless – now looks to become a war, with skirmishes and casualties and battle-plans, the first of which is to lift the network back into first place. The bar is raised. Nearly every department head is replaced. He's the new man in charge. He is The Boss.

And I am nervous.

I feel quite the child again in the face of this imposing new adult in the room. A plebe to a five-star general. But then I remind myself that I've survived worse office transitions, that I know I have a place in this town and at this network, and that while I fear The Boss's power and role, I don't fear the man himself. Mostly because I don't even know him. So two months into the bloodletting and re-provisioning, amid a period of relative calm, I ask for a meeting. Granted it a few days later, I sit facing The Boss's imposing desk, and I hear

110

myself say to him what I hope are three simple yet pointed sentences:

"We haven't really had any official one-on-one time yet. And I just want to introduce myself, so that you know about me from *me*, and not from anyone else, as you get to know people around here. And I'm looking forward to working with you."

With that, at it often does, as it does when I find myself talking back to my TV at age six and as it does when I attend college at home rather than out of state and as it does when I pick up a new movie-magazine during my senior year to handwrite a note to its editor and as it does when I'm 31 and I screw up the courage to ask a powerful producer for help in breaking into TV, life turns on a dime. And my executive career truly begins.

"I'm glad you came in here today," The Boss replies. "You're a gentleman. Your job is not in jeopardy; and I look forward to working with you, too."

Plain words from an imposing force. And the second I hear them, I'm both relieved and enervated. They encourage both motivation and loyalty in equal measure, a lifetime's worth. (In the management-lite world that is my Hollywood future, the exchange will stand out as my most valuable – and one few others in charge around these part even know to offer.) The meeting sets up a working relationship like no other I've had, a professional working relationship infused with respect that I hope (and sense) is mutual. New to the day-to-day machinations of a broadcast network, The Boss is unfazed about turning to me one morning and saying, "The details of Scheduling are something you [Scheduling guys] know; I don't. So tell me." To me, the confession reveals a wealth of information about him, about his style, about his success, and about what will be our future together.

My duties and responsibilities begin to expand, along with my profile (which is for both good and ill, given that it comes with my sometimes-abrasive dinner-table molded personality, often clueless to my effects on others). I'm encouraged to speak and to act more, to contribute more. I'm given permission to be the executive I came here to be – both by The Boss and by myself. I'm awarded a literal seat at the table and a role on the changing team. I'm also presented with another new office, this one permanent – I've had many on the third floor -- on the coveted perimeter, with its wall of windows. It overlooks the famed CBS red portico that fronts our Beverly Boulevard address, seen so long ago in the cartoon opening of the landmark Carol Burnett series that my family devote its Saturday nights to. The Hollywood sign can be seen in the distance from my desk-chair. And, at last, I also get an assistant.

I think of my mother as I settle in – her days of laundry in the Wellington Street basement, walking passed me day after day, night after night, as I sit staring at our small black-and-white set. She'd be intrigued by all of this. She'd be excited to talk about it, too – modestly -- to the co-workers at the Clover Customer Service desk where she'd no doubt still enjoy working. And she'd laugh as I do at the price tag that comes with the new office furniture ordered for me: A standard hardback guest-chair alone costs more than my first-semester tuition at Temple University. I send it back.

The office is a by-product of The Boss's restructuring of the Scheduling department itself, complete with a smart new guy he brings in to head it and to which I am now relegated full-time. The Boss wants me to apply the skills I'm hired for to this single post only. No more straddling of two departments. No more Current Programming.

I'll miss the creativity that comes with these duties, the direct access to writers and producers and to the process that is the building of a weekly TV show. But I remind myself that the whole point of the move to Los Angeles is about the connection to and interest in and need to be a part of television's Big Picture. To be part of programming an entire TV network. The Scheduling department is where that need can best be met and where I also hope I can learn the most and be the happiest, not to mention where I suspect I can be of most value. Current is fun, but on as many days as not it can also be equal parts thankless and unrewarding and anonymous. That a series becomes successful is seldom credited to a Current executive's not-insignificant role and influence. Plus the job requires special people who themselves have special people-skills, and I don't think I'm one of them.

Current can also be silly. As I wrap up my show-files for storage, I look at random notes I've been keeping as part of my role here, things I've heard or things I've actually said myself in the weekly attempts to affect change on various series:

(Dec 1993, about a western) *Make chicken noise sounds more distinctive*

(Oct 1994, about a comedy) *Reinstate Betsy's inner-dialogue*

(July 1993, about a new drama) *The show needs more hats*

(Aug 1994, about a family comedy) *Make the character of Scar more appealing*

(Feb 1995, about a lawyer pilot) *The story is in need of more reverse alchemy*

(Sep 1994, about a new family drama) *The expression on her face needs to connote divine intervention.*

Re-reading these, I sense that I'm likely meant to work outside this strange bubble.

I also recall some of what can come from the exposure to high-priced ego-inflated often-marginal talent, both behind and in front of the camera. The shenanigans and the carryings-on that have little to do with the output of art or even the practice of commerce. The middle-aged actor sleeping with the teenaged girl who co-stars on his series as his daughter (and whose 18th birthday is met with a round of applause at a CBS staff meeting), the actor who refuses to come out of his trailer because producers have hired the wrong kind of monkey for the day's scene (he'll work only with orangutans, not chimps), the actress who has a stipulation put in her contract that the network is to supply her with a local apartment while she's starring on a New York-shot series (despite the fact that she already lives/has a home in Manhattan), the actress who is said to have expressed her displeasure over a script by urinating on it in front of its writers, the actress who wields her clout as star of a successful sitcom to have all the promotion featuring her more popular co-star removed from the air, the actress who insists that she's to be the only female on her successful drama with below-shoulder-length hair, the actor who holds up shooting on the first day of his new show when he finds out that his co-star's dressing room is bigger than his.

It all tends to erode an executive's passion as it distracts from his time. I realize that maybe the more academic world of Scheduling is the better fit for me.

With The Boss's edict, I get to focus now full-time on helping to plan and to schedule the whole of CBS's prime-time. I long for more of the interaction the post gives me with most every department at CBS, from creative to technical, from Los Angeles to New York, from high-profile to no-profile. Our generation and/or confirmation of changes to CBS programming have ripple effects throughout the network and its many tributaries. Much of the day-to-day work of Sales and Marketing and Media Relations is in many ways jump-started by the announcements that come out of our department. I enjoy meeting and dealing with all these people.

Scheduling is also where many all-purpose complaints seem to be directed, too -- internal ones from Current Programming executives unhappy with their assigned shows' placements and external ones from producers unhappy with promotion or timeslots. And somehow, despite a whole CBS wing devoted to the concept, we're the recipient of viewer complaints, as well, from those unhappy with a favorite show's cancellation ("You people make me furious" writes a ten-year old when we drop the 1995-96 satanic serial *American Gothic*) or unhappy with pre-emptions of their favorite shows ("Please tell me the name of whoever took *Touched by an Angel* off for a basketball game; I need to know so that I can pray for his soul") or unhappy with newly announced projects ("What lesbian idiot thought it was a good idea to put dyke Ellen DeGeneres back on the air?"). They're joined by calls of concern from stars themselves, unhappy with anything from when their work is being shown to how, including ones from a notoriously high-demand personality miffed that her project is airing on

Passover ("when my people won't even be watching TV") and from a legendary other who actually calls CBS Master Control in New York as her show is airing to insist that its volume be lowered.

One afternoon, I'm stopped on my way into the men's room by the CBS executive in charge of our police-drama *Nash Bridges*, starring Don Johnson. One of the Current department's more over-zealous members — a bit too emotionally connected to the series he oversees, in my observation, a bit too aligned with the people associated with it on the production side — the executive has an all-too-usual look of deadly concern on his face. I try to look passed both it and him as I go to push open the bathroom door. He stops me.

"Jim, we have to talk," he says.

"Can I go to the bathroom first?" I ask.

"I'm serious," he says.

"Actually, so am I," I reply.

"But Don Johnson just called, and he's very upset."

"About me going to the bathroom?"

He sighs.

Not in a joking mood, I guess. Okay, I bite: What is Don Johnson calling you about, and why is he upset?

"Don's upset about *Providence*."

"*Providence*?"

"*Providence*."

A fairly new family drama, *Providence* airs on another network.

"NBC's *Providence*?" I ask.

"Yes."

"The *Providence* that airs on NBC?" I ask again.

"Yes."

"Don Johnson is upset about a show that airs on another network?"

"Yes."

I pause. Then:

"Why on earth is Don Johnson calling you upset about a show that airs on another network a full two hours before his own show airs on CBS?"

"Because that show has become a hit."

"Okay…?" I say.

Viewer letter (1996)

"And because it's helping NBC's ratings on the whole night," he says, "not just at eight when it airs but at nine and ten after it's over. And ratings for Don's show are falling off a bit at ten o'clock as a result because the competition has gotten stronger."

I'm bemused.

"Don Johnson is upset because a show that airs at eight o'clock on NBC is affecting his ratings at ten o'clock on CBS?" I ask.

"Yes."

"What exactly is he calling you to *do?*" I ask. "What would he have *us* do?"

"I don't know. I guess he wants us to, y'know ... " – he makes a lifting-up gesture with his arms – "beef up our Fridays at eight o'clock and nine o'clock so that our ratings are stronger leading into his show at ten."

And with this, I'm now fascinated. Don Johnson apparently wants us to work harder and/or to come up with better programming. I don't know how to respond. And then (forgive me) I do.

"Look," I say to the Current executive, "let me go to the bathroom first. But go call Don and tell him that when I'm done, I'm going back to my office to call NBC and I'm cancelling *Providence*. But I can't promise they'll do it."

W hat few here know – what few people anywhere know – is that around this time, amid the backdrop of the new hard-charging CBS steward and combined with long-standing personal pressures of varying strengths further attacked by a virus I can't shake, I begin a debilitating real-life fight of a whole other sort that overshadows everything else -- one with clinical Depression. (It merits the capitalization.)

Seemingly out of nowhere, induced by a seasonal flu that I cannot take time off work to treat (sickness equals weakness at the new CBS), worsened by days as a literal one-man network Scheduling department at this time of corporate change before the new department-head arrives (the presiding department head has long been relieved of his duties, leaving just me at the wheel), and stirred by endless nights of what becomes unbearable insomnia divined by all of it, I stumble and fall on the rocky path of mental health. My body and mind deteriorate on parallel tracks. I pass out twice in my office, alone, making sure though to get my office-door closed first each time so that no one can see.

Overworked and afraid, I endure long office days of desperation, crawling through each a minute, a second at a time, the duties mounting and the pressures multiplying. There is *so much* to be done. And literally *so little* of me to do it, which begets only more work to be done. I tell no one what's happening. No one. I just exist as I can, a collection of cells, fervently hoping for both inconspicuousness and relief – my condition likely exacerbated by the continued treks into the office each day, the skipped meals throughout, the self-torment and worry at night, and by the occasional visit I make, in secret, during my lunch-hour, to see a sick colleague who's dealing with the threat of cancer. (The colleague is part of the old guard at CBS that's currently being shown the door, and I fear that to affiliate with him is to be disloyal to the new guard.) A shrink I'll end up seeing will observe it as "one of the worst professional situations" she's ever heard of. I'm disappearing into a void I've never experienced. It is, however, one that I've seen before.

Which begs my joke:

Depression doesn't just run in my family, it stops.

My memory is clear. It's never spoken about as the seven of us grow up on Wellington Street, but Depression (capital D) is part of life here. Real actual certifiable clinical Depression. I don't know what it is or how it forms or where it either comes from or goes to when it goes away, but in seeing it in at least three extended-family members when I'm young, I know it's as frightening as it is unexplained. Hidden in plain sight.

When the genetic giant awakens in me at 35, though, invited by illness and fortified by stress, its familiarity is cold comfort as it reaches out from somewhere I do not see to pull me down to places I do not know. Down into what author William Styron calls in his book of the same name about Depression "darkness visible." What's once *of* me is now *in* me. Untamed internal wildfires, leaving scorched terrain. Physically painful. When I finally relent to confessing what's happening to me, to a few friends outside of CBS – when I know that as a man alone I now need help and attention -- I crib a description:

Depression is falling into a black hole, dropping deeper and deeper and deeper still, to a point where you can no longer fathom a way out – because you no long can remember the way in.

And then you *become* the hole.

Two weeks into the worst of it, office work is no longer an option. Thankfully, it's late December, a time of TV-autopilot. Colleagues have scattered. So no one at CBS is clued in as the fire consumes me. The friends take me in to their home, where they facilitate the medical help I clearly need. And where, fate has it, not seconds after swallowing sleeping pills that I beg to get prescribed for me the afternoon they do, I'm called to participate in a CBS conference call, hastily set up at the last-minute to discuss Christmas programming.

The picture: Me, in someone else's house, in someone else's bed, a flu and clinical Depression tearing at me, the tranquilizing drugs rapidly taking hold, discussing CBS strategy on the phone with colleagues none the wiser.

I can handle the indignity that is my dismantling for only so long under someone else's roof, though. I need my own space. So I return to my own home, left with little choice but to wait out the storm as Christmas 1995 collapses around me. Only the daylight chasing away the sleepless nights tells me that time is passing. My appetite gone, I shed more of the weight that the flu has already claimed, on my way to a total of 30 pounds lighter inside of a month. I'm hounded by the inside of my very own mind, a visit to madness I cannot leave. There's neither rest nor respite nor retreat. I pray for relief to find me, as I wait for the Depression medication to take hold.

I avoid reminders of the season however I can: If switched on at all, the TV is tuned only to old movies or vintage sitcoms. But there are times I can't stop from taking myself to the front window of my house, to look outside, and to see how others are exploring a holiday brighter than mine. Standing there, I'm reminded of how a friend and longtime depression sufferer once describes her own battle when it's at its worst: "I look out my living-room window and see normal people out there living normal lives. And I know that not one of them knows what Hell is." Today, I understand the words.

On Christmas afternoon itself, a friend comes by to suggest, gently, that I join her for a family dinner, and I struggle to find the words to beg off – to try to explain to her that I cannot even conceive of a way to get dressed this day, let alone to step passed my own doorway. I can manage just two words, with minimal eye contact: "I can't."

"I know," she replies, squeezing my hand with a reassurance that suggests she is familiar with the pain. "I know. And it's okay."

I fight how I can. I try to create as much structure as possible for myself in an all-too unstructured new world. I literally force myself into daily walks throughout my pedestrian-friendly Pasadena neighborhood. (I've fled Studio City in the wake of the 1994 Northridge earthquake, which damages my starter-apartment there. "We didn't even realize he left," says one former neighbor to another months later, who reports it back to me, "until we realized we weren't hearing his Sunday morning phone calls to his father through our walls.") I don't stray far from home, but I do make a point to walk a block, a house, a step, further each day. Any progress is some progress. And when my appetite begins to return, I paper my house with home-delivery menus, my every meal ordered in, cost be damned. I know that food I won't prepare for myself is the path to wellness.

I also simplify my life in every way I can envision. I try to regulate what little sleep I start to get again; limiting the daytime dozing helps support the cause. I pay long-dormant bills and balance my accounts. I even buy the washer and dryer that my rental bungalow does not provide, to reduce still more stress of Laundromat visits. To make my days, my life, incrementally easier. Big thing, small things, any things -- combined with a reduced strain at the office, all of it allows that I slowly, glacially, begin to find myself again, even if to my own amusement I find that an early and casual New Year's Eve dinner that I force myself to attend requires two hours to dress for.

When 1996 arrives, so does help at CBS in the form of the new direct-report – not just another body in the department but one to take charge of it. Complemented by the home-rest and by the medication, it offers some light so that I can slowly emerge from the hole. I get through more days. I'm a daily worker again, even if at the end of the day I still all but collapse from fatigue for the trying. I even manage an occasional night out after a while, unsure though I am of how long I can last each time I do. (The sweated-through clothing cues my return to home.) The mere effort is the new goal. My sleep returns to a semblance of normal. As does my appetite and mood. Then, standing in my kitchen on an otherwise uneventful Monday night at the end of January, six weeks since the curtain comes down, I feel what I can only describe as whatever is the opposite of life draining from me: I feel life coming back *into* me. With the awareness comes hope. And then comes me again.

Words can fail Depression. The latter months of 1995 and early months of 1996 are mine alone to remember and to learn from. And to be cautioned by. I know that I can never walk away from Depression. Not really, anyway. It's a genetic haunt. Years will come and go, but it will always be there, always teasing and threatening and looming just out of frame. All I can do is to be vigilant and to be ready for each unprovoked assault (of which there will be three in the next eleven years). It will inform all my days, good and bad. And though I'll try to avoid exposing it to my professional world, and certainly the world at large, I will out myself a decade into the fight by way of a newspaper article I write in 2005, fueled by anger and frustration when the topic of depression becomes part of a silly and ill-focused national debate on mental health initiated by caged-looking actor Tom Cruise.

Promoting his latest movie, Cruise will rant about medication and psychiatry in a way that I'll feel is both dangerous and ill-informed, obfuscating an important subject (at best) and hurting people who may need real mental help (at worst). So I'll write an opinion essay for *USA Today*, which editors there will entitle "Tom, You've Said Enough." And in it, the Philadelphia boy raised not to talk publicly, or at all, about family matters will prove to be the man who does just that across the entire top half of the Op-Ed page of the nation's newspaper. Tom Cruise's face, my name, a personal family story, the facts of my Depression – all there for the world and my family to see and read. Which it will. *USA Today* will be flooded with letters of thanks, the blogosphere swollen with responses of support. "Clearly you have touched a chord," my editor will say.

It'll be my proudest moment ever.

(Actually, in that it forcefully demonstrates for me the power of the written word, which fuels my life and career, it'll be tied for first with an essay I write in 1992 for the *Los Angeles Times,* about grief, on the fifth anniversary of my mother's death – if only because fully eight months after it runs, I find out through the most serpentine of paths that a local friend of a friend, whom I don't know, actually carries the article with him in his suit pocket to his own mother's funeral, handing it that day to a family member who asks how he's doing, saying, "This is how I feel.")

My professional world does re-establish itself as life's main focus in the wake of Depression. It's more and more demanding, the skirmishes of Scheduling and Planning more intense, so I am grateful to have a sense of normalcy to support me. Beyond the self-evident tasks that our department's name suggests – What shows airs when? What nights and time-periods need attention? Which series are strong enough to lead off a night or even an hour? Strong enough to go head-to-head with the strongest of the competition? Most compatible with what other series? Need help in the form of a stronger show either before or after it? What movies or specials are available to air to supplement or fortify a night or a week or a sweeps period or even just to fill a hole? – there's also a laundry list of items involved in our area dealing with details I never think about as a viewer. Or even *know* to think about.

Like what happens when a series is delivered to the network from the studio too short or too long for its allotted timeslot? (Studios make and pay for TV series; networks license the rights to air them from those studios.) Or when a series can't meet a delivery deadline at all? Or, what exactly is involved when prime-time is delayed by a live broadcast (sports or awards shows) that runs long? Or if programming is flat-out interrupted by breaking news or when transmission signals are lost or break down? And how is all of it resolved and communicated among the more than 200 affiliate stations that make up the CBS network on its way to our living-rooms?

As I see and experience it, the Scheduling department is a TV network's air-traffic-control tower: In conjunction with a host of unknown departments on the ground, as uncelebrated as they are indispensible, it coordinates the departures and arrivals of a fleet of planes in a process that involves an army of personnel, affecting air-travel nationwide. The primary concern and hope? Smooth flights, the avoidance of crashes, the swift tending to any that occur. It all begs mention of another huge part of the job I have no concept of until it presents itself and is explained to me.

Sometimes, not often but sometimes, a TV network is forced to pull from the air (or re-edit before it does air) a specific program in the wake of breaking news -- a high-profile death or a national tragedy or a world incident – when it's decided that the programming touches too closely on or is too reminiscent of the real event or would just be insensitive to air at that time. ABC, for instance, postpones the 1981 Oscars after the assassination attempt on President Reagan, which happens early on the day it's set to happen. In 1995, FOX scrambles to re-edit a bombing sequence shot for its season-finale of nighttime soap *Melrose Place* after the Oklahoma City terrorist explosion makes the idea problematic. The reviewing / reevaluation / repositioning / editing is done quickly, with the departments affected by the decisions (be it Movies or Specials or Current) working in conjunction with the network's Sales and Media Relations people and in accordance with the network head. (In the case of the 1981 assassination attempt, ABC also faces an additional dilemma: The lead character in one of its hit shows, a light superhero drama called *The Greatest American Hero*, has the same last name as that of the Reagan shooter. So, completed episodes in which the name is heard are looped; future scripts drop the name altogether.)

My first experience with this whole sub-world of Scheduling comes two years into the job when a Pennsylvania plane disaster leads to CBS pulling a TV-movie that features a small-plane crash. I sit in on the debate, confused: Though deadly, the real crash is a low-profile one, of interest mainly to those in Pennsylvania and the surrounding region. It doesn't seem to fit the "national-interest" criterion. But then the reason to remove it becomes apparent: The accident occurs near Pittsburgh, home to The Westinghouse Corporation, which owns CBS right now. In this case, the corporate parent is the influential motivating force.

Two other discussions soon after involve a matter of the actors starring in shows. An equestrian accident paralyzes Christopher Reeve, who has recently completed a series of movies for CBS in which he appears throughout on horseback. The first is about to be broadcast. Does airing it make us look insensitive? (With the approval of everyone involved, the movie remains scheduled.) And around the same time, the suicide death of actor Carroll O'Connor's son Hugh occurs just as an installment of the series in which they co-star, *In the Heat of the Night*, is about to run, which ends with a scene in which a murder suspect commits suicide. (It too goes on, without edits.) Other high-profile real-life events that prompt programming reviews run the gamut from the 1997 Princess Diana car crash and 1998 death of Frank Sinatra to the 2001 execution of Oklahoma City bomber Timothy McVeigh. Does any of our programming feature even a passing reference to the Royal Family? Or to Sinatra? Or feature a building exploding or a bombing of any kind or even a mention the word "execution"? Of "Oklahoma"? (No issues are detected in any of the cases.)

Silly sounding perhaps, these discussions and decisions become a prudent part of our day-to-day. More prudent on one day in particular.

In the morning hours of Tuesday, April 20, 1999, teenaged students Eric Harris and Dylan Klebold wreak deadly chaos at their Columbine, Colorado, high school by shooting and killing 13 people and wounding two dozen others before fatally turning their guns on themselves. It's a small-town massacre that plays out live on national television, including on all the TV-supplied desks of the third floor of Television City. As soon as I see what will become the iconic images of the day – the school's surviving students being evacuated single-file out of the school, mid-crisis, arms above their heads -- I make my way over to the Current Programming side of the third floor with an inquiry of its executives that I know will be met with eye-rolls but which needs to be made nevertheless. ("Jim, no one thinks the way you do" is something I hear more and more around here.)

The question: "Do any of the soon-to-air shows that you cover have storylines, scenes, or images that would be deemed insensitive to broadcast in light of today's breaking news in Colorado?"

The two most senior members of the department – a seasoned pair, each takes seriously the responsibilities of their jobs -- know the drill: As soon as they themselves see the news break, they review all the content of their shows, both completed and still-in-production. There are no scenes or images that needs cutting. Each is good to air. I move on. The next three Current executives I go to, each newer to the department, predictably laugh at my question ("Oh, Jim, here you go again, taking things too seriously"), but they nonetheless double-check their shows' storylines and scripts and rough-cuts as I wait. All clear.

My last stop is to the office of an executive who's no long-timer, but he's not brand-new, either. He's sitting at his desk talking with the department intern, CNN in the background. "Hey, guys," I say. "I'm just wondering if any of your shows scheduled to air tonight or in the next few days might have content that would be deemed insensitive to air in light of today's events in Colorado? Y'know -- just to be safe?" The executive thinks for a minute, then says no. His shows are issue-free. "Okay, just checking," I say. "You're sure?" The answer is yes. I thank him and walk away.

"Wait a minute, Jim," I hear, from the intern. I re-trace my steps, and I see her looking at the Current executive with a concerned expression. "We do have that episode of *Promised Land* this Thursday," she says to him. His eyebrows arch. "Oh, yeah -- that might be a problem," he says.

Might be? I wonder? It's a low-profile spiritually infused family drama. How much of a problem could it pose?

"Well, there's a mass shooting in this week's episode," he answers, casually. "At a school. Several students are gunned down."

I stand there, slack-jawed, staring at him.

Adds the intern, waving her arm at him as a prompt, "Oh, and the show *is* set in Colorado."

"Oh, yeah," says the executive. "That, too."

That, too.

With as much sarcasm I can muster (which is considerable), I reply, "Well, I *think*. That. Might. Qualify. I think that airing an entertainment show that features a mass shooting at a Colorado school just two days after a mass shooting at a Colorado school just might be seen by some as insensitive."

A repeat episode of the show airs on Thursday instead. (Typically under such circumstances, when a replacement episode is needed at the last minute, the network turns to the next original episode of the show on hand, as series can be one or two episodes ahead. But the only other original episode of *Promised Land* that's ready to air is one that also just happens to feature a child-related shooting, a fact also uncovered by the intern, later in the afternoon, by herself. The boss-executive has left for the day with the pre-emption issue unsettled. A repeat is the only option. Thus, the Colorado school-shooting episode of *Promised Land* -- titled "A Day in the Life" -- achieves a sort of television immortality as the lone episode of the series that never airs, ever, on the CBS network.)

Two years later, the events in New York on 9/11 invoke their own trials of the emergency system, though in this case there are no discussions about what to do when they occur: These are the times when a network's News division just breaks in to and then indefinitely preempts regularly scheduled programming, no questions asked or permission sought. It'll end up taking over the air for four days round-the-clock, just as it will at every other broadcast and cable-news network, the first time this happens since the Kennedy assassination in 1963. (In fact, the continuous coverage of this week will eclipse that of 1963, lasting a total of more than 90 hours.)

For me, the experience begins with a 6:45 a.m. phone-call at home from my direct-report, who asks if my TV's on (it's not) and who then explains what has happened in New York. "Thousands are dead," he says. He asks that I call the now-third executive member of our Scheduling department and that each of us gets to the office as soon as possible.

When I arrive, TVC is all but empty: Understandably, some employees have stayed home; some who've come in have been sent home. (Throughout the day, there is a perceived threat of attack directed at media facilities all over the country, including ours.) A skeletal staff mans the third floor. The News division has already commandeered our air. Three of the four planes are known to be down.

A key early issue: CBS, like the other broadcast networks, maintains a transmission tower atop the World Trade Center. It, of course, has been destroyed, and its technicians killed. Back-up towers are called into play. Then, on a much less dramatic scale, attention turns to the Emmy Awards presentation that CBS is scheduled to air in five days. It's quickly cancelled, a change handled by those in our Media Relations department, among others, as the madness plays out on our TVs.

Department heads from Current and Specials and Movies and other areas go about reviewing all content scheduled to air in the coming weeks. A new drama series set to debut in nine days -- *The Agency*, about the CIA – opens with a terrorist bombing. It'll need to be re-edited. A made-for-TV movie scheduled to air in three weeks begins with an airplane explosion. It's pulled altogether. All other series in every day-part are scrutinized for taste and sensitivity – even though we're not at all sure when entertainment programming will even resume.

All of this is happening as members of the network's Sales staff, in town from New York for the Emmys, sit in various offices of the executive wing, ears on the relevant discussions and eyes on the TV images that are documenting the destruction of their hometown. At one point, the head of Sales takes in the imagery and then shakes her head in disbelief as she listens to reporters' attempts to summarize the morning's events thus far and to estimate the death toll in lower Manhattan. "What are they talking about?" she says. "They keep talking about 'the missing' down there. What 'missing'?"

" 'Missing' is dead," she says, her wan voice fading. "Missing just means dead."

The sentence hangs mid-air.

On the more ridiculous end, the morning's events also stir a conversation with my direct-report about, of all things, the hold-music heard on CBS's telephone system. Several years ago, in one of those typical office encounters that find an employee (me, for instance) in the wrong place at the wrong time in the vicinity of the right person (The Boss, for instance), I'm put in charge of it. Vice-President of Hold Music, colleagues joke. This Tuesday morning, my boss turns to me and says, "Jim, first thing you have to do is take care of the phones." (*First* thing?, I wonder.) The I realize why the urgency: On the loop of music that callers hear when placed on hold is the song used for our legal drama *Family Law* -- Edwin Starr's "War." It's not an ideal selection for anyone to listen to for a while. The VPHM has it removed.

After four days of round-the-clock news overage, the powers-that-are at each of the broadcast networks agree that entertainment programming will resume with the start of prime-time on Saturday September 14. Fittingly for CBS, that means that the first show back on the air post 9/11 is the spiritual anthology *Touched by an Angel*, whose producer scrambles to film what she calls a "prayer for the nation" to open the week's episode, to be offered by its two angel-portraying leads. If it's one of the more awkward examples I've seen to date of the self-regard that's rampant in television – "We do acknowledge that they're not real angels, right?" I ask when the proposal is made and signed off on with the solemnity of a papal conclave -- the over-the-top gesture does make for a smooth transition from the real world back into the reel one.

For the bulk of the eleven years I work under The Boss, I'm part of a three-person team in the Scheduling department – a troika of executives who've each stepped into his role here through unconventional right-place-right-time means. (It's how it happens.) Together we program an entire TV network, each of us bringing complementary skills and personalities to the union -- two earnest Catholic Wisconsinites and a former altar-boy from Philadelphia. The Boss (Jewish) jokes that we're his "Christian Scheduling Team."

A fairly tight-knit group, we spend most every workday in the same one room – the department-head's office. I like to see us as an effective and efficient group, too, even if the head guy does have a tendency to leave the room without notice from time to time, mid-sentence (his or ours). We get along well enough to sit side by side all day, mapping out CBS, grateful and loyal to the Boss who is in return loyal to us, taking our duties much more seriously than we do ourselves. We socialize off-hours frequently, too. On occasion, we even car-pool since, by coincidence, we each end up buying houses in the same small oceanfront community southwest of L.A. – the head of the department literally at the ocean's door, me a mile inland, the third member a mile behind me.

"Yes, we each live at the beach," says the lower-rung third member of our ladder when asked, "but in proportion to our income."

We laugh constantly, helped not insignificantly by being in a creative business, often in the company of comedy writers and comedy producers, which likely makes our attempts at humor even more biting. The self-amusement permeates the small department: At one of the ubiquitous office gatherings on the third floor for the latest employee birthday / engagement / retirement / marriage, I stand off to the side next to the direct-report's assistant. "What's this one for?" I mutter to her with an eye-roll, as another candle-topped carrot cake is wheeled in for the person-of-the-hour. Mock-yawning, the female assistant dryly whispers, "She had a negative Pap smear."

I for one these days (and I sense that my partners feel the same way) appreciate knowing that while ours are high-stakes sometimes pressure-cooker jobs, which we more than respect, they're also the kind that make us feel very fortunate, very lucky. In many ways, we've won the career-lottery. Good jobs, good salaries, benefits and perks and stability, Hollywood allure. It also helps that these days, only a few years into The Boss's reign and thanks to a winning combination of leadership and timing and programming, the floundering CBS ship stands righted. We are now the lead network in prime-time-- not just resurgent but victorious. Respected and powerful again.

It's intoxicating to be back on top, to be part of this winning high-profile well-run administration. CBS is being more and more strengthened with each show, with each week, with each passing season. Fortified by the annual rites of spring.

Basketball has March Madness. Retailers have Back-to-School. Pet lovers have Westminster. The time of year when everything matters. TV's time is known as the Upfront, the single-word term that translates into the planning and then unveiling of a new fall schedule every May in New York, on the heels of weeks of screenings and meetings and discussions on both coasts. If LA is where TV is made, New York is where it's sold, providing the money that greases the chain. And the Upfront, or more technically the phase that follows it, during which advertising for the new schedule is sold, makes it all happen.

My first experience with it comes, of course, during the first two weeks that mark the start of my CBS job in 1993, watching the dozens of pilots that make up the list of shows eventually taken to and then chewed on in New York. Two years later, I'm invited to participate in the actual ritual itself, in person -- albeit from the sidelines, away from the room where the final decisions are made. (Truth be told, it's less from the sidelines and more from outside the stadium: My chief responsibility is to sit in my boss's Manhattan hotel room waiting on an IT tech to fix his laptop -- "Jim McKairnes, you're just the man I'm looking for to handle a special project" is, I believe, how he extends the assignment – which prompts a snarky call I make to a friend back in Television City to say, "I'm sitting here in New York trying to figure out which of the four new suits I bought for this trip best matches the décor of the hotel room I cannot leave.") I'm very much present, though, a few days later at the CBS offices when the new schedule is officially presented in-house, most of which is news to me and all of which finds me saying to myself:

They must know something I don't.

What's unveiled violates just about every tenet of smart scheduling, as I sense it anyway. Nearly a dozen existing CBS series are canceled, eleven new ones are to be introduced, popular long-running shows with loyal constituencies are moved to new timeslots, and the number of half-hour comedies on the schedule doubles to eight. In short, change is evident on every night of the week in just about every timeslot -- a disorienting recipe for viewer confusion and rejection. It's as though a large city's heavily used bus-line schedule has been re-jiggered in such a way that not only have the arrival times changed but also the route. Epic failure can be the only result: People will take one look and opt for their cars.

But another big TV lesson is underway: I pick it up when the head of CBS Sales points at the giant whiteboard at the front of the room in which all the executives have gathered here in New York, the one labeled **1995-96 SCHEDULE,** and makes a proclamation as sweeping as his PT Barnum hand-gesture:

"We can sell the hell out of this schedule," he says.

And there it is: The Upfront, the actual Sales process for which this time of year is named, the one to follow tomorrow's presentation of this new schedule and which involves getting advertisers to commit to and to buy commercial time for a new yet-to-air lineup (committing to money "upfront" of the season), is about selling the hell out of the schedule. Selling the *promise* of what's to come, under the guise of *new*.

In the case of CBS's 1995-1996 schedule, new is the watchword. It refers both to the shows and to the network. The mandate this year is to get younger by attracting younger viewers with more younger-skewing fare. And the eleven new series, if not the revised schedule as a whole -- wall-to-wall with younger stars and more half-hour comedies, which tend to attract younger viewers and thus premium advertising money – represents a massive effort to create new value and generate increased revenue for a network long derided as out-of-touch and out-of-date. It's about selling the specter of change in a business where sometimes even successful series, at any network, are denied renewals if the cast is perceived as too old. (I once hear a network head say on the eve of an Upfront presentation, when asked about a certain face from a popular previous year's series that's missing, "I'm not getting up there on that stage tomorrow to announce [proven but older sitcom lead] as one of our stars."

But there's change and then there's change. This is much too much entirely, I feel, standing in the back of the room and taking it all in. It's alienating. It'll drive away existing viewers, and despite what everyone in this room is telling

131

himself, it won't bring many new ones in to replace them, because the new shows just aren't that good. It's a lose/lose schedule. I know in my heart it won't last two months come fall.

But he can sell the hell out of this schedule.

And over the summer he and his staff do.

And come fall the new schedule implodes inside of two months.

As feared, longtime viewers of the network turn away; new viewers never show up. With a lone exception, every new series ends up being cancelled. *The Client, Central Park West, Courthouse, American Gothic, New York News, Can't Hurry Love, If Not For You, Dweebs, The Bonnie Hunt Show* -- all gone. Stars JoBeth Williams and Patricia Wettig and Gary Cole and Gregory Harrison and Mary Tyler Moore and Nancy McKeon and Elizabeth McGovern and Hank Azaria and Bonnie Hunt (again), franchises like John Grisham, a young cast of a new nighttime soap picked up to bring young people to the network – poof! CBS begins to sink under the weight of the failure. Not even *Bless This House*, starring Andrew Dice Clay, developed and launched as the hottest comedy prospect of the 1995-96 season, survives.

Or, in my viewpoint, <u>especially</u> not *Bless This House*.

From the outset of its development, I loathe the show and everything it represents -- star over story, concept over comedy, hype and manufactured expectations over reality. The script makes daily headlines all over town, hailed as TV's next big breakout hit, a show that will lift the fortunes of whatever network smart enough to get it. But this "vehicle for Andrew Clay" (it's announced that with this show he's dropped the "Dice" from his name, as well as the abrasive persona that goes with it) supports my growing contention that in Hollywood people see what they want to see, and then pass on that vision as reality, which reporters in turn print as fact -- which then informs future decisions.

The reality is that *Bless This House*, star or no star, is average at best – a middle-class everyman sitcom being done better on at least two other shows (on another network). And the star, in fact, makes it less likely to work, not more. Because he's not *likeable*. A fatal flaw on TV.

On the spring night the pilot shoots on the Warner Bros. soundstage in Burbank, where the whole of the industry assembles following weeks of hype, I watch and I just can't fathom its success (though, for the record, the bleacher-audience in attendance this night laps the whole thing up). To me, Clay, middle name or not, is neither likeable nor relatable, certainly not in the Ralph Kramden / Roseanne Conner way he's being pitched.

The following Monday, in one of many memos I send off in these early years that find me not yet confident enough to speak out loud, I tell my boss (not The Boss, who will arrive later in the year) that I just don't see it.

"You don't see it??" is the emailed response. (Two question marks.) He's incredulous. "I heard everyone laughing there last Friday night. This is the project *everyone* is talking about. This is going to be huge." Then he offers a concluding comment I'll never forget and which I'll learn to get used to hearing each time I reject any of the town-stirred Kool-Aid: "You're swimming against the tide on this one, Jim. And no offense but I hope you drown." (A nice guy, he doesn't mean it: He's just under the gun to turn the CBS boat around, caught up in annual pilot fervor.)

Instead, of course, *Bless This House* drowns, going under in half a season. Flat-out rejected. Not funny. Not interesting. Not relatable. Style, such as it is, over substance. Headline masked as story.

But typical for an industry that surfs on waves of generalizations and unproven declarations, the show's demise is summed up in-house at CBS by a colleague this way: "These country folk sure are hard-core anti-Clay" -- which seems to be some kind of reference to CBS's more traditional audience base. As if *that's* the issue with *Bless This House*. And despite the fact that through the years the CBS "country folk" audience takes in shows from *All in the Family* to *Two-and-a-Half Men,* characters from Manson to Hitler, and subject matter from transsexualism to the Holocaust to incest.

TV offices out here do not have shelves lined with history books.

I do seem to swim against the tide here, I guess. It'll likely be my legacy. But I like to think it's passion for TV and an awareness of both its power and our responsibilities that inform my approach. Still, it can be isolating, no matter how right I feel or tell myself I am – or maybe because of it, since I can be so lousy at articulating my positions.

In the fall of 1997, I'm walking passed The Boss's office when he sees and waves me in, to join an impromptu discussion he's having with the head of Comedy Development about a newly launched sitcom that's fading fast. *"Jim, we're just here trying to figure out what went wrong with [title of show]."* The development head – as gentle a soul as there is in the entire building -- turns to me with an earnest look on his face and says, "What are your thoughts? I mean, why do you think it didn't work?" With no small amount of impertinence nor any acknowledgement of his work involved in launching the project, nor even of his feelings now, I respond, "Um, maybe because it wasn't *funny?*"

The blank stares that follow tell me all I need to know about how my answer is received.

And then The Boss, whose leadership is so effective that he can impose rule with but a single syllable or look, offers me one of each. "Jim," is all he says, with a disappointed stare that makes me wither. Then after a long minute, he adds, "That was a bit impolitic, don't you think?"

The comment and disappointment sting. Once again, I have to remind myself that I'm no longer sitting at my family dinner-table, where cutting humor is the prevailing currency, spent with impunity. I need to remind myself that in the grown-up world, the working world, diplomacy and tact are part of the coinage. And in this case I know I just blew a good chance of exercising some of each, perhaps leaving a lasting imprint on me. It's a learning lesson I try to carry with me.

(I would have liked, however, to have had a real conversation about the show, to have zeroed in on the point I so awkwardly try to make, the one my flippancy obscures: The fading-fast series needs to have been better thought out, better worked out -- before it gets on the air, not after; we're wrong to have picked it up as it's delivered to us, and we misjudge the appeal of the star and of the premise. But this kind of analysis never seems welcome in Hollywood.)

It's for the first CBS Upfront under the aegis of The Boss that I'm given a real seat at the table in New York, in both the literal and figurative senses, to watch and contribute to the process as it plays out. To see the real east-coast machinery at work, with Sales concerns at its core. To observe the finesse and protocol accompanying decisions that involve hundreds, affect thousands, and mean billions. Beginning with this year and then for the remainder of my time at CBS, I'm there as part of the meetings and discussions and arguments and sleuthing and subterfuge and late nights and early mornings that go with setting a network schedule with him. There's pride and excitement and a sense of achievement felt each time it's wrapped up with the fanfare and folderol that greet the official unveilings.

The highlight of my every CBS year, it'll always jar an ancient college memory of my holing up in Temple University's Paley Library each May to read about the Upfronts in the *New York Times* – especially in May of 1982, ten days before graduation and with thoughts of my future at hand, studying the coverage of the just-announced 1982-83 schedules. (The hot titles are *Newhart, Cheers*, and *Tales of the Gold Monkey.)* Sitting there I wonder, *How does it all happen? What's it like to be a part of this?*

Not in my wildest of fantasies do I see myself one day able to answer.

A lengthy and complex process, the Upfront is brand-new each year, informed by the state of the just-completed season, with much at stake and multiple constituencies to acknowledge, usually above my pay-grade. Meetings beget more meetings. Morning dissolves into evening and weekdays into weekends, with very little awareness of the outside world among them. We're on-point and on-call and on-guard each day, which can be stressful and exhausting, though I stop short of seeing them as hard. With rare exception reserved for those in Hollywood who are on the production or physical-labor side of the entertainment business, few of the jobs here in TV are hard, not even the ones on an executive level. Intense, with high stakes? Time-consuming? Mentally draining? Yes. But they're not *difficult*. Unlike lay jobs in service industries, they don't involve *sweat*.

As is the case in boardrooms at each of the other networks here in New York, mapping out their own new schedules, inside the boardroom at the CBS headquarters in midtown Manhattan known as Black Rock, the screenings have been completed and the choices are becoming clear. Proposed new schedules come and go among the various representatives of various network factions. Sales, Marketing, Affiliates, and others each weigh in with thoughts on the pilots and on the perceived weakness and strengths of the schedule as is. Competitive intelligence scooped up on the street or whispered about in backroom conversations is evaluated. (It's interesting, even important, to know what the competition is doing – and to know what they think we're doing – but for the most part I find the clandestine stuff that's part of these many New York days of May quite silly, up to and including the "accidental" leaving of phony new schedules behind at various industry functions where both the press and the competition are to be found.)

There's a science and strategy and method at play, a deliberate structuring of a schedule designed to maximize profit and to minimize risk and to ensure long-term success for both the new shows and the schedule as a whole. But, like everyday life in Hollywood, there are moments when strategy gives way to anarchy. New series that seem to be sure things for pick-up based on successful west-coast screenings can easily be pulled from contention, gone as simply as the removal of their magnetized title-strip from the scheduling board in the front of the room, the result of TV vagaries from testing to hunches to personal dislikes. Some pilots are met with such derision that their title-strips become missiles launched to the back of the boardroom, to remain on the floor walked over and unmentioned for the rest of the week. Existing series can be renewed one day, cancelled the next, then back on the board the following morning. Schedules can be debated, decided and locked, then not.

Once, a successful producer is afforded the unheard-of luxury of a sneak peek of the top-secret just-finalized new CBS schedule. He stares at the board in wonder, points to various planned changes on it, and then notes a new drama attached to a 8 o'clock timeslot. "What's this one?" he asks, and then when told that's it's a new family-show starring a longtime TV-favorite in what will be his fifth series, he responds, "Really? *That* guy again?" The strip comes off the board, to be further debated.

In the early-round discussion phases, reams of research are brought out, about new and existing series alike, which offers internal data-based results and anecdotal focus-group opinions. Mocked and dismissed at times (including by me), research can and does play a significant and helpful role in the Upfront process. Personal ambiguities and guesses and in-the-middle scores can be assuaged by it. Another year, an amiable-enough comedy pilot featuring two proven TV actresses is in strong contention for the new schedule, to the point where it's not just on the board but also given a suggested timeslot. It's flawed – a bad pilot storyline is approved -- but there's a growing consensus that based on its cast and auspices the show should be ordered to series. Then the research comes in: Test audiences do indeed like the *idea* for and the stars of the show, but they're turned off by the storyline. The magnetic title-strip comes off the board.

As the selections dwindle each year and the new schedule takes shape, trailers for the new shows are put together, while in another room the network-head's speech for the upcoming unveiling is crafted. Both the cut-downs and the speech involve a myriad of iterations and many long days. (Once, a drama-pilot is actually pulled from contention based on its uninspiring trailer.) Then the whole thing soon comes to a head with the grand to-do for advertisers. Beyond closed doors, and above my pay level, there are also always more-private discussions held before and after the ceremony to mollify egos and to plan for contingencies and to offer promises and to secure or patch relationships. With billions at stake, it's all carefully calibrated and expertly produced.

The roughly two-hour show itself requires multiple rehearsals, both at Black Rock and at the presentation venue. Advertisers will be joined at the show by hundreds of other influential members of the TV community, as well as a phalanx of media. So a good impression is critical. Our show, these years anyway, is always held in glorious and historic Carnegie Hall. (NBC's and FOX's and ABC's are held at equally impressive sites on other days of Upfront Week.) Elaborate and expensive and celebrity-studded parties follow.

I'm not much one for the late-night reindeer games that go along with these long stays in Manhattan. I tell myself I'm there for the work, but the truth is I'm not the late-night type, and I rarely feel as though I fit in with the activities planned for any of them. But for those with the appetite or stamina or propensity or wallet – and given the average CBS-executive demographic (young and adventurous and male and well-paid) that means just about everyone I fly in with from the west coast -- there is fun to be had. I can only surmise what I'm missing the morning I see one of the younger colleagues, enjoying his first Upfront trip, struggle off the CBS elevator for an early meeting, looking like he'd rather be anywhere but work.

"Out with boys last night?" I ask, with a smirk.

His one-word response, delivered with a disbelieving shake of his head: "*Caligula.*"

It's during one of my very first Upfronts with The Boss that I have a true confidence-boosting breakthrough, confirming for me once again – I need the affirmation sometimes -- that I'm doing the work I'm meant to be doing, where and with whom I'm meant to be doing it. Telling me that I really do have something to offer here. It allows me to reveal another part of myself that up until now I keep somewhat shrouded at the office, if only because up it's often been the object of ridicule elsewhere. Affectionate ridicule, but objectifying ridicule nonetheless.

Like my mother's sister and a few other maternal-side relatives, I have a fondness, an affection, a *passion*, for numbers. And a sizeable capacity for remembering them. Dates, odd number-based facts, miscellany – they're all stored in my brain, stacking up, secreted away, ready to be downloaded whenever needed. Or even when not. I just see numbers in my head all the time -- especially if they're connected to TV, since that's where I've trained the quirk since I start keeping vigil in front of the set as a child. On Wellington Street, I'm the one in charge of remembering birthdays and appointments, yes, but my chief charge is remembering prime-time. ("Go find Jimmy and ask what's on TV tonight!")

As a magazine editor in Tennessee, in my immediate post-college years, I'm often called on by the fact-check department at the company to source dates for articles in production – told that it takes less time than rifling through reference books in this pre-Internet age or walking over to the library. Friends' wedding anniversaries and children's birthdays and other significant dates? "I'm not sure when it is, ask Jim," is the common response.

Sometimes it's a drag; sometimes it's fun. As an assistant in my early L.A. days, I share an office-suite with a guy whose boss is casting a TV pilot, for which a parade of middle-aged TV character-actresses (familiar faces to me, all) comes through the door every day for a week. As each does, I tell the assistant more about her, and more quickly, than he can glean from her headshot, to the point at which by the end of the week a game of sorts has evolved in which as an actress walks in and is seated, she's asked by the assistant checking her in, "Wanna see something funny?" He then points across the suite at me, and says, expectantly, "Jim?" And then I rattle off TV-show credits and their dates that sometimes the actress herself won't even recall.

At a CBS party once, a colleague comes up to me to introduce her husband, a well-respected national TV critic. "I just had to have you meet him," she says to me. Then, to the husband, "Honey, he's just like you -- he knows all these dates and numbers and can recall them so easily like you do." He and I shake hands. "It's weird, isn't it?" he says to me. "Why are these numbers so important? I mean, why do I even have them in my head? Like, why is it even important to know that the movie *Bull Durham* came out in 1987?"

"I know, I know, " I say, laughing, with what I hope is a twinkle in my eye. "Especially since it was 1988." (Trust me: It was.)

One May Tuesday in The Boss's Black Rock office, a group of us is gathered to discuss the latest competitive information picked up on the street. Someone mentions a certain actor's name as the star of what's supposed to be a hot pilot in contention at another network, and The Boss, a successful TV producer before becoming an executive, says he knows the actor well. "We were partners in a production company; he starred in one of the TV movies we made." Reflexively, I say, "Oh yeah, I remember that" – and then I name the movie and the date when it aired. In 1981.

The Boss offers me the signature over-the-rim-of-his-half-glasses look -- it can signal something good is about to happen or something very very bad -- stares at me for a minute, and then says, "You remember a movie that I made in *1981*?" A hint of a smile. "Sure," I reply, "It aired on NBC in late November. On a Monday. From nine to eleven." (*Doesn't everyone in TV remember everything about TV?* I think.)

His smile widens. "*You*," he says, "are a fucking savant." And everyone laughs. Me included.

But then, not wanting the exchange to end on a laugh perceived at my expense (early life at my family dinner-table teaches me better), I summon up the courage to throw the remark back at him, with what I hope is seen as respect. "Yeah, but boss," I counter, "I'm *your* fucking savant."

And everyone laughs even harder. *With* me, this time -- not at me.

"That's right," says The Boss. He points at me and repeats, "That's right."

And I have an awakening moment: In a business where knowledge is power, I have a source of my own:

I. Know. Television.

Knowledge *is* power here in the entertainment world. It's takes a more amorphous shape, befitting amorphous jobs in what itself can be an amorphous industry. But knowledge, and the clout that comes with it, is what moves you around. And Up. (You don't need to know TV to work in it. I've met many who really and sadly just plain don't. A department head at CBS once has a meeting with an actor who's come in to pitch his starring in a movie about a famous if not seminal TV personality from the 1950s, sits through and participates in the meeting, picks up the project for production, and then after the meeting privately asks an assistant who the seminal 1950s TV personality is.) If I have knowledge, I conclude, I might just as well make use of it. No more hiding. No more being semi-coy about what I know. I know TV. I'll show it on both coasts, everywhere I can.

Due either to the maternal genes or to my years of work at CBS, eventually I make my way up to a vice-president title. (The typical TV-network or TV-studio executive career-ladder has three rungs: manager, director, and vice-president, the last having several permutations itself; the rungs are cleared at varying speeds and for varying reasons, ranging from job-performance to offers-elsewhere leverage to if-she-gets-a-promotion-then-I-get-one-too to just plain time served.) I can't mail the notice of my promotion back home to my father quickly enough. It runs in an industry trade-paper, complete with photo, the story referring to me as a "scheduling wiz" who's becoming known in TV circles for "a near legendary knowledge of prime-time television."

Okay then.

See what happens when you learn the words to the commercials, too?

The Upfront experience each year is all goosebump stuff for me. I'm still the guy in my college library wondering how it all comes together. Still dazzled that this is part of my job. That this is what I do for a living. That I am part of this annual New York ritual, year after year. Out west and back home, however, several Carnegies into my role, routine and cynicism begin to chip away at the rest of the job itself.

It's 2002, and after seven years and hundreds of TV pilots, after helping to schedule multiple fall and mid-season and summer schedules, with CBS having been resurrected from the ashes to assume first place in the ratings under The Boss, with my profile and confidence and paycheck increasing, I'm closing in on ten years here. I do love what I do and, for the most part, whom I do it with. I value the education and the view of the industry it gives me. I've survived three CBS administrations and several personal crises. I feel as if I've found purpose and a mission in work that involves a powerful and influential and important form of communication. I've found satisfaction and clarity. I've found *myself*.

But like any long-term relationship the pluses of mine with CBS are being challenged by the up-till-now lesser, but accumulating, minuses, allowing a bit of ennui to creep in. I'm challenged, troubled even, by seeing how some of TV as a whole comes together. How the business behind the business works. How sometimes it's too much business, in fact, not enough art or creativity. And how the television viewer can be lost in the whole process, with the viewing experience soiled as a result. That lessens TV, in my eyes.

Or, I wonder, is this just more of me swimming against the tide and of thinking in ways no one else thinks?

Some of the backstage nonsense, the Altman-esque silliness, I don't mind. In fact, I enjoy it – the meeting called to decide how to handle a scene just shot for one of our dramas that features an obviously well-endowed actor in a Speedo; the June day a spontaneous line-dance of highly paid executives forms in the third-floor hallway when it's announced The Boss has finally left for summer vacation; the strategy-session with the network's Number Two, who stands up and walks out mid-discussion of a key and critical issue, muttering to herself, "I wonder if there's any licorice around here"; the conference-call hastily put together to discuss cancelling a show that I'm part of with my direct-report, who spends the time shopping on-line.

Or the the hallway conversation with the Business Affairs-department lawyer who asks me the name of the old TV comedy starring Dick Van Dyke ("Really, *The Dick Van Dyke Show*?" she responds when I tell her. "Well how about the one with Mary Tyler Moore? What was that called?"); the conversation I overhear by the third-floor elevator between two evidently disappointed lobbyists who've just left The Boss's office after petitioning for better programming ("I feel like I need a shower after being in there"); the afternoon I return from a seven-hour deposition for a Scheduling-related lawsuit leveled against CBS, hoping for gratitude from the colleagues who actually should be the ones spending this day with our lawyers, to see them at a desk leafing through the pages of the new *Maxim* to pick out potential dates; the week that David Letterman agrees to guest star on one of our lesser sitcoms in order to goose the ratings but only with mask over his head and only with the proviso that the network not advertise the appearance; the three-word email that goes out company-wide on the morning that CBS wakes to stellar ratings for a special that Disney-owned rival ABC tries to blunt at the last minute with a hastily scheduled special of its own ("Eat shit, mousefuckers"); the five-word memo passed down from on high after the miserable rating for our *Peter Rabbit* Easter special is reported ("That cocksucking bunny killed us").

Or the meeting that involves no fewer than five departments from two companies (CBS network and Sony studio) to negotiate the content of an episode of one of our medical series that's to feature a gay patient admitted with an entertainment-industry award-statue lodged in his anus (the script calls for an Oscar, the producers suggest an Emmy, the network rejects a Tony ... everyone settles for a Golden Globe); the internal game played amongst executives involving the re-naming of troubled projects (a failing Tom Selleck sitcom called *The Closer* is dubbed *The Loser,* a proposed mother-daughter-gynecologists sitcom pilot that we're pitched is referred to as *At Your Cervix,* a completed-but-never-allowed-to-air child-abuse movie titled *Not in My House* becomes known as *Not On My Network.)*

Or the realization that we mistakenly air promos for an upcoming movie about matricide on Mother's Day or the plan suggested that we herald the completion of our mini-series about Pope John Paul II by releasing Vatican-like puffs of white smoke over CBS headquarters; the reams of notes passed down from our Standards and Practices Department about the editing of feature films for small-screen broadcast (two favorites: "Please optically obscure the lower half of the frame in [scene] to conceal the lead female's nude loins" and "Please lower the volume of the orgasmic sounds throughout the lovemaking scene"); the frenzied frat-house reaction in the office one summer morning when words gets out that lesbian sex has occurred overnight in the on-camera-all-the-time *Big Brother* house ("Get me footage!! I need to see footage!!").

I'm game for all of it. To one degree or another, it's all part of the *Dilbert* life at any office, big or small.

It's the more Big Picture stuff that's starting to nag at me instead, about an industry I hold in esteem -- the diminishing quality of some of what makes it to air, be it in a rush to be trendy or to be controversial or to be competitive or due to a generally more casual acceptance in the industry at large of less-skillful writing and production.

More and more, it's *concepts* that seem to be being pitched (and bought), not scripts. Ideas, not series. From an increasing number of people not so much schooled in the craft and science of TV but popular in the town and hot at the moment or just connected to power. The sometimes inferior product that is the result is alternately becoming encouraged or just benignly accepted, which begets more still more inferior product, because that's what's selling.

And from what I can see there's little to no accountability to or responsibility for any of it when it doesn't work. Little examination of why a series doesn't succeed or what's behind a producer or writer who continues to disappoint -- yet is still sought out. I scratch my head. As success is examined -- What vein has been tapped that makes a certain show a hit? What is it doing that we should be doing and/or copying? – so, too, shouldn't failure, so that mistakes aren't repeated? Don't bad ratings have as much to tell us as good ratings? Don't bad shows?

Instead, press releases – *press releases!* -- are cobbled together around town to announce the signing of writers or producers who've just crapped out with their latest projects, sometimes in spectacular fashion. That they merely have gotten projects on the air supports the flourish – despite the fact that when they do they're soundly rejected.

"From the makers of Edsel comes...!"

Seriously?, I think. *What does it take to fail in this town?*

One morning, my direct-report sits in his office reporting to a top-level colleague about a new series underway for our air that by all accounts is a huge train-wreck in the making. Production has begun; scripts are coming in; money, a vast amount of it, is being spent. "Look," he says to the colleague, "it's *bad*. We got a problem here." Palpable concern and frustration in his voice.

"Yeah, well..." is the entirety of the response. And then the colleague gets up and casually leaves his office, the subject closed.

It is what it is, is the oft-heard mantra.

The perceived avoidance of responsibility and the disinterest in discussing consequence, throughout the industry, weighs on me. Moreover, when someone does voice concern or does make what seems to be a legitimate observation – a member of the press, for instance -- the critique is laughed off, its observer dismissed as an "idiot." "Oh, fuck *him*," is the reaction I hear most often in regard to one particular national critic. And I say to myself, *That's the extent of the dialogue about what we do for a living, with the public's airwaves? With all this money being spent?*

The angry dismissals aren't reserved for those perceived to be lobbing grenades from the outside, either. They're not all that welcome from anywhere. Woe to the person who dares pop the self-inflated balloons of grandeur from the inside, too, from among the ranks.

Me, for instance.

One afternoon a development executive invites the three of us from the Scheduling department to her office to watch a trailer that's been put together for a proposed reality series. It comes from a company outside of the CBS family, but here in her office, given the sell in her voice, it seems to be one that she herself is enthusiastically behind -- championing it as though its producer. But, whatever. We're game.

The time is about a year or so after *Desperate Housewives* hits it big on ABC (and several years before the invasion of the "real housewives" shows that will hit cable-TV in its wake). The idea being pitched is for a summer reality-series that hopes to tap those same viewers as it offers a look at the lives of a group of women-friends in their 30s and 40s, some married and some not, who under the guise of a once-a-week book club assemble to hash out the dramas of their lives. The trailer for it unspools. As the three of us watch, we see that, evidently, the lives of these women seem to revolve around extra-marital hook-ups and hot-tub soaks. The Algonquin Round Table it's not.

"Well?", we're asked when it's over, a note of exultation in the excitable colleague's voice. None of the three of us has much to say: We've seen both better and worse. We're not overly enthusiastic. But summer does seem to be fertile ground for this kind of programming. So we agree it's worth pursuing.

Which is when the executive, having struck oil, should stop digging.

Instead, she tries to stoke more of an interest from us, more of a passion for the project, picking up where the trailer leaves off, explaining to us how the show promises to be an examination of gender and socio-economic and marital roles in the decade of the 2000s, how it offers a look at where women born of a certain time find themselves when they're of a certain age and begin to wonder about their lives and about how far women in general have come since the liberation movement of the 1970s when they sought parity with men and –

Which is where I then feel the compulsion to stop her.

Because now I feel as though we're not only being sold but also talked down to. Rather than colleagues discussing the pros and cons of development, I feel as if the three of us are the network buyer being pitched to by the outside supplier – a process everyone involved on both sides of the equation on any given day in this town will acknowledge is theater. The room is filling with the stink of marketing mulch. (I feel the same way a few years ago when I remark to the colleague credited with bringing *Survivor* to CBS how impressive the ratings are for the new show. "Of course," he says. "I knew it would be. It's 'social Darwinism', Jim." And I think to myself, *social Darwinism? Is that why people are watching it? Are they are at home saying to one another, "Honey, is there any social Darwinism on tonight?"*)

The women's movement? Fallout from the 1970s? Atonement? This? Really?

"Oh, come on, who are we kidding?" I say with my admittedly becoming-all-too-impolitic tone. "Based on what you just showed us the show is a handful of hot women sitting in Jacuzzis talking about the great sex they're having with the guys who aren't their husbands." It may or may not be a TV show, I say to her, and it'll be fine for summer programming. We'll definitely find a place for it on the schedule. But it hardly suggests Gloria Steinem or Camille Lapaglia or third-wave feminism by way of Baumgardner.

A shot across the pitch-bow, evidently.

"Well," comes her indignant response, "*excuse me*, Mr. Not Married-Never-Has-Been-Married-and-Probably-Has-Never-Even-Gone-Out-on-a-Date."

To me, a colleague of seven years, in front of other colleagues (a sizeable no-no, which The Boss himself has taught us) -- who also happen to the members of *my* department.

And I'm 46 years old.

The meeting evidently over, I smile and stand up and return to my office.

If I'm too blunt in the meeting, I feel it's with cause. My colleague's retort is just as curt in return, but, in my opinion, without similar cause. And the bluntness is personalized, which worsens it. Another corporate no-no. But I move on, mostly unfazed. *The Tuesday Night Book Club* moves on, too: It's ordered, shot, aired – and then cancelled after one lone anemically low-rated and critically assaulted airing. Anemically low-rated even by summer-TV standards. Soundly rejected by viewers.

(For the record, the executive who assails me at the meeting does later apologize for her indiscretion, twice -- once immediately after, in my office, and then again the next morning. Both apologies seem genuine, though I suspect the second one has its roots less in my colleague's feeling bad than in her realizing overnight what I myself do about the exchange: In Human Resources terms, her words are actionable.)

The *why* behind the show's failure is, of course, never examined. It contributes to a growing itch that I just can't quite seem to scratch. About our roles here and about what we're doing with TV overall. I'm accused of taking my job, myself, of taking the business in general, too seriously. Maybe everyone's right. Maybe I do all that. Not everyone develops a *relationship* with and *connection* to TV as a child that instills feelings of commitment and responsibility to it in him as an adult. Not everyone is compelled to further mankind or to champion a cause. Some people actually get into the entertainment business with simple motives – for fun, for money, or *because it's just TV*.

In bed at night, I have dreams that underscore my rocky approach to the job. One finds me telling my direct-report that I'm quitting CBS over concerns about the quality of our programming. "You can't quit; you have a contract with us," he says. And with operatic indignity, I reply, "Yes I can too quit -- because I have a more important contract with the

American people!" (An embarrassing dream, it's also a ridiculous and funny one that I can't help but share with the direct-report the next day – who of course will go on to remind me of it often and lustfully as the years go on, folding it into encounters ranging from scheduling decisions to a lunch-menu selections. "Does that work for you, Jim?" he'll say, about an appetizer he's ordered at a restaurant we're seated at. "Or does it violate your contract with the American people?")

Another dream is more ominous. It comes on the eve of a new mid-season drama we're launching called *Four Corners*, a serialized Southwestern soap starring Ann-Margret of all people that on every level has been troubled from the start, down to a fiery fight between producers and CBS management over the show's main-title sequence. The series looks to be so awful that the whole project should probably be shut down and forgotten about before a single episode is completed.

But because that's not how things work in TV (rightly or wrongly), *Four Corners* stays in production and heads to air. The night before its debut, I have a dream that I'm on a remote beach with my CBS colleagues, each of us helping to load an enormous missile on to a massive warplane. As the bomb passes through my hands, I see stenciling on its side that spells out FOUR CORNERS. Frantic, I try to get someone's – anyone's – attention. I wave and point. I scream. I plead that we need to stop. But no one sees or hears me, and soon enough the plane is loaded and takes flight. And then explodes in the sky.

Four Corners premieres the next night. No one watches. It's cancelled the following morning, joining the exclusive single-airing club. One broadcast. Millions of dollars. And, again, no post-mortem of what went wrong. (More from the Supreme Irony file: Seemingly forgotten after its quick cancellation, *Four Corners* somehow manages an Emmy nomination later in the year, for Outstanding Main Title Sequence.)

A pair of assignments comes to my rescue as this ten-year itch spreads. Together, they remind me of what it is I fall in love with as a child and what in turn I want to be a part of as an adult when I move west. The first shows up in 2002 when CBS orders a thirtieth anniversary salute to its landmark Emmy-honored 1970s comedy *Mary Tyler Moore*. (It's actually 32 years since the show's premiere, but that's a quibble.) The plan is to reunite all surviving cast-members to talk about the show and to review clips of its best moments – all done under the supervision of CBS's expert Special department.

Normally, beyond random hallway conversations or email exchanges, those of us in Scheduling don't play much of a creative role in what we air. But when this particular project goes into production, the executives in Specials, familiar with my mental TV files as well as with my passion for *Mary Tyler Moore* in particular, ask if I want to be involved.

Here's the resulting image: Edward Asner, Valerie Harper, Betty White, Gavin Macleod, Georgia Engel, and Mary Tyler Moore in front of a camera for two days on a Hollywood soundstage, talking about their days on the classic sitcom of my youth; and Jim McKairnes a few feet away from them, watching and listening. On the second day, when the producers themselves clue in on my kinship with the show, they even turn to me to make sure no key highlights have been left out of the special, and then they ask if I have any specific ideas for how they should be remembered.

Next to stealing a seat alongside Moore and Asner at lunch on day-one of shooting, where I continue to feign my role as a grown-up executive rather than expose myself as the ten-year old who audiotapes their show for late-night re-telling, the highlight of the whole experience comes during a sequence that features actor Gavin Macleod recalling his role as Murray Slaughter, Mary Richards' newsroom colleague. He begins to recount a scene in which he and late co-star Ted Knight, playing Murray's foil, exchange a barb, but MacLeod can't remember the specific wording of the punchline that caps it. From behind the camera, I repeat the exchange verbatim, to cue him. Everybody laughs, including MacLeod, and I know that in this strange little world that I find myself there are few days better than this one – a day that comes to life for me courtesy of an amazing job. I find new energy for my CBS role.

About a year later, CBS is staring down at a milestone of its own – the 75th anniversary of its founding as a company. (It begins as a more-or-less TV network in 1948, but its roots as a company trace back to 1928.) A live three-hour special is planned, not just spotlighting the requisite clips from through the years but assembling for it on one stage just about every big name who's ever worked on the network – from Lassie to Ray Romano. For this, too, I'm asked to contribute. And as the countdown to the anniversary begins, my inner TV-geek also conjures up what I think is a good idea both to commemorate the occasion and to promote the special, borne of the success of the network's own memorable and successful on-air campaign called *Bicentennial Minutes* back in the mid-1970s.

Running for two years beginning in 1974 to mark the country's 200th birthday, *Bicentennial Minutes* is series of 60-second spots that recall significant moments in U.S. history from the actual date each airs. They run every night in the first hour of prime-time, and each vignette is hosted by a well-known American figure from a wide variety of walks of life. They become hugely popular and much discussed, both inside and outside the TV industry, going on to win multiple awards. A fan of the campaign as a teen, I wonder now if we can adapt it for 2003, creating a similar nightly countdown of great moments in the network's history as a lead-up to the anniversary special.

I pitch it to my immediate boss, a child of TV himself (minus the geek factor), and he likes the idea, saying that if we get CBS's Sales division onboard to recruit sponsors for it it'll be more likely to be approved from on high. We do. It is. The Boss signs off. A plan is struck to produce thirty 30-second spots showcasing 30 great moments in the network's history, under the heading of *CBS at 75*. They'll air once a night for the month prior to the anniversary show; a different celebrity will host each one. Just like *Bicentennial Minutes*. I'm beyond excited. My own personal idea is going to be produced for national TV.

In conjunction with a highly regarded colleague from our New York office, and with the help of a patient TVC talent wrangler, I end up spending several months in 2003 getting the project together. In what's probably a portend to my post-CBS life-to-come as a part-time teacher, I know part of my aim is to

remind audiences (and colleagues) of the contributions CBS has made to popular culture and to TV as a whole.

Some choices for the "moments to remember" are obvious; others, the ones I push for, are less so, forgotten through the years. I want all of them to represent what TV has been and still can be – a communications tool that makes a difference as it enlightens and entertains, programming spun from vision, predicated on character and story, emboldened by writing, built by craftsmen. So for every *Beatles On Ed Sullivan* (1964) and *Cronkite Announces the Death of President Kennedy* (1963) and *Tiger Woods' Win for the Ages* (1987), there's a spot devoted to *The Autobiography of Miss Jane Pittman* (1974) and to *Dick Van Dyke*'s *"Coast to Coast Big Mouth"* (1965) and to *The Carol Burnett Show* series-finale (1978).

By anyone's standards, it's an impressive collection that CBS is responsible for. We've been home to some extraordinary and influential TV.

The campaign runs every night for a month. It makes money and seems to make The Boss happy. It makes my producing cohorts and me very proud. Coming on the heels of my (minor) involvement with the *Mary Tyler Moore* commemoration a year ago – Imagine, I say to myself: a 32-year-old sitcom that still stands out as an example of what good writing can do -- I'm also stoked. I'm buoyed by the reminders of what TV is for and about: Comedy that endures, drama and characters and situations that compel as they connect, writing as craft, people and projects that *aspire* to something, television that unites. It confirms my reasons for being in Hollywood.

Sadly, when I look around Hollywood these days, I don't see a whole lot of anything like it anymore. There's good work and ever better intentions. But they seem eclipsed by a good deal of work that reflects bottom-line decision-making and benignly accepted mediocrity, not to mention a striking disconnect between those behind the TV screen making the decisions and those sitting at home in front of their TVs taking in the results. Even with my renewed optimism, I wonder if it's only a matter of time before I become the frustrated CBS long-timer I sit next to at the pilot- screening my first week here. ("A million dollars," he says, gesturing toward what he sees on the screen. "A *million*.")

Back in the spring of 2000, amid another cycle of pilots for another new fall schedule, there's a screening for a proposed new drama called *Cold Shoulder*, starring actress Kelly McGillis, a long way from *Top Gun* and *Witness*. She portrays a fallen alcoholic cop who, in the pilot, tries with varying degrees of success to salvage her personal life and professional reputation, which future episodes will continue to recount. As an idea for a weekly show, it's marginal at best. Average. It doesn't drum up much enthusiasm. (It's also hampered by what, in my opinion, is another horrible title – something that's also becoming commonplace these days. TV-show titles are as important as the shows themselves: They offer a convenient and easily grabbed handle with which viewers can both pick up a series and pass it around. From *I Love Lucy* to *The Sopranos,* most long-running series – there are plenty of un-read lists around that cite them -- have had titles that simply reflect a person, a setting, an activity. Not a metaphor or a concept or a saying that amuse only those in the room when pitched, such as *It's Like You Know* and *Wednesday 9:30/8:30 Central,* two actual titles for two very short-lived recent series.)

Following our executive screening for *Cold Shoulder*, the moderator-led evaluation is brief and passion-less, which is understandable given the wan reaction as we watch. But at the same time it's also surprising: The pilot features a fair amount of what I'd call gratuitous misogynistic violence. After all, I'm in a room half-filled with women.

As we're about to be dismissed, and with no one else having mentioned it, I can't stop myself from speaking up.

"Wait a minute," I say. "I'm just wondering. Am I the only one in this room who had a problem with the level of violence and sexism in this pilot, directed at this lead character?"

Blank looks and silence greet the comment.

I'm asked what I mean by "problem."

"I mean, am I the only one who thinks it's a bit over-the-top, not to mention alienating to viewers, the way this woman is portrayed and treated? By the physical violence perpetrated on her?"

Silence. More stares.

Then, the appearance of The Word. The one that's become the bane of my existence here every spring. The one that is every Hollywood executive's all-purpose go-to.

"But, Jim," says someone from the back of the room, "that's all part of her *journey*."

"Yeah, Jim," comes the group murmur.

I try a reply: "I understand all that; I really do. I understand arcs and journeys. I understand this is a fallen cop and that we have to see how far she falls to appreciate how hard it is for her to get up. To root for her. I get all that. But I think that the scene in which this drunk and unemployed and penniless and friendless woman merely *agrees* to get into the stranger's car to blow him for some quick cash to get another bottle of booze, only to change her mind at the last minute, conveys *all* of that without it going on to show the disappointed and angry guy in the car hitting her across the face with his tire-iron and then grabbing her head and forcing it into his crotch while we hear his pants unzip. Why do we need to see her physically assaulted, and so violently?"

An argument follows. An actual argument. Me against my fellow executives, in the CBS ground-floor screening-room. I genuinely can't believe that I'm alone in my reaction to the show, yet I seem to be just that. Apparently I'm just plain wrong, and it all ends with the sound of my concerns drowned out.

"No one out there thinks the way you do, Jim," I hear. (I wonder if I should be wearing a T-shirt with that expression by now.)

Yet when we finally do leave the room to go back to our offices — a few more *harrumphs* and chuckles tossed my way -- a female colleague sidles up to me in the hallway outside the screening-room and, actually looking around to ensure that no one's within earshot, whispers to me, "Thank you for what you said in there; thank you for standing up for women."

I mock-whisper a reply: "I appreciate your saying that, but I don't want your thanks. I want your voice of support in the room if you agree with me. If anyone should have been making my point in the first place, it should have been a woman."

Life goes on. No harm, no foul. It's only TV. The pilot goes away. But the experience with *Cold Shoulder* stays with me, and my jaundiced eyes open a bit wider. The CBS network is riding high these days, mostly with crime shows, admittedly a TV staple, one even that I like. But I start to pay closer attention to who tend to be the victims in them -- and who tend to be the killers.

On an October Sunday not long after, I'm at the home of a CBS colleague and friend. The conversation, as it usually does, falls to TV. "I just read the most disturbing script at the office this week – an episode of *Cold Case*," she says, referring to one of our newer and more popular crime dramas. "It's really creepy." I remind her that creepy seems to be the show's calling-card, but she says that this one's creepier than normal. As a mother of two, she says she had to stop reading it. "Someone should really speak up about this," is her conclusion. My curiosity is piqued. So the next day at the office I find and read the script. And she's right. It's creepy.

The darker-than-normal episode deals with eight separate murders of young women that go unsolved over a span of years, cases that are re-opened after a new killing is reported that reminds detectives of the older ones. The details of the deaths are identical: Kidnapped from the street at night, a woman is taken to a remote wooded location by a kidnapper, forced to strip to her underwear, and then told to run for her life, after which "the hunter" (as he's known in the script), armed with a rifle and employing night-vision goggles, spends the night tracking his running prey, until come dawn, exhausted from the hunt, she gives up, in tears. At that point, she's shot, beheaded, and buried.

Much of the killing happens off-camera, but the show's signature flashback scenes depict the ordeals of three of the victims, one of whom is a 14-year-old girl, who tearfully begs for her father in the final moments before she's shot. (The episode also features a flashback of another young girl, 10, hit across the face by her own enraged father. But -- spoiler alert -- he's not the murderer.) The sum effect is, in a word, disturbing, on any number of levels, from the sexualized violence to the beheadings to the age of the youngest victim.

When I go to the offices of the Current executives involved with the show to question it – the episode is about to go into production -- I'm once again met with quizzical looks. "I'm not quite sure what it is you have a problem with," says one. But to placate me, he invites me to watch the rough-cut of the episode when it's delivered in a few weeks so that I can weigh in again if my concerns aren't allayed. (I don't see how they will be, since the script is being shot as written, but at least he's acknowledging my concerns.)

A few weeks later, as promised, the rough-cut comes in and I'm invited to watch. The episode is what it's written to be -- underwear-clad and tearfully terrified young women hunted and beheaded. The scene with the 14-year-old girl is as disturbing on film as it is in script form.

Really? -- I ask again. This really is something we're happy to air? Beyond the basic elements of a TV crime show that involves murder, this is entertainment?

The response is the same: "Jim, "I'm not quite sure what it is you have a problem with." And I'm at once taken aback and disappointed.

The "Mind Hunter" episode of *Cold Case,* about underwear-clad young women hunted and beheaded, airs as scheduled on Sunday November 28. It's Thanksgiving weekend. (Interestingly, and I'm not sure what to make of this fact, given that it's written by two women, the episode is the first one from the hit show that ends without the killer being captured and stopped by the heroic crime-solving team at the center of the show. Maybe third-wave feminism is rearing its head in prime-time, after all.)

Whatever germ of a concern I have after the screening of *Cold Shoulder* mutates with "Mind Hunter," and I'm left with a viral chill. I take a look at our popular crime-drama-filled schedule – seven of 22 prime-time hours, one-third of the schedule – which in a TV-genre sense is fine but for the fact that the aggregate result that we seem to be killing an awful lot of people on a weekly basis – women, mostly, in the most heinous of tortuous ways. There are male victims among the line-up, to be sure. But while the men on the shows seem to be being killed as a result of being in the wrong place at the wrong time, many of the women seem to be being killed because of their gender. Kidnapped. Stripped. Tortured. Even, in the case of one series (in no fewer than three separate episodes), caged. *Caged.*

I find myself objecting to the on-screen violence with increasing frequency and volume, using my executive's voice to wonder aloud week by week, month by month, as time goes on, about the amount of sexualized violence on our air, about the differences in depictions of male and female victims. I make full use of whatever position that my now-eleven-or-so years at CBS have earned me. I write countless internal emails and memos, strike up hallway conversations one after another, as one show and one season literally bleeds into the next.

Mostly, it's met with eye-rolls and muffled laughter and accusations of being lost on some kind of quixotic crusade. "You're not still into *that,* are you?" a young Current executive asks me one morning when I try to engage him about yet another scene of torture that I've just screened, as though I'm touting the benefits of veganism or Scientology rather than suggesting to him that in his role as a network executive toiling with the public's airwaves he has a say in what airs on his show. And I become more and more baffled.

At the end of the day, I can't even believe it's a point of contention or debate, let alone derision. I'm not advocating for the cancellation of any of our series nor the reduction in crime that they show nor even the elimination of women as victims. I'm not suggesting CBS turn to revivals of *Seventh Heaven.* I myself love crime in both fiction and non-fiction form, I tell anyone who asks and who wants to pursue the dialogue. Movies, TV, books, whatever. I get into and get off on a good killing, too. As a guy, I'm fine with massacre and bloodshed.

What I'm advocating for, I tell them, or at least what I'm trying to draw attention to, is the loosening of the ties between gender and violence, a modification in the ways we conceive and depict crimes against women -- as their shows are being produced. As a network we have both the power and responsibility to do that. These are our series. They reflect our choices.

Can't there be just a simple recalibration of approach, by networks and studios and writers? If there's to be evisceration of women, can it just not be partnered with nudity?

If there's to be kidnapping of women, can it not be coupled with closed-fist punches to the face? If there's to be confrontation with women, can it not involve being stripped to their underwear? If there's to be a post-mortem shot of a female murder-victim, can it not involve five close-ups of her purpled bare chest? Can three suffice instead? Two? And perhaps, just perhaps, in this the 21st century, if there are to be any kinds of female crime-victims who suffer any kinds of harm, can they just not be caged?

Caged.

I'm reminded of a TV-interview that film director Peter Bogdonavich gives at the dawn of his career in the 1970s, defending the female-only nudity on display in his highly sexualized movie *The Last Picture Show*. "That," he says, dismissing the criticism with a chuckle that would never fly today, "is merely a reflection of the filmmaker's preferences." Conscious choices *are* reflected in both movies and TV. Maybe, just maybe, they can be run through the conscious another time or two, with consideration for the fact that people are *watching*, with acknowledgement that *signals* are being sent. The female *Cold Case* victims are seen pleading for their lives, about to be beheaded, while wearing their underwear. Why that particular choice? Beyond that, why our willingness to air it?

Does no one in this town have sisters or daughters or mothers?

Alas, I seem to be smacking my head against the cushioned walls of TVC. At the end of the day it seems to be a matter of asking something that's anathema to many Hollywood decision-makers, which is to look within, to think in terms of personal responsibility, to solve a problem with involvement.

I do know I'm not crazy in asking for it: When a trailer is created in May of 2005 for a new crime-drama that we're about to reveal to advertisers at our Upfront in New York – a hot prospect, it features a woman kidnapped, knocked unconscious with a blow to the face, then stripped to her underwear and, yes, caged – a high-ranking colleague cautions that the trailer not include any of its more violent scenes. He says it's too disturbing to show to advertisers.

But we're okay with airing it on our network? I ask him.

Avoidance being a substitute for responsibility, the executive walks away, laughing.

Criminal Minds is announced as the network's next big hit. The (full) pilot is distributed to critics later in the summer in advance of its fall premiere, and it's promptly assailed for its graphic depiction of violence toward women. A national debate is sparked. What I had feared and warned about is materializing: Questions are raised in *Entertainment Weekly*, *USA Today*, and other publications; "Has TV Gone Too Far?" is one of the headlines. Other CBS dramas, suffused with their own misogyny, are thrown onto the editorial pyres. Objections are raised at a national gathering of TV critics, primarily aimed at the (female) head of the network's entertainment division. The requisite self-inoculating responses of "We're only reflecting what's out there" and "The public will tell us enough is enough" follow.

I stand in the back of the room and sigh, audibly. Isn't she acknowledging that the press are right? And at the same time abdicating responsibility for what we air? (I also marvel at how "the public" is introduced into equations like this only at this *end* of the assembly-line – and as an excuse, at that.)

A few months later, a critic writes in his column, "What is it with CBS and its obsession with killing naked women?" (He's the often right-thinking one routinely dismissed in town with the swat of a hand -- "Oh, fuck *him*" – followed by a derogatory reference to his presumed sexuality.) I forward the article to the Current executive whose show is the critic's chief target, and this young guardian of television's future tells me to "get on the team."

Get on the team?

"Yeah, Jim," he says. "Get in line with the rest of us here. What are you doing, teeing off against our own shows?"

This, in response to my passing on to him a newspaper article.

"Besides," he adds, "Our victim in that show the critic's referring to was in her underwear, not nude, so he doesn't know what he's talking about." (The encounter stands out as both a high- and low-point in my perceived windmill-tilting this decade, ranking above "Jim, *someone* has to die in these shows" and immediately below what a female executive says with a laugh when told of an episode of one of our dramas that is to feature kidnapped women held in a subterranean chamber by a madman who dresses them in wedding-gowns: "Well, the producer *is* going through his third divorce, you know.")

I don't stop objecting, though. I think it's important not to stop. I want to be heard on this. I want the issue to be out there. And when after I leave the company in 2006 I hear from colleagues that to raise a concern about on-screen violence in a meeting is to offer "a Jim McKairnes note," I smile, even if the line is meant with scorn. Because at least they're aware.

My chief regret if any, I guess, is that I don't ever bring my concerns directly to The Boss, who I like to think would weigh in with fair measure. Even affect change. But he's managing an empire from New York these days. Instead, I observe the corporate protocol involving chain-of-command. The Boss is supposed to have people here in TVC to represent him. In this case, I'm not certain they do so all that well. The capturings and cagings go on. (And on and on: Fully six years after my last day at CBS I'll stumble across three separate episodes of a CBS crime-show over the course of as many weeks. In one, a kidnapped woman is trapped in a small underground cell that's slowly being filled with water; in another, dead women are literally stacked like cordwood by their assailant in an industrial freezer; and in the third, a young woman is tortured with her eyes taped open. Each is an episode of *Criminal Minds*, now almost a parody of itself and for my money the closest thing to snuff that prime-time will ever air. Evidently one of its stars agrees. Original lead Mandy Patinkin, who curiously leaves the hit after its first season without much of an explanation, presents one years later: He no longer could be associated with its level of female-directed violence.)

The wonderful irony of my alleged muckraking at CBS is that much of it occurs against the backdrop of the infamous and ludicrous Janet Jackson Super Bowl scandal of 2004. And the less said about this silly spectacle the better. I will suggest, however, that the real shame of it all isn't the incident itself, which is little more than a silly and childish pee-pee prank fueled by show-biz self-empowerment – a quick apologetic "my bad" from both of them afterward would have done a literal world of good -- but the apoplexy that comes in its wake and that will last for years, scalding industry leaders and eventually involving intrusion on to no less august a gathering than the Supreme Court of the United States.

The energy and outrage of this synod of self-interested politicians and self-regarding children's advocates could and would be much more meaningfully directed at realer issues instead – at media responsibility, perhaps, or at the notion of consequence, of understanding *int*ent as well as *cont*ent. So much more helpful than a frame-by-frame evaluation of an image of an areola, is my guess.

Me? My chief memory of the stunt is the six-word text I receive at home from a colleague as the game's halftime-show wraps up:

"Did I just see a nip?"

To me, that aptly sums up the whole silly thing.

The contretemps that follows, in turn, is best distilled by memories of a meeting I'm part of in the days after that's been called to discuss what to do about a scene in one of our series that features a glimpse of a naked backside. To offset any potential complaints about indecency, a decision is reached to blur the offending image for the nano-seconds it's on-screen.

The half-hour show is a *cartoon*.

The swimming-against-the-tide that is my so-called Violence Crusade does not bloody me, but it does wear at me. I'm still excited to be doing what I do and to be working for and with The Boss, but the recently planted seeds of unrest continue to take root. I continue to wonder what the fight is *for*, if my passion is shared here in the hallways and around town. CBS, like TV and Hollywood at large, is changing for a new millennium, incrementally but significantly. The future predicted for the medium back in the 1990s when I enter it, and then speculated about in the early part of this new century, is fast becoming a reality. Technology steers. Commerce reigns. Changes come. Rules bend. Creativity wanes. And a vulgar word -- *content* – is introduced to refer to my daily work. It's as dispassionate and impersonal a term as can be leveled against a creative process that should invoke neither.

More directly to what I specifically do here, I note with objectivity and no amount of self-pity that I'm beginning to sense less a need for or purpose to scheduling (and, consequently, to Scheduling), what I study as a child and the love of which I bring to CBS.

It's simply beginning not to matter as much, not really anyway. And the not-matter-ing seems like it's only going to accelerate.

The placing of shows in certain timeslots to win a night (and then a week and a season), the knowing of which shows go where so that they survive and thrive, the overall science and strategy of programming and counterprogramming, the zigging and zagging, is less important. Certainly less critical. Because these days TV schedules themselves are becoming less important and less critical. Thanks to DVRs and DVDs and (the beginnings of) online streaming, viewers are watching TV on schedules of their own makings.

The evolving broadcast-network business-plan, incorporating silos upon silos constructed outside of prime-time viewing, where other money is to be made in multiples of ways, is becoming such that Nielsen numbers aren't all that bottom-line crucial to revenue anymore. Shows are making money regardless of ratings, regardless of placement. The very definitions of *hit* and *success* and *failure*, of *good* and *bad*, in fact, have become quite fluid, almost relative. Unlike times of old – ten years ago? ten minutes? -- when ratings determine renewal and then profit, revenue can now be derived from shows that have limited (or even no) on-air audience by dint of the after-prime-time market. In general, there's less pressure to react to low ratings, brought on by whatever reason. These days in the world of TV two plus two can equal five. And it adds up to confusion for me. About my role here.

Scheduling plainly takes up less of my day-to-day, involves less of my thinking. Between CBS's dominant role in prime-time and the Changing Times themselves, there's a certain *de facto* algorithm to all of what we do, with some well-formed round-pegs of series all but scheduling themselves in matching round holes of nighttime programming and others left to live or die on their own in slots where they can do the least amount of damage to the week and to the company. One morning at TVC I sit with my Scheduling colleagues to hash out where and when a certain new mid-season show should air. After a brief discussion, a decision is reached, punctuation by "What the hell, why not?"

I get the thinking, but it hollows out my heart to hear it. A tourist at the Farmer's Market behind our building can make a decision based on a criterion of *What the hell?*

I'm not here for *What the hell?*

Scheduling is veering towards shelf-stocking. And even at that only certain aisles matter: Fridays and Saturdays are mostly ignored these days, by all the broadcast networks – and, as a result, by viewers, too. In 2004, for what seems to be the first time in the network's history, CBS's new fall schedule features permanent repeat programming as part of its weekly lineup: Part of Saturday will now be devoted to "encore broadcasts" of our many crime-dramas. The math bears out the logic: Reruns of popular shows generate revenue, too, and if Saturday is now a night that attracts fewer viewers, which in turn makes it difficult to justify airing expensive-to-produce original programming on the night, where fewer people will see its ads, then the airing of repeats is a logical if even prudent choice.

But which comes first, I wonder -- fewer viewers or fewer reasons to view?

In abandoning the night, I suspect that we and the other majors are beginning to do what a FOX colleague calls "teaching people how not to watch TV." Aren't we accelerating the night's obsolescence with this change -- and then perhaps our own? Does Saturday represent the first domino?

For now, I know it's smart business. And it is a business that I'm in, willingly, and from which I personally profit, nicely. Still, like every media empire in this decade of rapid change – one that will end with barely a hint of TV resembling itself as it begins -- orbiting around synergistic strategies and repurposed content and bottom-line thinking and second-windows and distribution pipelines, it seems that the networks are becoming just another streamlined business. Like the health-care industry. Networks are now Hollywood versions of HMOs. We're *EMOs* -- Entertainment Maintenance

163

Organizations, offering managed-care-programming with low-risk high-reward products and services.

If I take comfort in the fact that my boss, The Boss, a one-time actor and successful producer and highly regarded former studio-head who has a desk-plate in his office that reads IT'S THE WRITING STUPID, does value the creative tenets of television, who in my analogous EMO is the seasoned doctor who still values his patients, I'm left to wonder if one person is enough in this mammoth show-business practice. Especially one swelling with junior executives weaned on the concept of *content* and hired by business-people savvy to the changing industry but not to its history or to what really makes it work (story and character, for starters, which beget longevity).

Many of these ladder-sprinting TV kingpins of tomorrow, the children now beginning to run much of TV, know television only as product to push and not an art to curate. The next jobs, the bigger offices, the better titles, the power and the prestige are the pursuits. If a TV show he or she is connected to becomes successful in the process, fine. But it's not the goal. It's often really not even necessary.

A few years from now a broadcast network will announce an enormous investment in a high-profile series that has little chance of getting an audience at its outset, let alone enduring for several seasons. But it sparks headlines when announced, and then it generates worldwide sales in advance of its debut in the U.S. – which means financial and professional pay-off for all involved before a frame of the show even airs. That the advance word on the series is that it's all but unwatchable is irrelevant. Profit, both the real and symbolic kind, has been met: The show "got on the air."

Many track-records are similarly constructed of ceremony and headlines, of attention and affiliation, not necessarily success. But what happens to TV in the process? What happens to the actual product?

I try to cede much of what I see as just evidence of a naturally evolving business, alongside of which I am to evolve, as well. And I try. But still I wonder (because that's what I do, probably too often about too much and probably from too lofty a self-created perch): *Is* there a place in the changing landscape for those who value and appreciate the power of TV as a form of communication? Does programming still matter? Does the viewer? Do I?

So many big questions.

And then one gigantic answer, delivered in the most unexpected of ways, on a Friday night in 2006, at 6:31p.m.

Of the two routes I tend to employ each day for my commute home to Manhattan Beach after work, I opt on this Super Bowl-weekend night for the one with the perceived short-cuts, which incorporates side-streets and cut-throughs. Not that it matters: Traffic is merciless everywhere for some reason. Short-cuts add up to no cuts at all; little time is saved, even on these more navigable backstreets down around Hauser. In fact, when I finally dead-end on it at Jefferson Boulevard and then make the right turn that is supposed to take me swiftly to La Cienega and then to home, I see nothing but brake-light-red ahead of me.

But then the left-hand of the two westbound lanes that I'm part of opens up, and I maneuver into it and continue west along Jefferson at a surprisingly good clip, about to cruise through one minor intersection on my way to La Cienega-freedom. Just as I try, a fast-moving white-paneled van appears from the side-street to my right, intent on crossing both westbound lanes in front of me so that it can then head east on Jefferson to its own reward. The right side of my brand-new Ford Escape SUV stops it.

I won't remember much of the actual impact, but it's severe enough to separate the rear tire of my car from its axle and powerful enough to crush the entirety of the right side of the vehicle, shattering four of eight windows in the process. My brakes scream, metal crunches, glass sprinkles. And then it's over, as soon as it begins, my SUV made unrecognizable from within inside of a blink.

But then just as quickly, micro-seconds later, the shock of the impact nipped, the Los Angeles horizon in front of me begins to shift, me along with it. My car is flipping over.

My hands are clenched on the wheel; my right foot is pumping furiously in search of connection to wheels that themselves are no longer connected to the street. And any even-brief hint of relief I feel over surviving the collision is quickly replaced by feelings of white-hot fear and dull sadness as the car upends.

Because I know, I'm fully aware, that it's not the actual crash that will kill me on this February night; it's the revolution of my car across Jefferson Boulevard. *This, right now, is the beginning of my death, actually happening as I sit here, flashing on the waste and loneliness of it all, by myself on this dark street on this cold night.*

I remember thinking: *I just hope it doesn't hurt to die.*

I wait. I listen. I watch. I tilt. The left side, then the roof, and then finally the right side of the car, an unholy symphony of metal scraping blacktop. It lasts forever, the whole world slowly shifting. And then everything stops. I am upright again, strapped behind the wheel, facing oncoming traffic in a car that's straddling the eastbound lanes of Jefferson Boulevard. Alive.

I release myself from the seatbelt that has saved me and step out of the SUV, my lone injuries seeming to be a scratch on my left thumb and a wrenched back. I survey the scene: The contents of my car are strewn across the intersection of Jefferson Boulevard and Clyde Street here in this unfamiliar tract of Los Angeles, young locals stare at me from all points of the corner, the driver of the offending (and intact) panel-van loiters far down Jefferson, behind his wheel, evidently debating whether he should exit and walk back towards the wreck he causes.

"Mister," says a teenaged girl as she approaches me, "you better sit down on the curb, 'cause you got blood all over you." (Blood-smears, actually: Once outside the car, my instinct is to pat myself down, to see if anything hurts; the bloody thumb has left a trail.) Her fellow onlookers begin collecting the pieces that are my life from the street – cell-phone, briefcase, random files, spare clothes from an earthquake kit in the back of the car – piling the debris on the sidewalk near me. The other driver finally exits his car and walks towards me, but I shoo him away. "I don't want to hear anything from you right now," I say. (Or ever.)

Patting my pants-pockets again, I walk back to the steaming car and reach inside for the wallet I foolishly keep on my passenger seat when I drive, now on the floor. And then I go off to sit on the ground, increasingly more dazed, my lower-back beginning to seize. The young girl offers use of her phone since mine doesn't seem to be working, but in the moment I can only think that I will bloody it with my stained hands, so I decline. And there I remain seated, waiting out the police and paramedics that I'm told are coming.

What follows is an almost-enjoyable scene of absurdity lifted from a light matinee – Jerry Lewis's *The Disorderly Orderly*, maybe – that's more suitable for acting out than writing down. (So ask me about it when I see you.) Suffice it to say, though, that it pivots around two medics arriving at the scene, putting me in a cervical collar, strapping me first to a backboard and then to a gurney, lifting and rolling the gurney into the rear of an ambulance -- and then asking me where I'd like to go.

Confused, I suggest the hospital near my home.

"You don't want to go there" is the response.

I don't? I ask, strapped down and now freezing in the back of the ambulance. Naw, says one. Too far. " 'Sides, this rig aint got no shocks," he says. Then they ask for my other choices, a sort of 31 Flavors approach to triage, and I can only defer to them, which begets an argument between the pair about where best to leave my now-aching body.

Eventually, they settle on a Culver City hospital ten minutes away, to which we beat a fast retreat in a screaming ambulance that seems hell-bent on introducing me to every pothole in the neighborhood and on making hairpin turns that send my gurney on a tour of the inside of the vehicle, torturing my spasming back. Upside-down to me, the smiling medic raises his eyebrows and says, "See? No shocks."

I note that my feet seem cold and I express worry, to be told that it's just due to my socks being removed once inside the ambulance (which I don't remember happening). "Oh, okay," I say. "But it really is cold in here -- can I get them back on?" A bit reluctantly, he says he'll cover my bare feet with a blanket, adding as he does, "It's just that usually it's only the old people who have complaints like that."

If there's surrealism to the post-accident drama, it matches the wreck itself. But in that this night is evidently meant to be about a Very Real Life Lesson, it's summed

Remains of the day (February, 2006)

up twenty minutes after the impact, in the emergency room of the Brotman Memorial Medical Center in Culver City, when one of the two who've rushed me here pauses by my gurney on his exit, pats my shoulder, and says, "You were saved tonight to remind everyone you know to wear their seatbelts."

Okay, I think. *But why else?*

Los Angeles, with all its virtues, can be a difficult and soul-less place. Nearly 20 years a resident at this point, I think I can take or leave it. TV, in turn, the thing that brings me here, is becoming a bit of both, as well. In whole. Thirteen years into my dream job, do I now feel the same way about it as I do the city?

Businesses change as life does. I know that. I've studied it. But taking a quick spin around the TV dial, which I do a lot during my days at home recovering from the wreck, and in the weeks after, I don't see much that inspires or enlightens. Or even really entertains. I see that crime-shows out-gore one another, that the misogyny in prime-time as a whole seems to have mushroomed, that sitcoms peddle in juvenilia as the comedy-writing bar continues to be lowered, that game-shows feature the eating of cockroaches and bull-testicles, that felons are trading infamy for celebrity, and that people are fist-fighting while audiences cheer. It's a suffocating avalanche of vice and negativity and ugliness.

I know that TV has always had a mix of high-brow and low-brow – and even no-brow – but I don't ever remember it being this disposable, this contemptuous, of us and of itself. Where's the *life-force* that I know it to be?

I don't want to die upside-down in a car alone on the streets of Los Angeles breathing this TV air. I don't want to be in the same business as testicle-eaters.

My latest two-year contract with CBS is due to expire later this year, and while it pains me to think of leaving the company and the people and the security and The Boss, the thought is plainly here now, in front of me. I'm loathe to phone in a job, and I fear that's exactly what I will begin doing, as the importance of my role diminishes and as I teach myself to care less about the thing I generally love, television. That pains me even more.

I have to leave *sometime*, don't I?

To do what, I don't know. But perhaps that time is now. I spend a month thinking it over. Then, once again, life happens. I get a call with an offer for a new TV job. One with a higher level of responsibility and (it seems) influence. One that seems to bring me closer to that life-force. One that just might serve to answer some of the questions I find myself asking these days since the accident. (Little do I know it'll end up answering many more.)

It's 2700 miles away, back on the east coast I once call home. Another card dealt from a deck that I don't even know is in play, I take it. I'm going to leave CBS after thirteen years.

If I wonder whether the thus-far private decision I'm making is the right one, I'm helped at the office, in an indirect way, by a conversation I have with my direct-report. He confides in me one morning that he's been approached by the two other executives who make up the now-four-person staff of our department about receiving promotions. He wants to accommodate them, he says, but the result would be a top-heavy department, with three of the four of us holding a vice-president or above title, which would raise eyebrows and strain the budget. Mindful that my contract is up soon and that I've yet to make any noise about renewing it – a tell, to him -- he says, "All things being equal, if you're thinking of leaving, doing it soon would help."

I like my direct-report. I always will. In ways I'll likely never explain to him in person, he holds a real place in my heart and in my life. He means no offense by the meeting. His is a straight business question, if delivered in his inimitable way. I get it. But in hearing it I hear all I need to hear about my future at CBS.

I tell him I'm going to help him out of his dilemma.

The Boss, when I tell him in turn – or rather when I *ask* him, since my leaving requires an early exit from my contract – is gracious and supportive. He proves himself to be the ally I feel he's been since our first one-on-one in his office eleven years ago. We agree that this being April, the start of the Upfront season, I will stick around through the annual ritual and leave after it's over. Given the time of year I join the company, I find welcome symmetry in the plan.

My final New York Upfront adventure for CBS, as it is for the previous ten-plus years, is a haze of both formal and informal meetings and gatherings that involve the construction of a brand-new network TV schedule. As it is for the previous ten-plus years, it's mostly awesome. In that I am fully in awe that I am here. I allow my single yearly (over-) indulgence – taking advantage of the open bar at the traditional dinner overseen by The Boss for his staffs on both coasts (ahead of which there's always a shameful days-long negotiation with its planner to ensure a seat at one of the cool tables – which I always *always* lose.) But I spend the rest of what is now also a routine New York experience reminding myself that this trip is really anything but. It's my last. And each of the many days here marks a series of individual goodbyes. I will miss these days, this process, with these people. The camaraderie. Being part of a collective, making a difference. Contributing to pieces of TV history and to CBS's legacy. Not to mention the two weeks at company expense, my most-every need a card-swipe away.

Under the reign of The Boss, each of the CBS Upfront presentations held at New York's tony Carnegie Hall features a live musical performance of one kind or another that caps off the two-hour roundelay of speech-giving and trailer-showing and celebrity-presenting. It's usually tied either to a specific program the network airs (The Who performs one year, live, to celebrate the fast-growing *CSI* franchise, which uses its music for its main-titles; Gloria Gaynor reprises her 1970s anthem "I Will Survive" in 2001 to hype the recently launched *Survivor*) or to a New-York-only kind of experience (an operatic mock-aria befitting the historic venue or the cast of a Broadway hit, reworking some of the show's lyrics to make them about CBS). Little expense or creativity is spared, as a memorable Upfront experience is a springboard to a fortune in advertising revenue.

For this my final Upfront in 2006, intent on shedding the normal nerves and distractions of the day that we/I feel -- Will the speech sound as good as when we write it? Will the clips be as entertaining as when we privately screen them? Will the production itself run as smoothly as when we rehearse it? Will The Boss be unhappy with any part of it, and if so how much of that will trickle down and how far? -- I sink into my seat and try as best as I can to watch it as an audience member, enjoying the words and the trailers and the show as a whole as well as the role I play, however minor, in all of it. And I am first to my feet at the close when this year's live-act is revealed - - the four-man cast of *Jersey Boys*, just now breaking as Broadway's most popular new musical. I have little knowledge of the show nor even of the Frankie Valli story it celebrates, but the quartet's performance on this afternoon, twenty feet from where I sit, is jaw-droppingly good. It's easy to see why the show's a hit.

When the presentation is over and the stage clears, Carnegie Hall slowly empties; the crowd of press and industry executives, of advertisers and their minions, along with my CBS colleagues and the stars of our new shows unveiled here, make the ritualistic post-presentation march to Tavern on the Green restaurant in Central Park, where the real celebrating and glad-handing is to begin and to run for hours. In no hurry, I stay behind in the Hall. The Tavern portion of the day holds less and less appeal to me through the years. Too crowded. Too noisy. Too sweaty. Too much. Besides, I want to close the page of this particular Carnegie chapter more slowly.

So I wait for everyone to leave. I wait to be alone, then I walk to the center of the front row of the cavernous space, and I look around as I sift through eleven years of memories and the more than 300 pilots the bring me here– in the seats for countless rehearsals, backstage for late-night speech revisions, in the Green Room alongside actors and other familiar faces that thrill me in child-like ways I dare not show.

And then I look at the storied stage. I think back to all the appearances: The bipolar actor who stops dead-center after he's introduced, to drop his pants – it's unscripted -- for the crowd; the star who refuses to come out from the wings when he's told backstage the up-till-now secret timeslot for his new show, which he hates; the new-comedy headliner overwhelmed with emotion and reduced to tears as he stands in the spotlight and tries to convey to the crowd the impact of having his own TV series on his proud parents. Dozens of names, dozens of faces, scores of memories.

The grown-up version of the six-year-old boy from Wellington Street, hiding in the black-and-white of his basement, has been part of something special.

Outside Carnegie Hall, on 57th Street, a personal celebration seems in order. On a whim, I decide to skip Tavern on the Green altogether. I look at the time, and I know what I will do instead: I'm going to see *Jersey Boys*, damn the no-doubt prohibitive cost. So I walk the few blocks to the August Wilson Theater and join the long line at the box-office. "Any seats available for the tonight, by chance?" I ask when I make my way to the window 25 minutes later. My spontaneity is rewarded with what is literally the last seat for the night's performance. "It's sixth-row center," she says from behind the glass, almost with an apology. "Is that okay?" Sixth-row center is perfect, I tell her. Any closer and I'll be in the cast.

Inside, I enjoy four-dollar Snickers for dinner in the lobby, and then I go to find my seat. A curious buzz can be heard in the theater as I move down the aisle and then sit at sixth-row center. It doesn't seem to be just about the show. Then the buzz gets louder, the house lights still bright. I see necks craning all around me, toward the rear. People are taking to their feet. Next, they begin to applaud. At what, I don't know.

And then I turn around, too, to see why the commotion: Bill Clinton and daughter Chelsea are in the rear of the August Wilson Theater, tickets in hand, flanked by two security men. The applause is raucous now. I watch as the pair, acknowledging the cheers with smiles, comes down the very aisle I've just walked, in search of their own seats. Looking around, I see the only empty ones to be found:

Fifth-row center. Directly in front of mine.

Which is how on one night in May of 2006 I end up going to the theater with a President.

And how I end my eleven years of coming to New York for CBS.

(I've no idea what the show's about, by the way. My mind and eyes are elsewhere. But I can report that Bill Clinton does have one impeccably groomed neck.)

I return to Los Angeles the next day, and I use the four weeks that follow to settle office affairs, to make a brief recon trip to my future new east-coast home, to fly to enjoy the Jersey Shore vacation with various members of my Philadelphia family that we make in one grouping or another for the past 40 summers, and then to return to TVC to pack up my CBS life.

Among the last things I find to box up on my very last day is a small framed picture of me sitting on a reproduction of the 1960s living-room set for that decade's hit comedy *The Dick Van Dyke Show* -- faithfully wrought for a special that CBS makes in 2004 to salute it, from the louvered kitchen-counter shutters to the table-lamps and bric-a-brac to the iconic fabric-ottoman. When it shoots, I make sure I am there, even showing up early one day before anyone is on the set, to spend alone-time in the Petrie living-room, all these years removed from watching the show as a child. The opportunity is too great to pass up. Larry Matthews himself, the actor who plays young Richie Petrie on the show and who's been recruited for the special along with the rest of the original cast, is there. We chat.

"See that radio up there?" he asks, pointing towards the rear of the stage, near to the landing inside the re-created Petrie front door, where a large old-fashioned radio sits on a shelf, just as it does in the original show. "That's where we heard that Kennedy was dead." Running from 1961 to 1966, the CBS show finds the cast in rehearsal on a November Friday in 1963 when word of the assassination comes to the set. "We all gathered around the radio, up there on the landing, when we heard he was shot. In silence. Just listening. And that's where we heard that the President had died." I ask the actor to take a photo of me in the "real" Petrie living-room.

On this my last day at CBS, I look at the photo, of me at 46, sitting in Rob and Laura Petrie's house from the 1960s, and I realize that not many people get the chance to live out their dreams. I did that and more.

I stepped into mine.

Along the way through an amazing job this child of television has walked the backlots of every TV studio in town, large and small, cocking my ears to their whispered histories. I've stood alongside the real people who were the flickering

174

images of my youth – cast members of *The Dick Van Dyke Show* and *Gilligan's Island* and *Mary Tyler Moore* and *The Brady Bunch* and *I Dream Of Jeannie* and, yes, *Bewitched*. I've spoken with Carol Burnett and with Walter Cronkite. And I've witnessed the making of new history as well, alongside the stars of my adulthood – writers and producers and actors and more. Their world, I have been welcomed to it.

Two things seem to sum up my last day, if not the town. One comes in the form of a call from a long-time assistant on the floor. A stoic all-business professional, she phones to say she's out today and won't get a chance to say goodbye in person. She wants me to know, though, that she's enjoyed working with me. We chat. Then before she hangs up she stuns me by adding, "Well, I love you." It's sentiment I rarely if ever hear around here and definitely never imagine coming from her. I decide that a connection forging these three words is as good a reward as any for being here.

The other last-day encounter is an in-person one. I want to drop by a particular colleague's office to hug her goodbye, not just because I'll miss working with her but also because of what she says two months earlier, in private, when she hears I've given notice. "I'll be so sorry to see you leave," she says then. "You've been my ally, my confidante, my supporter, my nemesis, my colleague, my frustration, my friend." It's a nicely worded sentiment that humanizes her and humbles me. I hold it dear, especially the word *nemesis*, which I mentally circle in red. In a town of disingenuousness and bullshit and ass-covering, it stands out. So on this day I want to want to say goodbye. I find her and say how grateful I am to have worked with her and how meaningful her earlier comments are. "It's not often I can embrace being called someone's nemesis, but I thank you. It actually means we've had a real relationship here."

"*Nemesis?*" she responds, with an expression that connotes wood-rot. "I never said that. I'd never use that word."

Okay then.

Time to go.

I join a small crowd of friends and colleagues on this sunny afternoon at a favorite patio-bar behind CBS, and I say goodbye to thirteen years. I thank both the colleagues present and those *in absentia* who make it all possible. A few drinks, a

175

30 Fri Jun 2006

7:30	
8:00	
8:30	
9:00 AM	
9:30	
10:00	
10:30	
11:00	
1130	
NOON	
12:30	
1:00	
1:30	
2:00	
2:30	
3:00	
3:30	
4:00	
4:30	
5:00	
5:30	
6:00	

few photos, and then I'm gone. It's over. A confluence of factors – time and timing, desire and destiny, chance and luck, people and passion – comes down to this, a mission conceived a true lifetime ago, now a mission complete.

Thirteen years after finding myself in television in 1993, I leave CBS having found myself, in television.

*

CBS's 2006 Scheduling team:
Andy Kubitz, Jim McKairnes, Kelly Kahl, Noriko Gee
(Los Angeles, final CBS day, June 2006)

After

Teaching, DePaul University
(Chicago, 2010)

My gig at CBS lasts 13 years. It's the job of my dreams.

The position I leave it for lasts six months. It's the mistake of my life.

Three weeks in, I know the job won't work out. I know it's a bad match. Based on what I'm seeing, I know that if things don't change (and I know they won't) I won't be staying. But when I call a seasoned colleague for counsel and advice, she tells me flat out that no one can or should form an opinion about a new job for at least six months, and she suggests I ride it out at least that long before making any decisions. Fair enough.

Five months and one week after the call, six months to the day of my arrival, I announce I'm leaving. I cede to the mistake.

It's a mistake not because I leave CBS to take the job. I'm glad that I leave CBS. I *need* to leave the network when and how I do. Nor is it a mistake because in taking it I relocate across the country: I'm good with that, too. I like the east coast. And it's not a mistake because the new job finds me working at a TV network alongside people who don't seem to realize they're even *in* the TV business (news about which some glean from reading *USA Today*). Nor because in my six months there I attend literally 172 meetings, and in all those meetings in all those "strategy rooms" I am forced to listen to all those colleagues use the letters "i.e." in conversation as though it's a word and others who employ such phrases as *cross functional program alignment* and *monetizing the upside* and *incremental revenue driver* and *risk tolerance in a business continuum* and *road map for today's business discussion* and *pain points to dialogue about* and *seasonality as it impacts program attributes* and *topline review of a pipeline management problem exploring pillars behind the drivers associated with the deep dive* in their sentences. Nor even because of the one day a meeting is called to discuss the results of a new show's focus-group testing -- "*Viewers may not be coming to be entertained, but they are leaving having had an entertaining experience,*" we're told, with huzzahs -- and I see colleagues actually writing the conclusion down.

It's a mistake for none of these reasons.

Rather, it's a mistake because the job I'm offered while still at CBS, the position described to me in such rich detail and with such promise that it lures me to another city for a high-ranking well-paid position created just for me, doesn't exist when I get here. Three weeks in, I know it never will. (Sadly, it won't be the last time I allow a cloud of nebulousness to guide me in my career.)

It's never introduced as the new reality to the very employees I am supposed to be coming to oversee, one of whom, I find out later, sends an email just days before my arrival to his own sub-staff telling them that while the new guy (me) will be starting soon "he will have zero sign-off authority."

Okay then.

(I'm never to see the email, of course, but an anonymous supporter at the company slips it my way after I leave at the six-month mark, and then I then pass it on to my lawyer.)

No one ever as much as stands in front of any of the many strategy rooms at the place to say what I am told months earlier when the offer is made, that I have a specific role there as Executive Vice-President of Programming. All of it. In charge. For better or worse. So undefined and unsupported is the role that at one of the 172 meetings, after a colleague solicits and gets my input, he says to the others assembled in the room, "It's useful to have Jim's viewpoint here as an outsider."

I'd been in my role for five months.

Yes -- big mistake.

Still, as mistakes go, it really is the best I ever make. Because when I make it, when it does take me back to live on the east coast for six months for what's to be the start of my new life, it takes me to within a two-hour drive of my Philadelphia family, where one key member is facing what will be the final six months of hers.

My mother's never-married and childless sister Jane is known to everyone, not just to the fifteen nieces and nephews who use the title by birthright but to virtually everyone in the greater Philadelphia metropolitan region, as Aunt Jane. *Everyone.* Family, neighbors, friends of family, friends of neighbors, friends of friends of her nieces and nephews, even strangers who will never meet her throughout any of her 76 years but who often hear of her – she's simply Aunt Jane. No last name.

Aunt Jane is that one relative all families claim who are as memorable as popular, without whom no function is ever complete, the one who ends up its oft-talked-about main attraction, and about whom eyes roll in affection as the stories about him or her are shared through the grapevine, shipped across the miles, and handed down through the generations.

The lymphoma she develops in her 60s that she speculates is the result of her daily lifting of the heavy garage-door? The decades' worth of family photos she snaps that, to a one, seem not to feature their subjects' heads? The niece's wedding rehearsal she interrupts to whisper to the presiding priest that perhaps it's best not to have the brother of the bride in charge of the Communion wine at the service "what with him being in Three A's and all"? (The poor officiate is left to wonder not just who this woman is talking to him but also the curious connection between the blood of Christ and the Auto Club.) The legendary hospital visit following my 1980 surgery, when she arrives with a care-package of moist towelettes and Jergens Lotion that she hurriedly deposits on my bedside table -- directly on top of the small plastic tub into which I've been asked to deposit all my spit for the previous two days so that

185

doctors can determine the source of my post-op infection, which then falls to the floor? ("Oh, Aunt Jane, my sputum," I say, sobbing as I see my only ticket to release puddling on the floor. "My *sputum*." Further negating its use, she actually then drops to the floor, untucks the tissue forever kept in the fold of her shirtsleeve, and begins to push the spit from the floor back into the plastic dish, saying, "We can save it, Jim!") My cousin's California wedding, where her inability to find the thermostat in her hotel room – for the heat, in June – means that when I go to her room to fetch her for the service I find her standing inside wanding herself TSA-like with the room-supplied hair-dryer? On high?

Simply, Aunt Jane.

No last name.

Aunt Jane truly is the lifeblood of her family, as integral to the lives of her eight nephews and seven nieces as are their own parents. She devotes herself to them. We, in turn, venerate her. Always in our hearts, thoughts, conversations, and plans. If it's a deep connection for all fifteen, it seems even more so for the seven McKairnes children, given our mother's role in Aunt Jane's life as her lifelong best friend, always a short drive away from our Northeast Philadelphia home. When after 58 years and to her boundless sorrow she outlives Mom – never to be the same, which she tries to hide – Aunt Jane is our mother's always-present stand-in at McKairnes weddings and funerals and birthdays and holidays and even informal gatherings, which seems to keep them both alive. Even if it does mean that she introduces herself to strangers at each as "the dead mother's sister."

As providence has it, I fly east to begin my post-CBS life on Aunt Jane's 76th and final birthday. She takes ill the following week. Each of our journeys to follow lasts the same six months: Aunt Jane dies exactly 23 hours after I quit my new job, two hours south of her. But in that half-year we share, I'm able to drive up to Philadelphia periodically to join the family in an unspoken extended goodbye. To help with caring and feeding. To visit. To make calls to the doctor on her behalf. To sit with her in the small duplex she rents on her small bank-teller's pension midway between the house where she and Mom and their four brothers are raised back in the 1940s and the church that her adult life revolves around. A mile or so stretch of pavement that's been Aunt Jane's entire life.

The perennial Santa to our childhood Christmases, a grown-up child made joyous by the furtive shopping of the season and the secret late-night December 24 drop-offs at our house, Aunt Jane needs company on what will turn out to be her final Christmas Eve. I drive up to Philadelphia, and we spend a Saturday night watching TV -- repeat airings of *The Lawrence Welk Show*, a longtime favorite dating back to when she watches with her own aging mother during its original 1960s run. She makes note of every single cast member of the long-forgotten show who has since died (which is most of them).

After about six or seven of these mentions, I finally say with mock frustration, "Aunt Jane, we can't sit here on Christmas weekend watching TV and have you point out everybody you see who's now dead. It's morbid." She smiles and acquiesces. For the rest of the hour, she just clears her throat to get my attention each time an unfortunate appears on screen and then silently points at the screen with a thumbs-down gesture.

The next morning, I get to wake up early and beat a rush to the market while she still sleeps, intent on buying the makings of a favorite Christmas-time breakfast from her youth – the menu includes a very specific local brand of sausage -- which I cook and have waiting for her when she wakes. It makes her smile.

When the end comes three weeks later, fifty years to the day of the birth of the very first of the fifteen children who bestow upon her the revered title that all will come to know her by, I'm able to be there again for the farewell that follows. On the drive north for the funeral, I think of the days and nights of our Aunt Jane lives, from her visits to Wellington Street on Donut Day each February, her arms heavy with fragrant pink boxes, to the pain I see behind her seemingly frozen smile of acceptance throughout my mother's illness. (When one night right before the end I attempt to make sense of the tragedy unfolding around us, by suggesting that perhaps when finally Mom passes we can get some of our lives back, she looks at me blankly and says, "You don't understand, Jim -- your mother *is* my life.") I find comfort and relief in knowing I've been able to be nearby to my aunt these past six months, for a goodbye that would never be possible without leaving CBS to make the worst mistake ever.

Weeks after the funeral, back in my apartment near the nation's capital, I bundle up my short-lived east coast life, and I return to my never-sold house in Los Angeles. Still not a fan of the city even after twenty years, it does nonetheless seem to be home. I feel grateful, relieved, that the upheaval of the past year -- the near-fatal car wreck, the quitting of one job and the aborted start of a new one, the cross-country move made twice, the death of another family member -- does not up-end me. That it does not allow oxygen to be fed to the Depression that simmers inside.

Still, here in the spring of 2007, with no office-job to turn to in a city where profession equals identity, I am gnawed at by feelings of disappointment and failure. With ample time to scrutinize each, I begin to realize that they're likely rooted in something more personal. It's not my career that has stalled, not just the Depression I fear – it's me. The reality that *is* me. Maybe the time has come for me to untangle myself from some treacherous and knotted roots.

I do manage at least to begin the coming-out process a few years ago, baby steps, during my final two years at CBS. I do tell a few friends, the very first being a relative newcomer to my life, a long-distance pal in town on business, at the outdoor mall near to CBS known as The Grove. I accompany him to the Apple Store there one weekend afternoon, and then, seemingly out of nowhere, I just begin the conversation. It's easy. Unremarkable. Helpful. (The confession begets a joke that outing myself shall forever be known as *taking people to The Grove.*) Still, the ugly truth is that whatever I've said to him is something that I'm not sure I've actually said to myself yet. I'm not sure that I've even taken myself to the Grove.

How do I start talking to myself about something that I've spent a lifetime disallowing myself even to notice or to feel? What I ignore in my Philadelphia youth, what I distract myself from thinking about in my young adult days in Tennessee, what has been sidelined here in LA now into my 40s?

Surely, I conclude, the lack of *living* it and the inability to *do anything* about it are connected.

I try at times to deal with it, but I just can't seem to get next to it, be with it, share it. It's of me; yet unlike Depression it's removed from me, seemingly no longer inside me. My own fault, I guess, for anesthetizing for so many years, borne of knowing from a young age that something about me is just *off.* Something inside me, in a place that no one, not even I, can fully see. Point to. Get at.

Here's what I know: I am born; it's there; and then I am in my 40s. Alone. Thousands of miles and a lifetime from where I started, with a life that hasn't. Unable to hide from myself any longer. Unable to fight. Unable to ignore what I've been unable to face. I am lost. And I am tired.

Everything in between is a haze.

There's the 1960s middle-class Catholic rearing, all right angles and tight squares, the family and neighborhood as black-and-white as the news we read and the TV we watch. A time and a world in which This Is This, and where *that's* an aberration. An abomination. A time and a world in which boys are boys and those who aren't are girls. A time and a world in which a young son over-identifies with the mother he experiences as emotionally fragile, who finds comfort in the day-saving (male) heroes of the television he slips into and then never wants to leave. Then there's the vertigo and hyper-vigilance of adolescence, of going along and getting along, of not looking back or within, and the adulthood of accomplishment fueled by professional desire but with a secret shame that rides side-car to success.

A haze.

I do remember the word, new to me. Age 11. Sixth grade at St. Matt's elementary in Philadelphia. "Richard Taft's a *faggot!*" yells Margie Sims, hurling it across the parking-lot during recess in retaliation for Richard's knocking her books to the ground and then running off. Children being children, wielding grown-up words.

Faggot. An invective that's over most of our heads, it's a common go-to nonetheless around here, used to strafe the landscape of play. I remember the laughs that follow Margie's outburst -- and then the feeling of a sting I cannot find. Retreating within myself there on the schoolyard blacktop. Age 11.

I remember the day I have contact with the word again, a few years later, in high school. An age at which I better understand both the word and the sting. The tone behind it now is much more raw, its edges coarser, hate and separation and segregation behind it. Meant to hurt, not amuse, it's scrawled on a scrap of paper that's taped to the back of an oft-targeted unsuspecting freshman. A quick bump in a crowded hallway, followed by a "Sorry, man" and a mock-friendly slap on the back, and there it is. A dark and hostile word made up of dark and hostile letters, black letters on bright-white school-supplied paper, affixed to a student already maligned without mercy here for his unacceptably effeminate behavior:

FAG

A 14-year-old walking halls of bullies, unknowingly escorted by the word, trailed by laughter he cannot understand, his face burdened by the familiar hardened smile of appeasement that the harassed and outnumbered wear each day, the one seen above the sagging shoulders and the posture of defeat that telegraphs *If I am nice and I smile and I pretend to get it, will you stop hurting me?*

I hate his pain, hate those behind it, and hate myself for not reaching out to remove the paper and trash its offending word. But to do so is to risk being affixed with a tag of my own. So instead I retreat further into my own skin, and I walk on to class.

The vestiges of a Catholic education about compassion and love.

I remember, too, the upperclassman in the same school who targets me, on the other hand, one day not long after, at lunch, outside and across the street from the cafeteria, where we await the next period's bell. His signaling me to come over to the out-of-the-way area of the sidewalk where he stands huddled with friends, which I blindly do, only to see him point down, unzip, and then bring it out. Loud laughter follows among his group at my shamed and frightened reaction. I walk away that day confused, and then walk in fear the rest of the academic year that I'll see him or his friends again. I'll always wonder why my humiliation is their joy.

I also recall the ride to school still another day, in a stranger's car, at a more trustworthy time when hitchhiking is part of the daily Philadelphia school routine city-wide. A stranger whose manner and tone unnerve me from the minute I slide on to his bench-style front-passenger seat, my right hand staying true to the door-handle. A stranger who propositions me, at 14. For what, I have little clue. But I say no to whatever he seems to be asking, and he accepts my rejection with amusement. I avoid gold-and-maroon sedans from then on, too.

And I remember Friday afternoons in senior-year Geometry, last class of the day, last class of the week, where row after row of 17-year-old boys can be heard speaking of weekend plans that each hopes will involve a 17-year-old girl. And how odd and alone I feel knowing that mine ... will not. Because I don't want them to. Every Friday the same feeling of isolation, sitting there, calling on the Paul Simon lyrics I hear all the time these days on the radio that plays in third-period Study Hall, about what it feels to be "Slip Sliding Away." Every Friday, sitting there wondering how it has come to be that my life has begun without me in it, unfolding in ways I rather it didn't. How at 17 I already have days in which *I lie in bed and I think of things that might have been.* I remember how all of it further clouds a muddied adolescent mind, with me pushing against a pull I can't see. Slip-sliding away.

I remember tagging along as a teenager with Aunt Jane and her friends to a weekend movie. I hope that we're going to see the current hit *Dog Day Afternoon,* but in the car on the way I'm told that's been ruled out: It's about homosexuals. "Sorry, Jim, but I hope you understand," says sweet Aunt Jane, using the rear-view mirror to talk to me as I sit in the backseat of her white Signet, wishing at the moment that I were anywhere else but here if this is going to be the topic for the drive. "That's a grown-up movie." Then, ever the helper, she goes on. "Jim, do you know what *homosexual* is?" (Not *homosexuality* or *a homosexual,* but *homosexual.* Like diabetes.) I mumble a hurried "IdoandthatsokayAuntJane" to the mirror and then turn my

191

attention to anything at all outside the car window. And I retreat further inside myself.

I remember the close childhood friend who himself comes out, later, at 24, creating a family drama that finds him an asterisk in his own home. I want neither the fireworks nor the dismissal he experiences to be part of my world. So the hiding in plain sight continues, a fight now running on its own steam.

I remember all that.

And then suddenly, overnight, I am in my 40s, no fight left, the wall I keep trying to hold up to surround me overpowering my fatigued arms, collapsing under its own massive, punishing, demanding weight. On top of me.

The calls to my siblings begin. Because they have to. The youngest, number-four son and last of seven, now a family man, is first to be phoned. He lives here in California, as well, the northern part, so proximity and time-zone works in his favor. The conversation is life-saving – one that once again, like the first one at The Grove, tells me that the only real problem at hand seems to be one of my own construct. No one else cares, beyond the caring about me.

Making the call provides strength to make another. Which in turn feeds the next and the next. In all, six come and go over the course of a week, a sibling per night. (On the seventh day, I rest.) It's how I manage it. Elder sister Bernadette compassionately offers to take deaf Dad to the Grove for me, since the phone is less and less a part of his advancing years. (After Mom dies, we all try, no more so than he, to employ it, but his limited-and-lessening hearing just proves too big an obstacle as the years go on.)

They are effort-full, yet effortless. Age -- waiting so long to talk about it, that is – has its advantages: The responsibility-laden 30s and 40s are about so much more. "I'm sorry you are in pain, and I am here to help," says younger sister MaryBeth. "But call me when you have a real problem. I'm trying to pay my kids' tuition." We laugh.

There is only one real speed-bump on this particular familial road, when the drama dissolves into typical McKairnes-ian farce. It involves my final call of Coming Out Week, to younger sister Eileen, quite possibly and ironically the most forgiving and easy-going and live-and-let-live member of the entire family. Or so I think until the call. Born half-deaf herself, Eileen, unlike Dad, often refuses to acknowledge her disability – the quite-serious Gracie-Allen logic being "I can hear you just fine in the one ear I can hear you in." Well, sorta.

I dial, we swap small talk, and then I dive in. Prepared text at this point.

Me: "Anyway…Eileen…Look, I don't know if you've been talking to anyone else back there this week, but I have been making calls to everybody to let you all know about some stuff that's going on in my life."
Eileen: "Okay. I haven't really talked to anyone all week. I've been busy at work."
Me: "Good. Well. Look -- this is weird and hard for me to say and explain. I just want you to know that's there been some stuff going on with me lately. And I've been telling Dad and everybody else. I've just been doing a lot of thinking lately about my life and my future. And I realize that I just haven't been very happy for a long long time. I've had things bothering me. And I want everyone to know. I just have problems I am trying to solve and I haven't been very happy. But I really think it's time to try to solve them and to talk about them, because I want to try to be happy."
Eileen: "Okay. I get that. You should be happy. Whatever."
Me: "Good. Anyway, I guess what I am trying so hard to say is that, well, I guess what I'm trying to say is that my life is different out here and things are different with me. And I have different kinds of feelings from everybody else. And I'm getting older and I see that everyone around me is moving on with their lives and having kids and planning a future. And, well, look -- I want you to know that….I think I might be gay."
[Pause]
Eileen: "*GAY??*"

The tone is one of incredulity bordering on disgust -- from the last person in my family, the last person on the planet, whom I'd predict would have or express it. Eileen judges, condemns, criticizes no one. I'm speechless. Then I panic, stumbling through a response.

Me: "Well, yeah. I mean. Look. I just. I'm not happy. I haven't. I haven't been happy for a while. And I had to start asking myself why. I had to start figuring out what was wrong. I just didn't want to sit in my house afraid any more or for the rest of my life. I want to have a life and to have kids and to have a future and to be with people more. More open. I don't know -- more honest. It's been hard. I have had to do a lot of thinking. I just want to be happy like everyone else. And I've been alone too long. I just, I just, I just know I need to tell people I think I might be gay."

[Pause]

Eileen: "Gay? Who said anything about being gay?"

I pull the phone away from my ear and stare at it. Then:

Me: "Eileen, *I* just did. Just this second."

Eileen: "Oh. You did?"

Me: "I did."

[Pause]

Eileen: "Well, who cares about that? Do what makes you happy. I don't care."

And she's done.

And I'm confused, especially when Eileen begins to resume the small-talk.

Me: "Wait a minute, *wait a minute*. Eileen, back up. What did you *think* I said?"

Eileen: "When?"

Sigh.

Me: "Just now. Just now I said to you that I think I might be gay, and you said, <u>*GAY?,*</u> like you were offended or mad or something."

Eileen: "Ohhhh. No I wasn't mad or nothing."

Me: "I get that now. But what did you think I said that made me think you were mad when you responded to it?"

Eileen: "When?"

Sigh.

Me: "Just now!"

Eileen: "Oh, I thought you said you thought you might be dead."

[Pause]

[More pause]

Me: "_Dead?_ Eileen, I said to you that I think I might be gay. And you heard that I think I might be dead?"

Eileen: "Yeah."

[Pause]

Me: "Well, what would that even *mean?*"

Eileen: "I don't know. That's why I asked."

And that was that: Forty years of personal pain reduced to sketch comedy. She hears "dead" for "gay" and I hear "gay" for "dead." Neither of us picks up on the other's mistake. Then a conversation speeds along on parallel tracks.

Comedy = tragedy + timing ÷ family.

A huge burden is lifted with the week's calls, but the actual steps into a gay reality are still small and few. I finish out my years at CBS, and then, relocated on the east coast, I attempt more and larger ones. I guess I'm more open to it and to what may come of it. It becomes more of a way of life, or at least something I don't force from it. But it's difficult. At the end of the day this is just not the life I see for myself, or what is planned for or shown to me, when I'm young. And it's certainly not the one I expect myself to have at what statistics tell me is middle-age. I carry with me a burden of loss for time and for something that never will be, preventing me for years from living what simply is.

I recall a "Dear Abby" letter I read as a teen, in the now-long-defunct *Philadelphia Bulletin,* from the mother of an infant born with a life-altering handicap of which none were aware during pregnancy. She writes candidly and achingly of the disappointment she and her husband face upon delivery, its instant nullification of their life plans – and not, they knew, for the better. The future they map out through the long pregnancy, for themselves and for their child, is gone in a blink.

The woman writes that she feels as though she and her husband researched and then packed for a trip to Italy, boarded the plane with excitment, and then, without warning or explanantion, landed in France. No preparation. No real desire to be there. Or how to live there.

But she goes on to write that upon looking at their precious child, the *second* minute they see the newborn face, she and her husband come to realize that just because they arent where they had planned to be doesn't mean that they're nowhere at all, that though they may have packed and readied themselves for Italy only to land in France they were now -- look! -- *in France!* A place with its own promise, its own wonder, offering a new set of dreams and its own promise of its own future. She writes Abby that she wants people to know that she and her husband have not only come to celebrate France rather than mourn Italy, they've also found a better life there.

I've never forgotten the letter, and in the changing life that is my return to Los Angeles, I think of it, relating and identifying in ways I don't before. I seem to be in some kind of mourning, still, for a life that will never be. A life I consequenetly don't allow to be. Landing in France so long ago by what I say is a mistake, I sit on-board and I rue and I pretend and I distract. I never truly get off the plane. I never see past the first second of what my life *isn't* to the second of what it *is*.

I think perhaps it's time to let go of Italy.

Here in Los Angeles, commensurate with what are becoming frequent trips with friends to The Grove, the path seems clear for me to take my biggest step yet. It comes in the form of a first-ever male relationship, set up through a local friend. Like most, it has its good moments and bad. And it doesn't last. Twice, in fact. It's both an eye-opener and a heart-render. And when it's over, I don't really know how to explain the whole of it – a chance meeting of two people that progresses from hearing said *to* me "I'd rather hang with you this weekend than go anywhere else" to over-hearing said *about* me "Fuck that guy! Doesn't he know I've got other things to do?" in such remarkably short order.

This is how I try, in an essay I publish online when the dust-up(s) settle.

Let's call him Adam, since in the jungled Eden of my own creation he was The First. And let's call me naïve. Foolish, even. If not those, then certainly embarrassed.

We'd met through a mutual friend, Adam and I, at a time when evidently I was at last open and ready to meet someone, however late to the party. And we dated only briefly. But to a first-timer in his 40s, briefly is a lifetime: That's how long I'd waited for it and for everything that came with it. And Everything is what did. Affection, attention, attraction, inclusion, exhalation. Intimacy. *Company.* With someone charming and handsome, funny. Seemingly decent. Smart. And interested.

It was manna, from somewhere, for the starving. Daily contact. Laughter at every turn. A discussion of the future. *A* future. Singular.

Then, from nowhere, literally overnight, silence -- a long weekend's worth, after nightly calls (his to me, I feel the need to point out). Plans discussed went unexecuted. Messages left went unreturned. Nothing was said at all, yet Everything is what I heard. The end of it.

He finally reached out late on a Monday afternoon. From his car. Bluetooth. Nice touch.

"Look..." is how he began, his voice a world away, though barely five blocks from where I live, as he headed home from work for the day. And I knew. (The lone benefit of dashed first-love at mid-life: savvy.) "I'm a very independent person, and –"

I interrupted: "Adam, let me stop you right there." I paused. "Are you really going to do this on car-phone as your drive passed my house?"

Silence.

"Yes." Cold, detached, somehow angry. At me. For calling it.

And he did. In a strange and meandering and elliptical and blunt monologue that went everywhere and nowhere and that said much and nothing. *Snap*. Like that.

I just don't want to be around you anymore, he said.

"I'm also going to be totally honest with you here, Jim," he went on -- I steeled myself, curious: *Totally honest? What have you been thus far?* -- "I'm sorry that your father is sick; I really am." (A week earlier, my 82-year-old father, a continent away on the east coast, had been hospitalized, where he then lay dying.) "It totally sucks what you're going through. It really does. But it's too much drama to be around. I'm not having fun."

Is he actually saying this?

"I'm just being *totally honest* with you about how I feel," he said again, the italics his, as though the repetition and emphasis would both exonerate him and inoculate me from the pain the words were inflicting. "I just can't be around that."

As though I myself had opted to be.

Stammering, I could only manage to ask Adam if he literally was saying to me that he was ending our relationship because my father was dying. The answer: Yes. "Look, it's not you, it's me," he actually followed, although evidently it was both him and my Dad.

He said that what he needed at all cost was space and the autonomy to do as he felt when he felt it, what he wanted at all cost was a life devoid of attachments and responsibility, and what I represented was a threat to it all, even (especially?) at his own ripe age of 40. *Seriously?* I thought. You asked *me* out. You pursued *me*. You called *me* each night.

I was, of course, sad, but chiefly I was dizzy and confused from the impact of a conversation that actually came off like a collision from nowhere on a long stretch of what seemed like a deserted road. And I was crestfallen -- in a bigger-picture kind of way. I remember thinking: *Is this really what I'd been waiting for and wondering about? Is this how relationships between guys work, too?*

I did get an (emailed) apology from Adam two-plus months later, after my father had died, for, as he either sarcastically or pointedly put it (I'm still not sure which), "showing the maid at my hotel room last week more respect than I showed you on that phone call months ago."

"Jim," I was told by a friend later that day, "no one *ever* gets an apology." So that seemed to help me to move on. Closure and all. Out of the picture, Adam was now out of my life.

If only.

Eight months later (and it's only fair to confess that it was with my permission if not encouragement), Adam, at first through email, followed in short order by phone calls and then a dinner and then a long conversation made up of a politician's promises of change, worked his way back into my life and then into my heart.

"I wasn't ready last time; I'm ready now." Those were the words Adam used in a long conversation. I took it in, along with him: I liked the guy; I liked being liked by the guy. He really was all those positive adjectives I used after first meeting him.

But *now* was a relative concept to Adam. Ten days into our rapprochement, he subtly discouraged me from attending one of his office functions so that he could have "fun" alone with his (young) friends. A Friday after that he suggested bringing a (21-year-old male) pal along on our date. Two more weeks later, Adam scotched our Sunday plans because, he said later that night, he'd woken up earlier "resenting" that a relationship dictated his schedule for the day. And then a few days past that, he detailed for me a litany of plans he was making for himself for the coming *three months*, including those for New Year's Eve – none of which included even the mention of my name, not even New Year's Eve. Not one.

It was all-too-familiar. And once again, I knew: The guy is downright allergic to what I represent -- adulthood, living life from the inside out rather than the outside in, committing to *something*. No matter the protests of change nor his professed willingness to embrace the word "relationship" this time around, the now 41-year-old Adam had a compulsion to avoiding one and all that came with it.

When I pointed that out one afternoon, an eruption followed. Verbal volleyball. Anger. Muddled communication. "Why the drama, dude?" he wanted to know. Why can't we just have fun?" And on its heels came Break-Up Number Two a few days later – on the phone of course, with Adam, allergies flaring, reclassifying our relationship as "just hanging out" and saying that all things being equal he'd "rather just have fun with my friends."

The door that Adam didn't want to close is a door that I slammed shut. And that was the end of Adam. And us. Again. And for good.

I've told myself that *Adam 2.0* gave me a sense of relief and confidence that my first encounter with Adam didn't: The earlier break-up made me wonder what I'd done wrong; the second one suggested that it was nothing at all. I was far from perfect as a partner to Adam, new to the world that I was, but I was never less than decent. I did nothing short of just *trying*. It really was him, not me. So there's that, I guess.

Gay romance, it seems, is, or can be, just as rudderless, just as childish, just as painful, as the straight kind. I wish I'd known that years ago, though. Maybe I wouldn't have spent so much time, wasted so much time, convincing myself that a certain ideal awaited the me I was working so hard on. Maybe I would have dived in sooner. Maybe I would have learned about the drama earlier, too. And gotten the first hurt out of the way. At what perhaps is an age that's easier to do so.

Embarrassing to admit, but finally, to myself at least, I'm just being *totally honest.*

Related side-note:

My father is a good and kind and smart man for all of his 82 years, but he's never a fount of emotional profundity. Occasionally, though, some wisdom does trickle forth. In his final years, for instance, his days numbered and of late spent so alone, he looks among the children who have gathered for a birthday visit and points out that those among us still without partners need to find one. And fast. Not because a life without a union is an un-lived life, he says, but because of something much more practical.

When you're old, he says, "You just want someone around at three o'clock in the morning when you're sick and you need some aspirin." You want, he says, "a person to sit and hold your hand until you feel better."

Adam ... is not that person. For me, anyway. At best, Adam is the person who would tell me where the nearest pharmacy is and then how best to get there, so that I can find my own aspirin -- and then offer to hold my hand later when I feel better and can have fun again.

Dad would disapprove of Adam.

But meeting and experiencing him is a necessary and important, enlightening and painful, first big step for me. After a lifetime and wondering, and despite the particulars of being with Adam, dating a guy seems a no-brainer. It's fun. And once said and done aloud, it involves little to fear or to be embarrassed by, other than the peculiarities of dating in general or my own issues with intimacy and affection in particular.

When we're seeing each other, I take Adam to the Emmy Awards, and I'm asked by red-carpet reporters and photographers who my guest is, should the photo be published and in need of an identifying caption. I offer the name and then actually find myself saying, with ease, "Write whatever it is that's usually written to describe a date -- because that's what he is." It's huge for me to say it. Beyond this, if the subject comes up at all it's usually *part* of one rather than the *point* of it. And it begins to be part of many more.

Against this life-expanding backdrop – the fully coming out and the relationship it spawns and the dying parent and the refinement of perspective that all of it yields -- I find myself back on familiar professional ground. I return to the CBS family, at the invitation of The Boss. I'm offered a whole other kind of position (a creative one, in Comedy Development, rather than the more academic one I know in Scheduling) in a whole other part of the growing empire (the studio side of CBS, the division that produces programming, rather than the network side that licenses and airs it.)

It's another job created from scratch, a dubiousness that I stupidly tell myself to look passed, since the supply side of the business is one I do want to explore and with this job I'll have a closer-than-ever look at, and input on, how it all comes together. I tell myself that maybe it'll at least lead to making some kind of a difference in what's developed for prime-time. Mostly though, I look passed it to work with and for The Boss again. Not because his legend and power and his own position at CBS have increased monstrously in the 12 years I've known him or because he has established CBS as the winning and profitable and talked-about center of media that it is or because being associated with him is to be associated with solidity and victory, but because of Cher.

In January of 1998, Sonny Bono, the ex-husband and ex-singing-partner of singing superstar Cher – not to mention former mayor of Palm Springs and current House Representative from California -- is killed in a Lake Tahoe skiing accident. That spring, a TV special is conceived for Cher to host that will pay tribute to him and to her days with Bono when they were known worldwide as the stars of a self-titled 1970s variety-series on CBS. The Boss wants the special to air here on our network, so a meeting with Cher is set up, planned for his office at 4 p.m. on a Friday.

At 3:40 on the afternoon of the meeting, the phone in my office rings. The Boss wants to see me. As I do with each summons to his office, I grab all the at-a-glance TV-reference materials that I tend to carry around with me in the hallways and head to his corner office of the executive wing. Inside, The Boss says, "Tell me everything there is to know about *The Sonny & Cher Show*."

He knows TV as well as anyone, but for this meeting he wants details, background, a fleshing out of Cher's TV career. A refresher. And he knows I know. It's what I do.

I welcome being called on like this, for background, for trivia. One day, I'm summoned to the office while he's chatting with a famous comedian whose resume includes writing for *The Smothers Brothers Comedy Hour* in the 1960s. The guy can't remember the dates for when he worked on the show, and The Boss knows that I will. When I tell them, the comedian looks at me quizzically, and he says, "Really? 1968? I would have sworn it was later." About his own career.)

I spend about five minutes with The Boss this Friday afternoon summing up the history of the act known as Sonny & Cher, taking him through their early music success, their being discovered by a TV executive who brings them to prime-time, how long the resulting show runs, what night and time it airs. He thanks me, looking at this hour every bit the company head who's coming to the end of another long and pressured week – jacket off, necktie loose, hair slightly mussed, face made heavy with the day's details. In a word, The Boss looks a bit spent.

As I'm about to leave, he suggests that I come back for the meeting itself, and when I do, before a waiting Cher is brought down to be introduced, a completely different executive greets me inside his office: The jacket is on; the tie, squarely knotted; the shirt seems all but pressed; the hair's not only groomed it looks trimmed; even the complexion is changed. In the course of ten minutes, he's transformed himself into The Boss. Imperceptible or insignificant to some, the morphing is nothing short of remarkable to me. It's *business-time*, is the message. And this is how my business is *done*. For The Boss, this one meeting, happening right now, is the only meeting in all of television that matters.

And over the course of the half-hour that follows with Cher – I sit silently throughout, and all I see are leather boots sculpted around long black-stockinged legs that end at the waist-length hem of a denim jacket, and then massive amounts of dark hair – he does it with skill. He's solicitous, deferential, charming, slyly aggressive. He casually drops into the conversation *every single nugget* of information that I pass on to him only minutes earlier, every bit of minutiae about Sonny & Cher and about their TV history, so organically it seems like he's known all of it – and her – forever.

"CBS is the place for this special," he says. "We'll shoot it downstairs in your old studio. We'll put it on the air in your old Wednesday time-slot. It'll be great."

I'm floored by the ease of the sell, by the polish. It'll be one of my most burning CBS memories. And it's why I accept the offer to work at CBS again two years after leaving the network-side in 2006. To work for The Boss. To be a part of that approach to our TV world.

(*Sonny and Me: Cher Remembers* airs in May of 1998. On CBS.)

Sadly, while I am re-hired at CBS to work *for* The Boss, I am not hired to work *with* The Boss. And what a difference a preposition makes. The newly created post -- at the company's just-built headquarters on the Studio City lot, where it has recently moved following a half century in its original location (no more "From Television City in Hollywood!") -- proves itself to be that amorphous role I skirt over when it's offered. (Several people, including me, are to blame for allowing this to happen, but thankfully The Boss isn't one of them.) It's not even really about TV as I know it, about what I'm looking for or needing; there's no direct connection to the team that I'm part of before. This new one is team-lite.

Worse, within days of joining it I'm actually warned by no fewer than seven people, from both inside and outside the company, to be cautious of a fellow member on it. This colleague *"does not want you here."* Be careful, I'm told. ("You mean, like, it'll be casually mentioned to people that I had a lunch one day near a bar, with the insinuation that I drink on the job?" I ask. No, I'm told: "There'll be no insinuation. It will be flat out said that you had lunch *at* the bar because you have a drinking *problem.*") I'm incredulous. And sad.

I make the best of my short two-year CBS contract. When it's up, with a bit of a kick in my ass as I head out the door from some I once see as supportive colleagues, even friends, there's another valuable show-business lesson to be picked up: Here in Hollywood, when you're run over in the street by a speeding car, the driver of the car gets out and blames you -- and then his car. More avoidance of and misdirection about responsibility.

I actually learn a whole lot more about Hollywood at large from my brief stint as a development executive, gleaned from meeting after meeting and lunch after lunch, conversation after conversation. Suspicions I once have on the buying-side seem all-but realities up close here on the selling-side. Vague concerns then begin to be cemented now.

Children seem to be pitching and writing ideas for other children. Worse, there seems to be even less awareness today of the big-picture behind the TV business – the creative end of it, not the money end. Awareness that story and character are key to it. Or should at least be *part* of it. I wonder if some don't even understand the very basic notion of what a TV series is (**S***eries, n.* – a connected set of television program episodes that run under the same title, spanning many seasons), based on the number of ideas I see and hear and read about that are pitched, bought, developed, sold, and aired that are more concept than anything else. As many days as not, I feel as though I'm swimming in waters chummed with inexperience.

And I'm conflicted. Am I just feeling old, envious of the next-generation guard rising to power and strength behind me? Should I just surrender to the new normal as I age out of it, the *content* one that says good enough is now good enough? Or am I right to think that good enough can and should be better? That an ill-conceived piece of recent comedy-development called *Let's Rob Mick Jagger* (which neither I nor CBS are affiliated with) is emblematic of a modern-day problem as it's announced to fanfare brought on by a headline-worthy title and then collapses before even making it to air due to its lack of foundation? That it just shouldn't even have made it passed the front door of the network that bought it (ABC)?

Coming from where and inspired by what, I'm not sure. But like-minded title-heavy concept-driven notions are driving the train of Development these days – both Comedy and Drama. Some do work, the product of singular visionary writers and producers, who bring to them legitimate sensibilities. But most, those that aren't and which seem only to want to ape the *sensibilities* part (the town's new In word), do not. The result is a cancellation graveyard cluttered with series after series that just should never be, because they *never are*. Ushered in on a wave of "new" and "cutting edge" and "envelope-pushing" and "format-busting."

Meanwhile, amid the *Sturm und Drang* that accompanies the rush, the quite conventional *Two and a Half Men* and *NCIS* are TV's most-watched TV shows.

It drives me crazy. Makes me sad. The expense and waste. Even in a business where failure is not just a given but an expectation, the higher rate behind these oft-ill-conceived projects seems folly. And again: No one seems the wiser for or interested in connecting the dots of the failures. As I look around, only that the *selling* of these shows, the *getting picked up*, seems to matter. The getting-on-the-air is what makes and then improves a career.

It's the biggest contradiction of all in this City of Contradictions: Being successful here doesn't necessarily require success itself. I ask myself, *Shouldn't* staying *on the air matter more than getting on it?*

It begs other questions that nag at me: Where is the apprenticeship in the craft? The time spent in the minors before being called up to the Show? Where is the learning? In a 2002 *Hollywood Reporter* article about the coming-to-an-end success that is *Friends*, longtime writer-producer Shana Goldberg-Meehan, interviewed with writing partner Scott Silveri, jokes, "The first spec scripts we ever wrote were a *Mad About You* and a *Friends*, and our first job was on *Mad About You* and our second job was on *Friends*. We don't know if we can write anything else." She laughs at the confession, but truer words are never spoken. The track record for each that follows is abysmal -- which, of course, never dents their esteem in town.

For that matter, I ask myself, as I see the dismantling of the once powerhouse testament to TV sitcoms that claimed her show, NBC's Must See TV Thursday, now a collection of self-impressed projects each with more producers than viewers, where exactly is TV in all of this? Or the TV viewer?

My business-card these days during my second go-round at CBS says "Comedy Development," but even it doesn't reflect reality: I'm told that what I actually am is a "multi-platform content provider" for the new media landscape and its changing pipelines of distribution.

Okay then.

Times change, and TV is changing with them. Fair enough. I get it. It's a business. The idea is to sell and to buy and to make money, however you can, with as limited a risk as possible. The EMO transformation continues. And maybe that doesn't have to be a bad thing. But I do wonder where it's all heading, given what seems to be a diminishing regard for the output. Where's the something for viewers to latch on to and to experience a *relationship* with that keeps them coming back to a show, to its network, to its syndicated reruns, even to TV itself? Where is the building of TV's future? Is it like most construction these days – made of parts and pieces that fulfill their basic functions but with cheaper grade material that just doesn't last as long? Aren't as reliable or durable?

Does TV really have to fall apart as easily as my dishwasher?

Life continues to offer perspective. Around this time, I go home to Philadelphia, where, at 82, my father is in his final days. We've chosen home hospice-care. He lasts a week, dying on Thanksgiving morning, taking with him his humor and smarts and stories of his own days working at the dawn of Philadelphia broadcasting. It's a more natural and explicable loss than that of Mom twenty-one years ago, but unlike her death in the hospital his in his living-room is actually more disorienting, even monstrous at times to watch.

The only comfort I take from any of the seven-day ordeal – and I have to scrounge to find it – is that through the final haze of his end-stage imaginary conversations we're forced to witness, directed at the wall next to his bed, this man who has come to view his mid-life deafness as a curse utters not single "What?" or "Huh?" to any one of the people he seems to be talking to. Dad once says to me that he doesn't want to die without ever hearing again, that he'll hold out for either a miracle or a good doctor. It's not too much to wish for. The seven of us will never know for sure, but here at the end I sense he got his wish. And I hope it offers him relief and the promise of a better hereafter.

In a fit of bravado on what will turn out to be our final night of the hospice vigil, my next-oldest brother says he will stay alone with Dad until morning, so I leave my post there around 9 p.m. to return to my hotel for much-needed sleep. At 10:20 p.m., I'm called back for a two-man shift that lasts all night. Dad dies in the morning, on a quiet and sunny November Thursday. I retreat outside, to a small grouping of trees along the Delaware River that his living-room faces. And I weep. It's another loss, during another autumn.

My mother dies on a fall day, too, in a long-ago October. When I fly to Philadelphia from my Tennessee home some months earlier, in June -- one of several times this year that seem to mark the end -- I think it's to say goodbye. And when I land at the airport, I steel myself, making the decision to keep it together while with my family, vowing to wait until I return to the comfort of my Knoxville house to deal with the feelings I am about to experience.

The plan almost succeeds. But after a week of bedside sittings and of doctors' meetings and of discussions of both hospices and burials, of witnessing but not shedding tears, of staring at the sad eyes that are my mother's, and, ultimately, of saying what I gather is a final goodbye, I board the all-but empty plane for my return flight to Tennessee, find a seat by the window, sit down with a heavy heart, press my face to the glass, and dissolve into tears.

Thankfully, the cabin-door has closed, and the only seat next to mine remains vacant. But there I sit, 26 years old, sobbing heavy hard tears – through the pilot's welcome and the attendants' instructions, backing from the gate, rolling onto the runway, and on into the air. It just keeps coming.

Once in the air, the flight-attendant politely and repeatedly passing me by with just the quickest of sympathetic nods that I can see from the corner of my eye, I also notice a woman across the aisle -- a passenger -- periodically but unobtrusively glancing at me. Each time I turn my head, carefully, to see if she's staring, she just as carefully turns away, to avoid my eyes. It continues like this for about ten odd minutes, but I can't make much of an effort to care. My thoughts keep returning to my mother's bedside – to her confused and frightened face, her fading hair, her own tears.

No sooner do we get word from the front about reaching cruising altitude, though, telling us that we can move about the cabin, do I hear the distinctive metallic clink of a lap being freed. And before I know it the woman across the aisle eases from her seat, crosses the aisle, and quietly slips into the empty seat next to mine. In silence.

After seconds that seem years, with me trying to dry my tears, to appear as composed as I can, the woman – 40s, dignified, maternal, soft – finally speaks. "I'm sorry, but I couldn't help but notice you're very upset," she says. She pauses, eyeing my reaction. Then, "Do you want to talk about it?"

Grief. It's a strange and curious emotion, one that we all face and feel yet few know how to handle. To be with, whether it's our own or someone else's. Take, for instance, my

210

Knoxville boss at this time, at whose office doorway I appear earlier with a request for time off to be with my mother, whom he knows is dying. "Well, if you think you have to," he says, "but you know this is a busy time for us." (*Yes,* I stand there thinking: *That's my concern, too.*) Or take his boss, whom I check with as well, and who offers the compassion and sympathy I need to hear, apologizes for my pain, tells me to take as long as I need to be with my family, then when I get up to leave his office blindly says, "Have a nice trip."

Others, however, do seem to know what to do with the emotion, how to be in the same room with it, such as another colleague who will see me in the hallway at work the first day back from the funeral. She'll stop the conversation she's having mid-sentence, walk over to me, look me in the eyes, and then embrace me tightly. "I have no idea what to say to you, so I'll just say that," she'll whisper. She'll show she's one of these few who do seem to know what to do.

Like this unfamiliar woman next to me on the plane.

"I'm sorry but I couldn't help but notice you're very upset. Do you want to talk about it?"

I hear the words, and my embarrassment somehow dissipates. I'm strangely overcome with relief, in fact. I manage to explain to her the simple truth in simple words -- that I'd just said goodbye to my dying mother. And then with the words released I begin to sob again, even harder, my head falling on this stranger's shoulder, which she offers without hesitation or recoil. She doesn't reach out. She doesn't embrace. She doesn't even speak. She just offers the shoulder. And sits. And I cry.

When after a minute or so I lift my head, she looks at me and asks two questions in succession, with directness: "How long does she have?" ("Not long") and "Is your father a strong man?" ("I think so"). Brave, blunt questions. And somehow just the right ones to ask. They prompt an easy conversation for the remainder of the entire two-hours-plus flight, about my mother's life and my own, about our family and about what I imagine we will all be like without her. Her prompts, my answers. Who will hurt the most? Who will be the strongest? What will the funeral be like? How would I handle her absence as my life goes on? They're remarkably insightful and, it turns out, helpful questions – the answers to which she listens to intently, offering reactions and suggestions, crying a bit herself. The time races by. The encounter is consuming.

Before I know it, we land in Nashville, which she calls home and where I am to board a connecting flight to my own in Knoxville. As we stand to collect our overhead bags, I take her name and ask what she does here. Then I thank her, walk off the plane with her, and, at the end of the Jetway, hug her. "I think I'm okay now," I say. "I can take it from here." I tell her know how grateful I am for her having sat down next to me. Away from the gate, she disappears into the airport crowd, her bright red hair lost in a stream of weary travelers. Never again for me to see.

Four months or so later, my mother finally passes. When I return from the Philadelphia funeral, I look around my Knoxville house for the scrap on which I scribble this woman's name and job, look up its address, and I sit down to write a brief note. "I'm not sure if you remember me," it begins, and I re-introduce myself to her, recalling for her our airplane conversation. I tell her that I feel compelled to let her know that my mother died at last, but that my time with her, a stranger on a plane, months in advance of the ordeal, somehow makes it easier to handle. So I thank her again. I do not ask for, nor do I receive, a response.

Two years later, on an October Thursday, at my new address across the country in California, I find a letter in my mailbox, forwarded from my former Tennessee office, to which it's initially mailed. The postmark is stamped Nashville. I open it.

"Now it's my turn to re-introduce myself," the letter reads. And the Airplane Woman does, thanking me for writing to her two years earlier and for telling her how our time together helped me deal with my mother's death. Then she explains what she doesn't on the plane – where the courage comes from to approach me in the first place, which she admits is out of her character.

She says that not long before we meet, she herself buries a parent, her father, and as a result she's acutely aware of what grief and pain look and feel like. And she knows that they sometimes need to be shared. Seeing me across the airplane aisle, she says, she wanted to share mine, with the hope of lessening it. Loss, she says, is all the worse when it's felt alone.

"This being October," she concludes, she wants me to know that she knows the anniversary of my mother's death has come around again and that she is thinking of me, in turn. "May the fall be a time that you realize how important people are to your life, and that you tell them."

On a fall day nineteen years after reading the note, as I stare at the Delaware River that is my father's treasured view for so many years after losing his wife, his own death just minutes old, I hear the Airplane Woman's words again. I realize how important our father has been to the lives of his children. And I hope that we have told him.

A week later, I return to Los Angeles. I have a bit more time left on my two-year CBS contract, a bit more time to spend here on the CBS Studio City lot, a legendary one that dates back nearly a hundred years. Opened by filmmaker Mack Sennett in the 1920s, it's where Saturday-afternoon serials of the 1930s, B-westerns of the 1940s, and early TV-series like *Leave It To Beaver* in the 1950s are made, before CBS Television become its chief tenant in the 1960s, producing the crush of TV that I lose myself in as a kid. *Gunsmoke, My Three Sons, The Wild Wild West, Gilligan's Island* are among the titles that come to life here. (The small *Gilligan* lagoon survives the show itself by more than thirty years, until not too long ago when it's emptied out, filled in, and – *sigh* -- paved over.)

In the 1970s, the studio is chiefly known as the home of MTM Enterprises, formed at the dawn of a new and revolutionary TV decade with the launch of the *Mary Tyler Moore* show, named for the actress herself, and run by husband Grant Tinker. MTM is responsible for what's likely the best collection of prime-time television in the medium's history; it's a veritable writers' factory that yields benchmark programming of the time such as its namesake show and spin-offs *Rhoda* and *Lou Grant*, the two long-running Bob Newhart sitcoms, *WKRP in Cincinnati*, masterful ensemble dramas like *Hill Street Blues, The White Shadow*, and *St. Elsewhere* -- most all of which are shot on the premises. Now both its lot and its

Bernard J. McKairnes, Mary Julia Mallon (soon McKairnes)
(Philadelphia, 1953)

Our memorial, years after our parents' deaths,
in gratitude for a lifetime of summer beach memories
(34th Street Playground, Ocean City NJ, 2009)

building are mine (MTM headquarters was housed in the main administration structure just inside the front gate, where my own office now is), at a time when what "MTM" stands for seems long gone.

Like Television City a decade ago, I know that I work alongside TV history in coming to work here each day, and I'm grateful for the forces and people who make this happen. And like there I make a point to explore the expanse of the place as often as I can, during free lunches and office breaks. After-hours, too, since many shows still shoot here, for CBS and other networks. I enjoy the energy when there are live audiences on the lot.

I walk along its make-believe streets and neighborhoods (including the New York Street that doubles as Manhattan for exterior scenes in *Seinfeld*). I wander up and down roads actually named in honor of the lot's legacy. Just off My Three Sons Street, for example, there's the intersection of Mary Tyler Moore Avenue and Gilligan's Island Road. I stand there. Often.

I weave my way around the many soundstages, their walls hiding decades of TV secrets. The *Big Valley* stage. The *thirtysomething* stage. The *Will and Grace* stage. But I always come back to the best stage on the entire small lot, Stage 2, facing Radford Avenue itself, outside of which hangs a commemorative plaque.

ON THIS STAGE A COMPANY OF LOVING

AND TALENTED FRIENDS PRODUCED

A TELEVISION CLASSIC

THE *MARY TYLER MOORE* SHOW

1970-1977

I wish for everyone working in TV today to be able to stand where I'm standing and to understand the significance of both the memorial and the show – how it celebrates not just a character and the times she comes from but also vision and writing and the times we still live in. I stand there, and I remind myself: I'm front-and-center on the Wellington Street orange shag when the show premieres in 1970; I'm there in our basement for its famous finale 168 episodes later in 1977; I'm around for it as a executive of the network that pays tribute to its memory in 2002; and now I'm here for it as an employee of the same lot where it all comes to life in the first place. (And I'll be there the spring evening years later when the surviving cast assemble for a reunion steps away from this very spot, for what will likely be the last time, in support of one among them, sick and dying.)

With the daily walks around the lot complete, thoughts of Thomas Wolfe stirring in my head with every step, I always return to my Admin Building office by way its front door rather than the more convenient rear one. This way, I can take my daily look at the names and titles immortalized in cement pavers just outside the entrance. It's a Studio City version of Hollywood Boulevard's venerable Walk of Fame – except here it's famous TV shows that are shot at the studio through the decades being celebrated rather than famous movie stars.

Some are memorable; some are silly; some are brilliant; some are long forgotten and perhaps best that way. Some air on CBS; many do not. But unlike some (or is it much?) of what I seem to see on TV these days with increasing frequency, none of the titles enshrined in concrete out here for all eternity *bother* me. None *offend* me. None insult or embarrass me. None make me wonder what their existences in TV says about *me* and what I *do*.

With anywhere from 140 to 200 weekly series in any given TV season, on innumerable outlets for both scripted and unscripted shows – a number that will mushroom still further in only a few years with programming made for all manner of distribution, including the Internet – I can set aside as much as twenty percent (upwards of forty TV series) as shining examples of excellence -- brilliant work from brilliant people at the top of their brilliant forms.

What I'm left with makes me either blanche or cringe, in whole or in part. The TV that used to represent a curtain rising in our homes each night to reveal a stage of inspiration and imagination and information today, on a bad day, can amount to a window-shade flipped up to allow a peek at a back-alley. TV used to make me (us) feel *good*. More often that not, it doesn't seem to anymore. It seems more a spotlight on aberration or crudity, a celebration of mean. "The meaner and flakier the better" is how I once hear a producer gleefully refer to it.

Again, I think, maybe it *is* just me. Too much thinking on my part. Too much navel-gazing. Too much being dead-set on what's right even when I'm wrong. ("Frequently wrong but never in doubt" is how someone once sums me up with what I hope is an affectionate smile.) TV is changing and I need to change with it -- and change my assumptions about it.

Who knows? Maybe.

Maybe the serial killing of women in prime-time and the freezer-stacking of their bodies like cordwood *is* art and its writers should be *commended* for their concerted Hollywood backroom-effort to Give the Public What It Wants. And maybe scenes in TV dramas these days such as those that take place at urinals while characters appear to be using them *do* elevate the form, do provide the verisimilitude that viewers are saying they yearn for more of on TV. Maybe these and other images *don't* subconsciously reflect how little producers think of viewers. Or their own work. Maybe I *don't* feel disregarded or disrespected when I watch them.

And maybe prime-time dating-shows are made *better* -- are more involving and entertaining, more informative, speak more to today's audiences, are *real*-er (another buzzword on the rise) – with the inclusion of night-vision-camera footage of contestants engaging in oral sex, complete with captions ("slurp" and "gulp") that help clarify the fuzzy imagery, or the inclusion of a conversation between the father of a female contestant on another show joking with its love-seeking bachelor about how his daughter "went down on you" to win the competition. A father. About his daughter. Maybe this really just is part of a TV's evolution. A *necessary* part.

And maybe daytime television really *is* service television after all. Maybe it provides vital information for a challenging world. Maybe "The 15-Year-Old Who's Had Sex 500 Times" and "On-Screen Bikini Wax" and "Fat Kids Slaps Own Mom" and "I'm Happy I Cut Off My Legs" and "Hot Blondes Who Use Nerds For Sex" should be watched by families *together*, for educational purposes. For a better world. A real-er one.

And maybe sitcoms offering jokes that revolve around morning erections and pubic hair and crotch-grooming and male-ejaculate-being-mistaken-for-clam chowder and vaginas (both the dry and moist types) really *are* funny and really *do* reflect a grasp of the craft as it's been honed for sixty years. Maybe these jokes, especially the one in which a sitcom lead says "I did fart myself awake a couple of times last night," *will* last as long as ones in comedies from *I Love Lucy* to *Everybody Loves Raymond*. In fact, maybe the classic episode of *Seinfeld* about masturbation – the one that opens that floodgates of ribald humor to lesser scribes in 1992 -- would be even *funnier* if the writers opt to use the actual word and all its high-school euphemisms rather than slyly writing around it for subtle and clever comedic effect.

And maybe it's neither interesting nor significant that two of the most popular and influential and zeitgeist-shaking sitcoms at the turn of the century, *Friends* and *Will & Grace,* amass more than 400 episodes between them by the ends of their long runs, resulting in a combined 146 Emmy nominations for excellence -- and that just three of those 146 nominations are for writing. *Three.* (No wins.) This despite such envelope-pushing storylines and/or jokes throughout their seasons as one character's horniness during pregnancy or another's see-through shirt revealing her breasts or a gay character's confusing the words "cook" and "cock" on an apron he's purchased or a wife mistakenly concluding that her husband tends to masturbate while watching videos of whales or a character having oral sex with her ex-boyfriend-dentist at his office where they can make use of the "handy" spit-sink. (*Cheers*, 13 nominations for writing; *Seinfeld*: 11 nominations; *Frasier*, nine nominations; *Everybody Loves Raymond*, six nominations. *30 Rock* and *The Office*, 18 nominations between them before their runs even end.)

Maybe all the TV from these changing times really *will* hold up and really *will* be venerated twenty, thirty, forty years hence, offering testimony to art of its age, their cast-photos framed and hung in the hallways of fame.

And maybe Murrow and Minow have it wrong in their historic dawn-of-the-industry speeches about television's future – about how the powerful new medium will require curating so that it doesn't become mere lights and wires in a box, so that it doesn't turn into a vast wasteland.

Which I'd ask, were it not for the fear that so few here in town would know either the names or the speeches.

Maybe. Whatever.

The television that my father connects me to by birth and that calls out to me as a child and that my teacher explains to me in high school and that brings me to Los Angeles as an adult is harder to find -- the ties nearly threadbare. I try to understand it all. In newspaper articles, I read that musical legends Joni Mitchell and Elton John are among the veterans decrying fraying connections to their own changing art-forms and vocations. I read that politicians are leaving a Capitol Hill that has disappointed them. I read that a successful movie-studio chief opts to leave his post in protest of what he realizes is an output of "cynical" hits his company is releasing. I do sense there is a conversation to be had. But when I examine my feelings out loud or I try to open a dialogue about it with peers, multiple fingers on multiple hands point me to all the amazing work being done on television by all the amazing people toiling in it.

I see it: They're right. There is amazing work – funny comedy, moving drama, exceptional razor-sharp writing, actors in front of the camera and craftspeople behind who are working at the peaks of their trades and talents, informative and stirring and entertaining non-fiction and fiction alike that celebrates or spotlights the human condition or just plain entertains. Still, add it all up – in 2013 the very best of the best comes to be about fifteen shortened-season titles found across multiple cable networks (despite the fact that forty year ago one lone network claimed *five* such series on a *single night* year-round) -- and it really is a fraction of a fraction of what comes at us on a given day, in a given week, during a given year.

And all the great work still doesn't make the TV blowjobs go away.

(Not so incidentally, that fraction can mostly be categorized as what the film world calls *art-house* successes --

primarily independent auteur-driven projects that are given money and time and leeway to attain excellence on their own terms, damn the inevitable lower numbers; so-called experts should avoid lumping them in with or allowing them to be used as the bar for comparing multiplex big-screen projects of broadcast TV. By their very definition, art-house projects are *supposed* to be golden – they're *art.*)

"You just want everything to be *Little House on the Prairie*," a CBS colleague actually says to me one night at an office party when I lament another sitcom joke along the lines of a man flirting with an attractive woman by saying that "my velour pants are the only things about me that's soft right now." (Cue the giggles in The Writers' Room.) I have no clue how to respond to her or to have the discussion that I know should follow.

I want to quote Meryl Streep from a scene in *Postcards From the Edge* in which she argues with her dysfunctional and alcoholic mother about the less-than-healthy Hollywood upbringing provided her, with mother Shirley MacLaine defending herself by saying, "How'd you like to have had Joan Crawford for a mother, huh? Or Lana Turner?" (Please, says Streep's character, "these are the options?") But I think the reference might be too erudite. Or I want to bring the conversation closer to home to home by citing the brilliant *Seinfeld* episode in which Jerry complains to a rabbi about a mutual friend's sad attempts at Jewish jokes, prompting the rabbi to question, "And this offends you as a Jew?"

Responds Jerry, "No, it offends me as a comedian."

I want my colleague to know that I'd be all over adult humor and body-part jokes if they were only *clever* and *smart* and *well written.*

Mulva, anyone?

But I'm not sure I can get through to her. So I move on.

This I know, or feel: Once a handful of classy and well-defined department stores in the 1950s that morphed into a glittering if gaudy mall of entertainment and information choices in the 1980s, the television networks as a whole today resemble an enormous open-air flea-market. They display interesting and valuable items, but they're to be found only by sorting through stall after stall of bargains, cast-offs, trash and leftovers. *The Sopranos* are competing for space with The Kardashians.

In the not too distant future a new kind of half-hour comedy will pop up on HBO that sets critics and its small-in-number-but-passionate viewers in search of new words for excellence, winning all kinds of awards for its approach to comedy and to the younger people it courts. One episode ends with a man anally penetrating an unwilling date and then ejaculating on her chest, the results of which we see. An blogosphere debate follows, with those defending the episode accusing those who object to it as being out of touch with "kids these days." And I'm saddened that a generational divide has come down to those who are pro-onscreen-ejaculate and those who are anti-onscreen-ejaculate.

Yet that seems to be the issue.

As I phase out of my CBS post, I know I don't want to be one of those elder statesmen who lament young people's loud music or the cranky old-timer who rails against the blasphemy that is lights in Wrigley Field, but I'm struggling. Struggling to understand the changing ways of the business I love, struggling to be heard about quality and durability, struggling to find my role in all that I look around and see. I turn away, but I can't seem to *run* away.

I read an engrossing book called <u>Ladies and Gentleman The Bronx Is Burning</u>, by Jonathan Mahler, that helps me understand why, a bit. It's about the rollercoaster ride that is living in New York City in 1977, its steep drops and sudden curves the result of a boiling-hot summer-stew of backroom politics and bankruptcy and blackouts and baseball, all leading to a World Series game played out on national TV while fires ravage the borough named in the title, as quoted by Howard Cosell during the start of the prime-time broadcast. It actually speaks to me about TV, not baseball, with a chapter that begins with a quote taken from another earlier chronicle of Manhattan life called <u>Report From Engine Co. 82</u>, by Dennis Smith.

> "New York City is simply too big. I have
> lived in it for too long to hate it, but I know
> it too well to love it. I am still a part of it, yet

221

I feel removed, like a broken jockey who
grooms horses. I earn my living caring for it,
but I feel helpless because I know that I can't
train it, or ride it, or make it win."

I substitute the word "television" for "New York City."
It pierces my heart. I do still love TV. I do still love its
possibility, its promise of connection. But it really has become
too big, and I do feel helpless knowing that I can't train it, or
ride it, or make it win. My relationship is faltering.

Enter: Chance and fate.

Again.

In my two-year role at CBS as a Multi-Platform
Content Provider, I'm lucky to meet and get to know a talented
writer from Chicago, who, it turns out, is also an instructor at
the city's DePaul University. At one point in our many
meetings about a script that he wrote, he asks if I'd ever
consider coming to the school to talk to students about the TV
business and about my roles in it through the years.

A visit to the city where *The Bob Newhart Show* is set? A
chance to talk about myself? The answer is a quick and
emphatic yes.

The talk that follows comes in front of a friendly and
respectful crowd of both students and educators on the
school's Loop campus. It seems to go well – well enough,
anyway, for me to be approached afterward by some powers-
that-be about the possibility of turning the talk into a class, one
that I'd teach there in Chicago. I'm flattered. And intimidated. I
talk a good game, I think. But I've never taught, anywhere or
anything, let alone on a college-level.

The idea grows on me when I get back to Los Angeles
and I ponder it. No longer at CBS, I do have the time. And
with all the questions and concerns I have about TV and with
the changing industry issues circulating in my head the past few
years, maybe this the chance I need to address them, to present
an overview of the TV business to its practitioners of
tomorrow, themselves about to join one of the EMOs out here.
Maybe with this class I can remind them that there's still

8

Wed Sep 2010

7:30
8:00
8:30
9:00 AM
9:30
10:00
10:30
11:00
1130
NOON
12:30
1:00
1:30
2:00
2:30
3:00
3:30
4:00
4:30
5:00
5:30
6:00

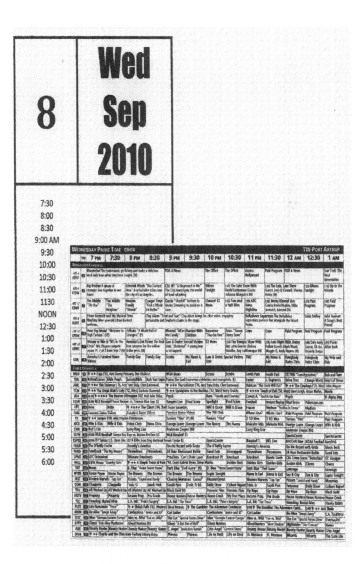

medicine and patient-care at its core. I agree to the offer. I begin with the new term in September.

The result is a strong gust of wind in mid-career sails, ten weeks spent with smart and challenging film-and-media students, talking about television's beginnings and its pioneers, the early visions and efforts, and a look at how it all works today, and involving whom. I try to avoid making the "history" part of the class the kind of yellowing history I myself tend to avoid when in college, but I know that groundwork is important and relevant. The founding of TV is fraught with passion and ambition and yearning, high hopes and dashed dreams, life and death and even suicide. The experimentation of the 1930s? The introduction that is the 1940s? The expansion of the 1950s, the revolution of the 1960s and 1970s, the innovation of the 1980s through to the start of a whole new century? It's all connected to today.

My course has a generic name in the university catalogue, but I think of it as an updated version of The Written Word and the Moving Picture, since each seems to be what brings us to this room in downtown Chicago. My approach is a basic one, focusing on those two elements. I try my best. At the very least, I hope students walk away from the class with the realization that TV isn't just another appliance that comes with their house. After the term, my evaluations are kind enough for me to agree to come back when asked. It becomes an open-door invitation.

I focus much of each term on breaking in to Hollywood, since so many students have their eyes on that prize. I talk about how I manage it so long ago, and I hope that the story offers encouragement or direction or clarity, which I know they need when arriving in Los Angeles from Someplace Else. I explain that while it's natural to be afraid of or intimidated by the specter that is Show Business, it's not all that necessary. To be aware and to be smart is enough.

As to whether they're smart enough, I remind the students that in their lifetimes for every *Homeland* or *Curb Your Enthusiasm* or *Modern Family* or *The Wire* or *Frasier* or *Downton Abbey* or *Damages* or *Lost* or *Game of Thrones* or *Breaking Bad* or *Daily Show* or *Louie* or *Children's Hospital* or *Seinfeld*, there's also

Cavemen and *Coupling* and *Carpool* and *Rock of Love* and *Married by America* and *Viva Laughlin* and *Celebrity Boxing* and *I Hate My Teenaged Daughter* and *Joey* and *Stacked* and *The Swan* and *Celebrity Diving*. And that the list of bad or failed titles grows by zillions when looking even further back, from *My Mother the Car* to *Dad's a Dog*.

I remind them that through the years there are powerful seemingly infallible people in the industry who actually try to make TV-series versions of *Steel Magnolias* and *Driving Miss Daisy* and, yes, *Fargo* (twice), not to mention shows based on car-window signs (*Baby On Board*) and on singing police-officers (*CopRock*) and on the survivors of a nuclear apocalypse (*Woops!*). And I point out that these and hundreds and hundreds (and hundreds) of other half-baked or just merely questionable projects are conceived, written, read, bought, approved, financed, and produced by people who are paid enormous salaries to do so. For a living. And who not only emerge unscathed from the wreckage each becomes but also are often promoted for it afterward.

I never want to parrot my old friend's warning that "they're all idiots." The class does give due credit to the medium's achievers. But I do want to frame the business in such a way that those wanting to join it know that most anyone can do what is done out here, with the right combination of luck and timing and skill and passion -- or in some cases simply savvy and proximity to other people's success. I want them to know they, too, really can succeed. That I know that, even if they yet don't.

My teaching may or may not do something for the students, but it definitely does help me. It helps me to recall why I fall in love with TV in the first place, and it does help to confirm for me what I still think it's capable of doing. The past that I introduce to students and the present that the students end up introducing to me adds up to a celebration of the whole. I end up wanting to be more a part of it than ever, more a part of TV's day-to-day, in its trenches, even as a changing TV landscape speeds scarily along on a current of pipelines and distribution platforms and ecosystems. Or maybe because of it.

One night after class, a student asks my opinion of a just-launched series. I tell him that I haven't seen it yet, but that

I want to. "When's it on?" I ask. He screws up in face in confusion. "When's it on?" he says. "What do you mean, professor? It's on when I *turn* it on." And so it goes.

(I may learn as much as I hope that I'm imparting, but despite valiant attempts on their parts my students do not succeed in talking me out of my purist preferences for live-audience multi-camera sitcoms – I still like to share my laughs – and for watching TV as it happens, live. Putting wrapped gifts under a fake tree in your living room in June doesn't make it Christmas. To me, it's Christmas only when it's Christmas everywhere. Live TV, today as when I'm young, connects me to an outside where others are watching as I do. It's a link as vital to my life as the air I breathe. In fact, I once find myself racing to get home in time to watch a re-broadcast of a landmark old TV pilot on a retro cable channel, despite owning the episode itself in disc form, which sits on a shelf next to the TV. So, no DVR. Sorry.)

At the end of each term, I offer a commencement address of sorts that I hope incorporates what I've lectured about the TV business and my road to working in it:

> *I hope that you have come to know that TV history has value, and that it amounts to more than last night's ratings and tomorrow's headlines. That the medium is a force so powerful that it led to nothing short of a seismic shift in the way human beings communicate... 1960s FCC chairman Newton Minow is famous for a speech that decried "when television is bad, nothing is worse." But in that same speech he also said, "When television is good, nothing is better." We all should remember that sentence, too. ... Your own roles in that goodness, your own successes in TV (or in film) will come through unexpected means and at unexpected times, the result of both what and who you know, tapping you on the shoulder from behind, as you stand in a curious intersection of Ability, Passion, Chance, and Timing ... And as is the case with my career, it all will be perfectly planned and absolutely not.*

Like life itself.

*

Epilogue

$\mathbf{E}$very few months, I check in by phone with a longtime friend and onetime CBS colleague who, like me, is an east-coast transplant here in Los Angeles, for what seems like forever now. (Given that we live in the same city, you'd think catching up in person would be easier and more likely, but such is the contradiction that is L.A. I rarely see him.)

During these long calls, borne of a need to offer mutual support and to hash out our respective projects – me, dealing with writing and teaching and TV-executive work; him, about his representation of writers and directors -- the conversation routinely devolves into a much more fun free-for-all that finds us trading a litany of complaints and raised-brow observations about the latest TV- and film-world news. Usually unable to fathom the thinking behind much of what we hear announced or see produced, we're merciless in what we think is our noble and well-meant evaluations.

We lament that we're even part of a business that can be so poorly managed. We question how its many elements can survive when run by those whose chief qualification for their jobs seems to have been *availability* and how the other -ilitys (accountability and responsibility) are rarely part of the math, how creative types seem to be able to make deals but not shows, how conclusions are often drawn based on assembling the wrong set of facts, how *still* no one in TV circles has explained or apologized for *Viva Laughlin*.

We also commiserate about each other's experiences with friendships and relationships out here – about the limitations of personal ones and about the rudeness and stiffness attached to professional ones, people we befriend and think we know and in part give ourselves to, people whose self-inflated balloons of importance disallow room for us in their lives when we're no longer part of their everydays. We exhaust our respective vocabularies in search of synonyms for words like frustration and befuddlement. (He's frustrated; I'm befuddled.) And we out-threaten each other's plans to bail on our careers entirely so that we can open a fishing lodge or a bookstore or join a Target stockroom team, if only for the health-plan. And do it Anywhere But Los Angeles, anywhere with manners. Where we can develop lives that don't frustrate as they stimulate, break hearts as they leads to scratched heads.

And then at the end of the calls we each bemoan that we're each not busier doing more of any of it, more immersed in all of it. Which is the part of the conversation that always brings us to the scene from *Annie Hall*.

> **Alvy Singer** [addressing the camera]:
> There's an old joke. Two elderly women
> are at a Catskills mountain resort, and
> one of them says, "Boy, the food at this
> place is really terrible." And the other
> one says, "Yeah, I know; and such small
> portions." Well, that's essentially how I
> feel about life - full of loneliness, and
> misery, and suffering, and unhappiness,
> and it's all over much too quickly."

This also describes our phone-calls: Complaints of horrible Hollywood food – and such small portions.

And then we hang up and return to our work.

Me? I do it with full knowledge that having been invited behind the scenes so long ago I can't seem to get enough of even that which disappoints me, because it compels me, it's part of me. That's why I continue to commit myself to it, in one form or another, despite the grousing.

A TV documentary I once watch that celebrates the 100th anniversary of Fenway Park offers a behind-the-scenes tour, introducing us in the process to an aging maintenance worker who's lovingly toiled there his entire adult working-life. Why? Baseball isn't just something the man knows, the narrator says. It's something he feels. A line-drive to my heart. TV is of me. It's in me. It's something I feel.

Television and I are a couple. We marry long long ago, introduced to each other in much younger and simpler days. We change and grow over the coming decades, but we do so side-by-side – each finding our feet in the black-and white world of the 1960s, each seeking independence and identity in the 1970s, and then each finding ourselves living in and adapting to the changing world of the 1980s and 1990s and beyond -- emerging out of all of it in ways we never foresee. Some good, some bad. I survive several moves and jobs, loss and love, two literal near-death experiences. TV survives *The Brady Bunch Variety Hour.*

And here we each are, still.

I like to think that what it's gotten from me is loyalty and appreciation and support. I know that what I have gotten from it is not just connection to the outside world but also an education about it. Lessons small and large. About having children (*The Dick Van Dyke Show*, "That's My Boy") and about responsibility (*The Andy Griffith Show*, "Opie the Birdman") and about justice (*The Fugitive*, "The Judgment") and about grief and death (*Mary Tyler Moore*, "Chuckles Bites the Dust") and about saying goodbye (*MASH*, "Abyssinia Henry") and even about accidental drowning (*Mary Hartman, Mary Hartman*, "Chicken Soup").

I've learned about the Civil War (*The Carol Burnett Show*, "Went With the Wind") and lesbianism (*Charlie's Angels*, "Angels in Chains") and the physical sciences (*WKRP in Cincinnati*, "Venus Explains the Atom") and addictions (*Little House on the Prairie*, "Home Again, Part 2") and dating (*Cheers*, "Showdown") and the afterlife (*Magnum, P.I.*, "Limbo") and self-pleasure (*Seinfeld*, "The Contest") and childbirth (*ER*, "Love's Labor Lost) and terror (*The X-Files*, "Home") and self-acceptance (*Ellen*, "The Puppy Episode") and Judaism (*Frasier*, "Merry Christmas, Mrs. Moskowitz") and parenting (*The Sopranos*, "College") and denial (*South Park*, "Trapped in the Closet") and bullying (*Law & Order*, "Loco Parentis") and even the Fine Arts (*Everybody Loves Raymond*, "Marie's Sculpture").

Through TV I've come to know about everything from devotion and betrayal (*The West Wing*, "Two Cathedrals") to the Holocaust and humor (*Curb Your Enthusiasm*, "The Survivor") and the changing face of the American home (*Modern Family*, "Pilot").

The lessons stay with me.

I still have daily hope for TV, for its ability to inform and to entertain and to instruct. I still yearn for its company even as I question whether it deserves mine: Love is strong like that. I hold out a hope for others to love it too – the way, for instance, Gale Sayers in *Brian's Song* asks a sports-crowd assembled to see him awarded the Heisman Trophy to support his dying friend Brian Piccolo. ("I love Brian Piccolo, and tonight when you get down on your knees I want you to ask God to love him, too.")

Yes, *everything* is framed by television.

I know that we in it will all have to change as it does, but I hope it's not for the worse. I hope that evolution brings with it people who care about it as much as they care about what it can do for them. I hope TV doesn't fully become what it's slowly threatening to turn into – a mere monitor. I hope that the search for "enhanced second-screen television experiences" doesn't mean those involved with it will disregard the need for a first-screen one.

Any specific tips or advice or guidance to offer as we weather the ongoing revolution of the early part of the 21st century are likely to be obsolete before the sentences in which I offer them can even be punctuated. Change is coming that fast. But I know this: As film gave way to radio, as radio weathered the arrival of TV, as AM bowed to FM and as both small- and big-screens yielded to home-video and then to streaming, TV as the 20th century knows it can survive this high-tech transformation of the new one. I just hope it keeps in mind the value of the written word and the moving picture.

Those in it, in charge of it, broadcast TV especially, however it's defined, would do well to keep those as their aims. I know I try to. They'd also do well to know what viewers (and consumers) *think* and *feel* in addition to what they watch. To know what writing and story and character are, as well as to know the difference between a TV idea and a TV series. Even in an age of disposable YouTube content, they would do well to familiarize themselves with a list of TV's 100 longest-running shows, from *Ted Mack and the Original Amateur Hour* and *What's My Line* and *I Love Lucy* to *The Real World* and *CSI* and *The Simpsons,* and ask themselves why these hits last as long as they do and how that knowledge can inform what they themselves do. Even 100,000,000 YouTube views for "Annoying Orange" has significance, should anyone care to search for it.

They would do well to evaluate both successes and failures equally. To know that almost every huge TV mistake and small-screen misfire from *Rhoda*'s wedding to Jay Leno's prime-time *Tonight Show* merit review and analysis and conversation and even admissions of bad decision-making, not just write-offs or write-downs. The pages of failure shouldn't just be turned, so that everyone can move on: The staining ink on the other side of the paper does bleed through. Viewers see it. They care.

They would do well to wonder how scrambled schedules and re-purposed series and how the rush to cash in on other platforms affect TV as a whole. To remember their patients as well as their practices in the giant EMO that is TV. To retire lamentable broad-stroke brushes like "Viewers want comfort-food at troubling times" and "People don't want to see stars on TV, because TV *makes* stars" and "No one wants to watch westerns or period-programming" and "New and cutting-edge and envelope-pushing are the only things that are getting attention out there" and "Big comedies aren't possible anymore" and especially "Viewers don't' watch networks, they watch TV shows." (Tell that to the folks behind TNT and USA and AMC and HBO and Showtime and FUSE and IFC.)

Because each mantra is absolutely true, except for when it's not. And then what do you have? And what do you know? They'd do well to remember all of that.

And if in the process one less woman in prime-time is stripped, tortured, and then caged, all the better.

A CBS Development executive takes me to lunch one day in the early 2000s, on the eve of another pilot-season. She wants to talk about what our Scheduling needs are and whether her latest development slate reflects it. I point to our new and growing spin-off drama called *NCIS,* which looks like it's turning into a mainstream hit of its own, one that people seem to want to come back to week after week, even in repeats, and that in success allows us in Scheduling to launch new hits behind it and to promote other shows within it. It's everything a TV show should be, I say.

"Oh I can't stand the writing on that show," the executive says of the routine police procedural. "I'd never develop anything like that." (*That* being a series that goes on to become one of the longest-running in CBS history.)

This kind of thinking can go, too, because it's not about the executive's wants, it's about the viewers'. So removed from the equation, the viewers' allegiance can't and shouldn't be taken for granted, underestimated, these days.

These days ...

These days, thirty years after leaving, I return to Philadelphia more a visitor than a resident. Five siblings still live in the area, four near the same Mayfair neighborhood in which we're raised. Each lives with the big challenges and the small triumphs and the kids and homework and laundry that make up their own family dramas now.

I often find myself driving through all the familiar streets of my childhood, each smaller and narrower. The same but different. There's the endless one that threads its way to Father Judge High School, where the blue-and-red flag is still flying just outside the second-floor classroom where Father Connery opens up the world to me with a senior-year English class. There's the busy commercial one that connects both of my first teenaged-era part-time jobs, the earliest at the pizza place where I discover it's wise to avoid ordering a pie ten minutes before closing, when the ovens will have just been cleaned for the night (the cook will take out his anger on your order), and the other at the first fully automated McDonalds in all of the city of Philadelphia, where I learn that the middle of the three-piece Big Mac bun actually has a name of its own. (It's called the club, to go with the sandwich's self-evident heel and crown.)

There are the four quiet residential streets, too, that form the perimeter to St. Matthew school and church, the six-acre tract around which my parish and family revolve in the 1960s and 1970s, the dual-winged elementary-school where all seven of us are taught, the imposing church that sees each of my three sisters married and my mother eulogized, the mile-wide parking-lot that hosts mercilessly long grade-school May Processions each spring, the rectory and convent standing sentry on opposing corners, each too intimidating and mysterious for any to get too close to. Even today.

One of the four borders is Wellington Street. *My* Wellington Street. The name that signifies home to the McKairnes family. I drive the two blocks towards our specific hundred, always circling it first, rebroadcasting in my head the play-by-play of days and nights of Out Back long ago. And then I pull around to the front, to the middle of the block, near to 3220, where I idle by the curb. I stare up at my old house and at the three concrete-grey identical rowhomes east of it. Four houses, four families, 33 children, a million years.

Seven of eight parents and at least three of the 33 are now dead, the rest scattered to the winds of their adult lives. All gone, overnight. To me though they're all still here, and it's all still then. On the far left of the group of four it's still New Year's Eve, and Mr. Gravlin is still outside on the small patch of grass we each call our front-lawns, launching his usual holiday fireworks into the midnight sky, while three doors down inside our house Dad still rolls his eyes in response.

Next-door to the Gravlins', at the Clarks' house, I'm still ten years old, and Mrs. Clark is carefully ministering to my scalp, bloodied by her own 8-year-old Jimmy after he becomes so incensed that I've borrowed his family's steel rake that he's grabbed it from me and promptly leveled it on my head.

To their right, the Quinns can still be heard screaming shouts of joy through their living-room window, roaring in both unison and relief as the latest draft-notice lottery announcements come on the radio and son Jackie's number is passed over. There'll be no Vietnam for Jackie. He'll be around to sing along with the rest of the Quinns for my next birthday come August.

And then there's our house, my house, site of one of the last dreams I ever have about my mother, three weeks after she dies. In it, we stand in the living-room, me beyond sad over her being gone and her trying to apply a balm to the grief, offering a reminder of where's she's going *to* rather than where she's leaving *from*. Confused, I ask, "What do you mean? Where are you going?" The soft reply: "I think you know."

I don't, but then I think for a moment -- and I do.

"Oh," I say, feeling both increased sadness and great relief, realizing that her Heaven waits. "You're going home, aren't you?" She smiles, nods, and then her image begins to fade, right in front of me in the living-room of my childhood -- a light literally and slowly dimming before it's gone forever.

From the car, I crane my neck to look up to the top-floor bedroom, the one facing Wellington Street, where I'm still in bed listening to an endless TV loop under my pillow courtesy of the reel-to-reel. Looking down, I still hear jokes echoing off the walls of the main floor -- from the kitchen, no doubt, even from the corner of the room where the portable dishwasher still rests, a place-setting for Paul always at the ready on top. (Don't bring it up.) And I still see myself at the front windows, parting the curtains on a Monday night in the winter of 1976, looking out as the clock nears nine to see nothing but emptiness on the streets in the minutes before the start of another chapter of *Rich Man Poor Man*.

Below the main-floor, the glass-block windows still front a basement where so much washing and drying and ironing is still being done by a parent who still walks passed her fourth-born to tend to it. Embraced by the black-and-white reach of a small TV, he's still staring at the screen, wondering what life is in there -- and Out There -- for him, not knowing that just out front, steps away, his elder self sits in an idling car, a TV executive.

Bewitched and star Elizabeth Montgomery are each as long gone as the neighbors and my parents, but down in the basement in the middle of the 3200 block of Wellington Street in Northeast Philadelphia, it's still on. It's always on. And I'm still watching it. Propelled into the TV world, and into the TV business, by a need to be part of a shared experience. I still long for that connection. Even as, or maybe especially when, fewer and fewer are sharing any TV connection at all anymore.

TV is still talking to me. I'm still listening. Because in TV I find life.

In TV, I find myself.

*

Born and raised in Philadelphia, Jim McKairnes is a writer, TV executive, and college instructor who lives in the Los Angeles area. At least as of this typing. He has held the posts of Senior Vice-President, Program Planning and Scheduling, CBS Television Network (1993-2006) and Senior Vice-President, Strategy and Development, CBS Studios (2008-2010), among others in broadcast- and cable-television. He has also served as an adjunct faculty member at De Paul University in Chicago and a guest-lecturer at colleges nationwide. Go figure. And he is author of **103 WAYS TO GET INTO TV (BY 102 WHO DID, PLUS ME**). His birth and rearing, his East Coast education, his West Coast career -- and everything else from Philadelphia to Tennessee to Hollywood -- have been due to the efforts and support and help and guidance of many people, who should know who they are. He thanks them with a very full heart.

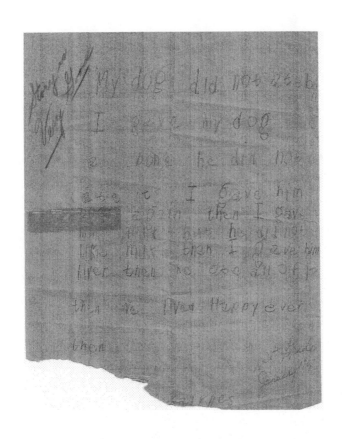

A writer's beginnings …
(First grade, St. Matthew School; Philadelphia, 1967)

Made in the USA
Lexington, KY
26 March 2014